Heartprints of Hope

A Healing Path for Tiny Hearts Carrying Deep Hurts

Break the Cycle. **Heal the Roots**. Raise Wholehearted Kids.

JASON AND GWEN CLARK

*Because what heals early doesn't have to
be carried for a lifetime.*

Scripture quotations marked (NIV) are taken from The Holy Bible, New International Version®, NIV® Copyright © 1973, 1978, 1984, 2011 by Biblica, Inc.® Used by permission. All rights reserved worldwide.

Scripture quotations marked (ESV) are taken from The Holy Bible, English Standard Version®. ESV® Text Edition: 2016. Copyright © 2001 by Crossway. Used by permission. All rights reserved.

Scripture quotations marked with (GNT) are from The Holy Bible, Good News Translation®, © 1992 American Bible Society. All rights reserved. Used with permission.

Scripture quotations marked (NLT) are taken from The Holy Bible, New Living Translation, copyright © 1996, 2004, 2015 by Tyndale House Foundation. Used by permission of Tyndale House Publishers, Inc., Carol Stream, Illinois 60188. All rights reserved.

Scripture quotations marked (KJV) are from The Holy Bible, King James Version.

Scripture quotations marked (AMPC) are taken from The Amplified® Bible, Copyright © 1954, 1958, 1962, 1964, 1965, 1987 by The Lockman Foundation. Used by permission. All rights reserved. www.lockman.org.

Scriptures marked (CSB) are taken from The Christian Standard Bible. Copyright © 2017 by Holman Bible Publishers. Used by permission. Christian Standard Bible®, and CSB® are federally registered trademarks of Holman Bible Publishers, all rights reserved.

Cover Art and Illustrations by Jason J. Clark

ISBN: 979-8-99957-370-4 paperback

CONTENTS

INTRODUCTION

Dear reader,

If you are holding this book, you probably have a strong concern for a child's heart, whether it's a young person in your ministry, a student, or your own child. Perhaps you've noticed their emotional struggles and wondered how you can support them. Or maybe you've seen in their eyes some of the same pieces of your own childhood trauma.

Whatever the reasons that brought you here, you are being invited into a different approach to shepherding young hearts. This was a collaborative effort between my beautiful wife, Gwen, and me, so throughout this book, you will read both our voices and viewpoints periodically.

In these pages, you will find stories that may move you to tears, truths that can change how you view emotional healing, and practical pathways for connecting children to Jesus' peace. You will discover how emotional wounds can be healed early, before they shape identity and destiny. Most importantly, you will learn how to foster peace and wholeness in tiny hearts that last a lifetime.

Our journey together isn't about doing everything perfectly, perfect parenting or raising perfect kids; it's more about being intentionally present and connected. It's not about controlling behavior or fixing our children, and it's not necessary to have all the answers. Gwen and I are continually learning as we go, and really, it's ultimately about knowing whom to turn to when hard things happen. Take a moment and just breathe. You're reading this book, and that alone tells me something powerful: God's already using you to leave a heartprint of hope in a child's life. You are in the very place where God can begin to plant something new.

Heartprints?

Fingerprints leave evidence of our presence. Footprints mark where we've walked. But heartprints reveal what's been imparted.

We all leave marks on each other's hearts at some level. Some are light while others run deep. As we will learn later, these heartprints shape how children see themselves, others, and even God. These marks don't fade with time like skinned knees or pencil sketches; they stick around. They create a lens through which love is received and pain is handled. Whether we notice it or not, every interaction with a child leaves a lasting impression: the sharp word that escapes us in frustration, the gentle hand guiding them through disappointment, and our consistent presence that calms their anxiety. It's the way they watch us navigate our own storms and celebrations.

Some of these impressions can lead to buried hurts (see Chapter 14), distorting a child's perception and limiting their capacity to receive love. Others create fertile soil where peace, joy, and genuine connection can grow.

As we walk through this together, I hope that you'll begin to see just how powerful your presence can be in a child's healing. You'll learn to notice the heartprints, both the tender ones and the troubled ones. And more than that, you'll discover how Jesus meets us in those very places, helping us turn pain into peace, not by pushing it away, but by walking through it with Him.

Every prayer of forgiveness, every moment of yielding to peace, every connection with Jesus in them creates an inner engraving that says: "You are seen. You are loved. Jesus is here."

The emotional memories you create today, especially during moments of vulnerability, can shape and define the story they hold for a lifetime.

As you continue your journey, my prayer is that you become increasingly aware of the heartprints you're creating and are intentional about making them ones of hope. The kind that point to Jesus, the ultimate Healer of hearts.

It's important to note that as you journey through this book, you'll come across some terms and phrases associated with emotional and spiritual healing, like "Bible-heart," "Spirit-led," or "bitter roots." To help with this, I've included a **glossary** near the end of the book to clarify these concepts. Think of it as a helpful companion tool you can turn to whenever something feels a bit unfamiliar. I genuinely hope it supports your journey and enhances your reading experience!

(JASON)

This is the resource our hearts have longed for, the one we wish had been given to us years ago when we were quietly drowning in questions, trying to navigate pain we didn't know how to name.

Not because we've figured everything out perfectly, but precisely because we haven't. We've learned the hard way, through personal struggle, real-life pain, and the messy yet beautiful journey of healing together. We want to share these lessons clearly so you won't have to learn them the same way we did.

The hard truth? Most of us don't realize just how much our childhood shapes us. Especially the kind of hurts we never really talked about. You know, the really painful ones. I know, because I've lived it. There was a time I almost lost everything, my peace, my joy, my identity, even my very life. But God wasn't done with my story. He stepped in and started a deep restoration, almost like a reformation of my soul that I never saw coming.

(GWEN)

When Jason and I met, I could see he wasn't just *talking* about emotional healing; he was actively walking it out. What drew me to him was his authentic pursuit of wholeness, something I'd longed for myself. As our lives intertwined, his journey became mine, and together we've discovered something compelling:

Children don't have to carry wounds into adulthood. Healing can begin early, right now, even in the youngest hearts.

As a mom, I've felt the urgency to recognize hidden hurts in our children early on and walk them toward healing. We've seen firsthand how quickly unresolved pain can become more profound. Still, we've also witnessed the miraculous, transforming power of emotional healing when we step in with intentionality and compassion.

We wrote this book not only to share our story but to offer a practical, biblical, Spirit-led method you can use immediately with your household or in your ministry.

(JASON)

We've dubbed it The *Bible-Heart Model*, inspired by Jesus' promise of living waters flowing from our innermost being (John 7:38). In simple terms, it's a clear method for recognizing, addressing, and releasing emotional pain, leading children toward forgiveness, peace, and their true identity in Christ.

You'll learn about the simple steps we call the Forgiveness Flow, which are practical enough for daily parenting yet impactful enough to leave a mark on future generations. You'll hear real-life stories, uncover hands-on wisdom, and, most importantly, discover how quickly healing can come when we recognize the signs early.

(GWEN)

You'll hear something, maybe a few times throughout this journey, but it is because there's something we want you to keep close to your heart: This is about seeing and hearing beyond the surface, learning to recognize when a child's behavior is actually the voice of their heart asking for help.

We will create space for Jesus to meet them right where they are, in their anger, fear, shame, or hurt.

But perhaps most importantly, it's about *your* healing journey. The atmosphere of your heart shapes the environment where your children grow.

(JASON)

Before we dive into the specifics, I'd like to mention that you're not holding this book by accident. You may sense God leading you to some of your own unresolved emotional hurts. Or maybe God has placed children in your life whose hearts need tending. Whatever brought you here, there is hope.

So here's our invitation to you:

Heal the roots. Break the cycles. Plant peace.

We are so honored to walk this out with you.

THREE WAYS TO JOURNEY THROUGH THIS BOOK

A Practical Guide for Parents, Teachers, and Ministry Leaders

Before You Begin

Heartprints of Hope isn't meant to be consumed like a typical parenting book. It's designed to be experienced slowly, prayerfully, and with your own trusting heart wide open to God. The greatest healing moments you'll guide children toward will flow through you first. So, as you read, take a timeout with God when something stirs. I want to encourage you to let Jesus meet you in those tender places before you attempt to shepherd others there.

The Personal Path *(Start Here)*

I encourage you to read Part One and Part Two with your own heart as the focus. Let the nine foundational lessons work in you first, as best as you can. Many parents, including Gwen and me, discover their deepest healing happens while learning to help their children. Your emotional wholeness creates a safe atmosphere where children's hearts can trust and be open to Jesus.

Recommended pace: One lesson per week, with time for prayer and reflection.

The Family Application Path

Once you've walked through your own healing, move to Part Three. Each chapter builds on the previous one, so resist the urge to skip ahead to "quick fixes." The Bible-Heart Model works because it's relational, not formulaic.

Key chapters for immediate help:

- Chapter 13: Where Is Your Heart?
- Chapter 19: Forgiveness: Our Heart's Healing Medicine
- Chapter 27: The Bible-Heart Model (Forgiveness Flow steps)

The Ministry Leader Path

Use this book as a family discipleship resource. The "For Teachers & Ministry Leaders" sections in Part Three provide group activities, but the real transformation happens when you help families implement these practices at home.

Essential Tools for Your Journey

Create Space for Encounter

This book focuses on **creating opportunities** for children to experience Jesus. Gwen and I have observed that some of the most powerful healing moments often occur during ordinary daily routines: bedtime, car rides, and after conflicts.

Learn the Forgiveness Flow *(Chapter 27)*

These five steps become your family's emotional GPS:

1. **Feel the Feeling** (acknowledge what's inside).
2. **Open Your Bible-heart to Jesus** (invite His presence).
3. **Forgive** (release others, yourself, even disappointment with God).
4. **Give Jesus the Yuck and Receive His Peace** (exchange).
5. **Fill Up with Love** (receive His truth and presence).

Practice these steps yourself first. Children learn more from watching you model emotional authenticity than from hearing explanations.

Adapting for Different Ages

Although the application section is generally intended for ages 3-8, feel free to adjust it for your specific situation and age groups. We love to hear from parents and teachers who implement new and exciting ways for children to experience Jesus.

Speak to the specific needs of each age:

Ages 3-6: Keep it Simple

- Use physical touch (hand on tummy).

- Tell stories and use object lessons.

- Focus on "yucky feelings" and "Jesus hugs from inside."

- Celebrate with the child in every small step toward emotional awareness.

Ages 7-12: Build Understanding

- Explain the "why" behind emotions.

- Introduce the concept of bitter roots.

- Help them recognize patterns in their feelings.

- Teach them to pray the Forgiveness Flow independently.

Teenagers: Go Deeper

- Address identity lies and comparison.

- Connect emotional healing to their spiritual journey.

- Respect their growing independence while staying available.

- Share your own stories of healing when appropriate.

When You Feel Stuck

If a child resists, don't force it. Create safety first. Sometimes, the most powerful healing occurs when we simply stay present without demanding participation. Trust the Holy Spirit to open their heart in His timing.

If you feel overwhelmed, return to your own heart. Sure, you can guide kids in the Forgiveness Flow steps and see great results. The greatest heartprint you can make on their tiny spirits will be made when you walk the walk first. You can guide, but ultimately, you cannot give what you never received. Take time to connect with Jesus, receive His peace, and then try again from a place of rest, not striving.

If family members don't understand: Focus on fruit, not methods. Let the transformation in your children speak louder than your explanations. *(See Chapter 25 for navigating relationships)*

Most Important Reminders

- **Progress over perfection.** Every step toward emotional awareness matters.

- **Connection before correction.** Address the heart before the behavior.

- **Presence over performance.** Your calm, steady presence teaches more than perfect words.

- **Jesus does the healing.** You create space; He does the transforming work.

In Your Daily Routine

Healing doesn't require hour-long sessions. Build these heart-check moments into your regular routine:

- **Morning:** "How's your Bible-heart today?"
- **After conflicts:** "Let's take this to Jesus together."
- **Bedtime:** Simple forgiveness prayers and heart connection.

Remember, this isn't behavior modification. We're guiding children who know how to bring their authentic selves to the Living God, Jesus, and find His peace in every circumstance. I promise, it is a journey worth taking, one heart-print at a time.

Think about this, you're about to embark on a journey that will change more than you ever thought possible, for you and for the children you love. *"Let the little children come to me, and do not hinder them, for the kingdom of heaven belongs to such as these"* (Matthew 19:14, NIV).

For additional resources, troubleshooting guides, and family tools, visit www.heartprintsofhope.com.

PART ONE:
The Story

CHAPTER 1:
Crafting an Enduring Legacy of Hope

Every moment with a child creates an invisible impression, a spiritual fingerprint that shapes how they see themselves, others, and God. The question isn't whether we're making these marks, it's what story they're telling.

This book is about **raising wholehearted kids from the inside out**. It's about learning to **heal the roots** of emotional pain before they distort a child's identity, to **plant peace** that sustains them through life's challenges, and to **grow a legacy that lasts** far beyond our years because the **seeds you plant in their hearts today shape the story they'll carry forever**, a story of connection, healing, and unshakable hope.

Kids remember what we do when no one's looking more than anything we teach them with words. Our goal is to forge timeless imprints that far outlast our words and become the very foundation of their identity in Christ.

The Seed of Bitterness

Imagine a child standing quietly in a garden, small hands pressing a tiny seed into the soft earth. But this is no ordinary seed. It isn't going to blossom into bright sunflowers or sweet carrots. Instead, it's something much darker, planted not in soil, but in the tender soil of their heart.

This seed begins with a moment of pain. A careless word. A harsh glance. An unkept promise. A sudden loss. A hidden fear. Something whispered or shouted, something felt but rarely spoken of again.

And every time that hurt goes unnoticed, dismissed, or buried, it's like rain soaking the soil, causing the seed to swell and grow beneath the surface. At first, nothing seems to happen. The garden looks unchanged, peaceful, even. But beneath the surface, unseen and silent, roots begin to twist downward, anchoring themselves more deeply into the heart.

That, dear reader, is what Scripture calls a root of bitterness.

Hebrews 12:15 (ESV) sounds the alarm with a solemn warning: *"See to it that no one fails to obtain the grace of God; that no 'root of bitterness' springs up and causes trouble, and by it many become defiled."*

A bitter root isn't simply anger, sadness, or disappointment; it's an unresolved emotion that quietly takes on a life of its own. It lives and grows unseen in the shadows of a child's heart, shaping their thoughts, beliefs, and even their understanding of who God is.

The roots whisper lies, convincing lies that sound too true to ignore:

You are unlovable.

It's all your fault.

You are alone.

It's too late; God can't help you.

From these insidious whispers comes a harvest no one desires: anxiety, perfectionism, shame, rebellion, addictive behaviors, crippling fear, and isolation. Reflecting on it now, I didn't have the words for it, but I began collecting what I now call 'Hell Flags' (see glossary), those toxic emotional warnings like fear, shame, and guilt that indicate when something isn't right deep inside. They accumulate. They take hold. And when they remain buried too long, they begin to shape how you perceive everything: God, yourself, and the people around you. The effects of this may not always appear immediately; roots can quietly grow for years before fully revealing their true nature.

These roots never stay small either. They expand and intertwine, becoming part of the foundation of who that child becomes.

But here's the hopeful reality and the reason you've picked up this book today: Heart wounds that fester can be uprooted. No matter how deeply they've grown or how long they've been there, they can be pulled up, releasing you from pain and freeing you to heal. I know this because I've experienced it firsthand.

Let me take you back to a moment when I was trapped by my own roots of hopelessness. It's a story I've titled, "Caught in a Trap," because that's exactly how I felt: stuck, hopeless, and desperate for freedom.

And here's how it happened…

Caught in a Trap

I sat on the cold linoleum floor, my back pressed hard against the edge of the bathtub, trembling as the sound of splintering wood echoed through the walls. The crash still rang in my ears, sharp, violent, and final. Then came her voice, slicing through the air with a fury that felt almost otherworldly. It didn't even sound human. My breath caught. I froze, my body locked in that in-between space where fear and instinct collide, like prey trying not to move, hoping not to be seen.

A moment ago, Lana's bare foot had smashed through the center of the hollow-core door I had locked myself behind (I've changed her name here, but every detail of what happened between us is true). Shards of the doorframe littered the tiles around me. My heart pounded in my chest like that of a frightened child. How had it ever come to this, I wondered, with my knees pulled tight to my chest?

When It Looked Like Love

There were moments early on when I thought I had outrun my past. Lana was magnetic; she made me laugh. She saw the "good boy" in me and applauded it. For a while, I honestly believed this could be the redemption story I'd been

13

waiting for. She was passionate, intense, and emotionally expressive—everything I thought I needed to shake off the numbness I'd carried for years.

I didn't see the warning signs. Or maybe I did see them but mistook them for chemistry. What I didn't realize back then was how deeply my desire for connection blinded me to danger.

We had some great days in the beginning that felt real enough. Lana seemed perfect: sweet and silly, charming in all the right ways. I fell hard for her innocence and light. In those first few weeks, I genuinely believed she might be "the one." I even called my dad, eager to tell him I'd met someone amazing. I felt hopeful. Alive. Like a man stumbling into water after years of wandering through a desert.

But I was building a house of cards.

And it collapsed faster than I ever imagined.

The Dream Turns Dark

The hope I once carried had curdled into terror. My dream girl had become my captor.

I wasn't just hiding in a bathroom.

I was hiding from the woman I thought I loved.

And I was trapped, not just behind that door, but in a life that had become a nightmare in real time.

I squeezed my eyes shut, and for an instant I wasn't a grown man at all—I was a little boy again, maybe six or seven years old, small and scared. I could almost feel the scratchy carpet of my childhood bedroom under me instead of those cold tiles. I was hiding back then, too, hiding my tears, hiding my needs, trying so hard to be a "good boy" so that no one would leave me. Even at that young age, I had already learned one terrible lesson: if I wanted to be loved, I had better not show how broken or needy I felt inside. I had to be perfect. I had to pretend everything was fine.

Back then, Dad was a beloved pastor of a growing church. To everyone else, he was a spiritual hero, compassionate and strong, always available to lend a helping hand. But to me, he was always busy, always tucked away praying, or just distant. I knew he loved me, yet I longed for more of his time and attention. I remember sitting in the front row every Sunday, hands folded, the dutiful preacher's kid. Outside, I smiled and behaved, but inside, I often felt lonely and unworthy, as if I had to earn the love that flowed easily from him to others. I never admitted it, but I wondered, "Am I not enough? Would Dad (or even God) care more if I were better?" I was unsure if I truly understood what it meant to be a "good boy." What defined a "good boy," anyway? Yet, I believed that distinction would always be just out of reach.

Those questions planted something in me, quiet yet corrosive. I didn't know it at the time, but a bitter root had already begun to grow: the belief that I was on my own. That if I didn't hold everything together perfectly, I'd be left behind. So I buried the ache and built a mask: a straight-A student, a helpful son, a polite church kid. I figured if I was "good" enough, I could outrun the sting of rejection.

But secret pain doesn't stay buried. It twists. It grows like a vine, slowly choking the life out of who God meant you to be. By the time I was a teenager, anger had started to emerge from that root. I didn't understand why I was so angry. But beneath the surface, I resented my dad for things I couldn't articulate. I was bitter toward God, too, for feeling distant when I needed Him most. I stopped praying, except when I was in trouble. Church became a performance. Inside, I was a storm of guilt, shame, and rage. By the time I left home, that storm had begun pulling me far from the faith I once knew.

I cannot believe, looking back, how quickly I made Lana *my everything*. It wasn't just love, though I desperately needed it. Deep down, the little boy in me was whispering, "Don't give up. I told myself, "Don't let her go, whatever it takes to keep her. If she leaves, you'll be alone again."

I never expressed it to anyone, but that particular thought seemed to drive every aspect of my life. I ignored all the red flags and downplayed any concerns. "I *need* this relationship to work," I told myself. I needed her to stay with me.

My stomach turns every time I remember how I told everyone she was "the best thing that ever happened to me." Yikes. I was terrified she'd leave; I felt this was my last chance at true happiness, but there was that nagging fear. And that fear gave her more control over me than I ever imagined.

At first, it was subtle. There were a few small lies here and there that I willingly chose not to challenge, stories of mistreatment from exes, and particular health challenges. I felt uniquely called to care for her as my rescuer instinct took over. All my life, I've felt valuable when I was needed. Lana gave me a full-time role in her crisis story, and I played it like my life depended on it. I wanted to be the one who healed what others had broken, but in trying to save her, I was losing myself.

Then the cracks began to show.

Once, she told me she was at work, but her "Find My Friends" location said she was at a Subway down the street. My gut twisted when I found out, but she had a story, and I wanted so badly to believe it that I let it go.

Then came the messages, late-night texts to an ex. I wasn't looking for them, but there they were, and something inside me just sank. When I brought it up, her reaction wasn't guilt or apology, it was rage. Accusations spat out through the tears and soon turned into threats. And somehow, within minutes, I was the one apologizing for all of it.

I can still taste the shame as I asked her to forgive me...for catching her in all the lies.

Writing it now, it sounds absurd. But when your deepest fear is being abandoned, you'll do anything to keep the ground from falling out from beneath you, even if it means apologizing for having set proper healthy boundaries.

I wish that moment were the exception, but it was quickly becoming my new normal.

The sweetness that initially drew me in began to fade, replaced by something unpredictable and potentially dangerous. Although laughter wasn't common during those times, Lana could laugh with me over pancakes at breakfast, only to become completely unhinged by lunchtime. It didn't always add up. Sometimes it was a word I said or the way I looked at her; other times, it was something I couldn't quite identify. Then the storm would hit: tears, yelling, blame that didn't fit the moment. And there I was, as always, right in the middle of it. Because that's what I did. I stepped in. I tried to fix it.

I'd hold her as she fell apart. I'd whisper reassurances I desperately needed to believe myself: "It's okay. I'm not leaving. I love you."

I meant it. Or at least, the scared little boy inside me did, because leaving wasn't an option. Leaving meant I failed, and I would be alone. The very thing I had spent my life trying to avoid.

So I poured every ounce of energy into making it work. Not just to convince her that I was enough, but to convince myself. That I was worthy. That I was lovable. That I could make someone want to stay with me.

Lana figured out how to use that fear like a lever.

She was a master at it, emotional manipulation that felt like love. One minute, I was her everything. Next, she'd threaten to disappear, or worse. She'd say I was too good for her, that maybe she should end it all because she was ruining my life.

All of a sudden, she'd paint herself as the victim with such conviction that even I started to wonder if she was right.

You know, when your reality is rewritten so many times, you stop trusting your own thinking.

And I was in a deep, thick fog.

I was living two lives. On the outside, what little of the outside world I was still allowed into (work), I pretended everything was fine. I did isolate myself, as I mentioned earlier, partly from shame, and partly because of Lana's influence. If my dad called to check in, I'd slap on a cheerful, over-the-top "Yeah, everything's great!" while Lana stared me down from across the room, eyes sharp, silently warning me not to say too much.

At home, I walked on eggshells from morning till night. Although a faulty plan from the start, perfect responses became my survival strategy. If I could anticipate everything, do the dishes exactly her way, respond to every text the moment it arrived, speak in just the right tone, I believed maybe, just maybe, I could avoid the next eruption.

It was like I was on a tightrope, tense, exhausting, impossible. And no matter how well I performed, it was never enough to combat her unexpected reactions and outbursts.

The emotional abuse didn't stay emotional for long. It eventually escalated. And during any number of these escalations, she'd claw at my face, and sometimes hit me with whatever was within her grasp. Things were thrown at me, too, once, even slamming a whole can of crushed tomatoes into my head. Of course, that sent me to my knees.

I recall purchasing makeup to hide the bruises.

She always had explanations like: I stressed her out, exhaustion, or misunderstandings.

She cried, apologized and promised it would never happen again…almost every time.

And I let it go.

Because I had convinced myself that's what love was supposed to do.

Deep down inside, I knew there was something really…*really* wrong. My breaking point didn't arrive all at once; it rose slowly, like water behind a dam.

One chilly evening, that dam nearly burst.

Angry words poured out like shrapnel. I remember the way her spit hit the inside of the windshield, catching the headlights, tiny flashes, like angry little stars. *I have to get out.* I thought. I pressed up against the passenger door, trying to disappear, trying not even to breathe too loudly. Tears were coming whether I wanted them or not, hot, silent, and burning.

My chest was a war zone, rage and fear crashing into each other. And then, just like that, "thwap!" Fist to nose contact.

Instant pain. The shock of it sent me directly into a state of clarity. Not confusion, clarity. *I have to get out.* I didn't need to think it through. Something in me screamed: *I need to get out. I have to get out NOW!*

Not metaphorically. Literally.

I slipped off the seatbelt and reached for the door handle.

In my panicked mind, "out" meant leaping from a speeding car into the dark, because that felt safer than staying in it.

The Moment Everything Changed

The roar of the wind exploded into the cabin. Lana screamed, slamming on the brakes and grabbing for me in a panic, yanking me away just in time. She pulled over to the shoulder. We sat there in silence, both of us breathless, trembling, our hearts pounding so loudly it felt like they might shake the car apart.

I was shaking uncontrollably. My eyes locked onto the pavement just outside — only seconds before, it had been a blur I was ready to disappear into. And that's when it hit me.

I almost did it.

I almost ended everything right there on that dark highway.

March 29th. The date is burned into my soul. The night I nearly chose oblivion over one more moment of captivity. I couldn't know then that years later, God would reclaim this very date, transforming it from a marker of my deepest despair into a day of profound joy. Where death nearly had its way, new life would eventually enter the world. But standing on that roadside, salvation seemed a world away. All I knew was that I couldn't keep living this way.

The weight of it collapsed over me like a tidal wave. I was a grown man with a good family who loved me. I had a faithful God who hadn't given up on me, and yet I had been reduced to this, a whisper away from jumping into the night just to escape the prison my life had become.

That moment pierced the fog that had clouded my thinking for so long. It felt like a bucket of ice water thrown over my soul. For the first time in months, maybe years, I saw my situation for what it truly was: not just painful, not just unhealthy.

It was deadly.

And if I didn't find a way out soon, I might not survive it. Whether by my own despair, her escalating volatility, or the sheer exhaustion that had begun to eat away at my body and spirit.

That night, the question wasn't whether I could fix the relationship.

The question was whether I could stay alive.

The Phone Call

I didn't speak a word to her when we got home.

Lana collapsed into bed like nothing had happened. I sat in the guest room, back against the wall, staring into the dark. My head was pounding. My chest felt pressured. I could still feel the wind on my skin, the blur of highway in my memory, the rush of being one second away from never coming back.

And then, finally, I broke.

I picked up my phone with shaking hands and called the one person I knew would answer.

"Dad, " I whispered, "I need help."

There was a pause on the other end, just long enough to scare me. Then his voice came, calm and clear. "We've been praying for this call, " he said. "Just come home."

I was in my late thirties, but in that moment, I felt like a kid again. Like maybe, just maybe, I didn't have to hold the world together on my own anymore.

Dad gave me instructions. Simple, firm, practical. "Call the police tomorrow morning. Request a stand-by. Don't try to leave without them knowing."

I took a breath and promised him I would make the call to the police station first thing in the morning. My voice cracked. My hands wouldn't stop shaking. But I committed to following through.

And when I hung up, something in me exhaled for the first time in months.

I hadn't escaped yet, but the decision was made, and it felt like hope.

But something told me this couldn't wait.

So I called the police, right then and there.

Fifteen Steps to Freedom

The police knocked just before sunrise, the sky still inky black outside the windows. Lana jolted awake, suddenly realizing what was happening. She exploded in anger and panic, screaming and crying, but the officers firmly held her back while one walked me to my car. I will never forget that surreal walk—fifteen short steps to freedom, feeling Lana's anguished eyes burning into my back, she screamed, 'What do you think you are doing? You can't leave me! You can't do this to me!' Her voice echoed in the darkness. My hands were shaking so badly that I fumbled the car keys and dropped them on the pavement outside. I felt utterly pathetic in that moment—a grown man reduced to this. But I kept going. I picked up the keys, slid into the driver's seat, and with a final acknowledgment to the police, I started the engine.

I pulled away with only what I had on, my phone, and a beat-up laptop. Dawn was just bleeding into the sky as I rounded the corner and left that apartment, leaving Lana behind. Something cracked open inside me then, a ragged sob from deep down in my gut. It was a mixture of pain and relief. A cage door had swung wide. I was free. The road ahead was a big question mark, but for the first time in months, I was breathing air that didn't taste like fear.

By nightfall, the adrenaline faded, and my eyelids felt like sandpaper. The white stripes on the highway were gradually smearing into one long blur. I knew I had to stop, but the idea of signing into a motel under my real name shot a pulse of panic through me.

Would she start dialing every front desk between here and nowhere? Maybe?

Then I spotted the exit sign: Metropolis, Illinois. It felt oddly fitting, and, somehow, safe. I flicked on my blinker and took the ramp.

And there he was, fifteen feet tall, standing in the town square as if he owned the place. Superman. With his hands on his hips, his gaze conveyed that he was completely in charge. I pulled into a parking lot across from him and just sat there, staring up at that incredible jawline I wished I had.

I couldn't help but laugh a little under my breath. After everything, all the years of feeling drained, stuck, and here I was, finally out, finally free, and wouldn't you know it? That's the night Superman decides to make an appearance.

The motel clerk didn't ask any questions. She took my cash, handed me a real metal key on a plastic fob, and sent me to a room that seemed like it hadn't changed since the Reagan administration. Wood paneling reminded me of my childhood home in Pennsylvania, complete with faded artwork on the wall. That night, I felt safe for the first time in months; I actually slept, deep and dreamless.

Before sunrise, I slipped the key under the office door and hit the road again. Superman slowly disappeared in the dust in my rearview, silent proof that sometimes rescue comes from the most unexpected places.

With renewed spirit, I continued my journey toward my father's house, and toward whatever healing awaited me there.

A Father's Welcome

The journey itself passed in a blur of highway truck stops, gas station coffee, and moments of paralyzing doubt that I forced myself to push through. I drove as if escape itself were fuel, stopping only when necessary.

Even after a good night's rest, I still found myself changing routes several times, half-convinced Lana might somehow be following me. Paranoia doesn't disappear overnight, even when the threat is miles behind you.

Two days and a thousand miles later, I pulled into my dad's driveway. It was Easter weekend—a fitting time for what felt like resurrection. I felt utterly drained, running on the fumes of adrenaline and heartbreak. Dad and Jennifer came out and enveloped me in the kind of hugs I hadn't realized I needed so badly. In their embrace, I broke down and wept, body shaking with months—no, years—of pent-up agony. To my astonishment, they didn't scold or lecture me.

They just held me, my father's tears wet on my shoulder, matching my own. It struck me that I had feared facing him in my shame, but here he was, embracing me like the prodigal son returned home. In that safe place, the little boy inside me finally felt seen and held.

The Real Trap was Inside of Me

Over the following days and weeks, I began the journey of untangling the twisted roots that had wrecked my life. It was not easy; I had to confront the fact that Lana was not solely the problem. I had to face the truth that I had carried deep wounds and false beliefs since childhood that made me susceptible to someone like her. I believed I was unworthy of love, so I tolerated abuse. I feared abandonment, so I let myself be controlled rather than risk someone leaving me. I clung to false responsibility, so I tried to "save" a profoundly broken person at the cost of my well-being. These were the bitter roots that had grown unchecked in me for decades. They nearly destroyed me.

Even as I write this, I feel emotional thinking about that scared little Jason who still lives inside the grown man. In many ways, my healing journey has been about reaching back in time to comfort and heal that little boy, finally giving him the love, truth, and voice he needed. I often wonder: What if someone had helped me acknowledge my pain and lies when I was young? What if I had learned as a child that I was worthy of love, that I didn't have to earn affection or fear abandonment? What if I had been taught how to bring my hurts to God back then instead of hiding them in shame? If I had received inner healing in my youth, maybe, just maybe, I would have recognized the warning signs with Lana early and dared to walk away before things got so dark. Perhaps I wouldn't have wandered for twenty long years in the wilderness of anger and toxic relationships.

I share this story not to wallow in its darkness, but to shine a blazing light on a critical truth: the harbored hurts of unhealed childhood pain will grow and strangle a life if left unchecked. I paid a high price for neglecting the wounds of my inner child. The cost was nearly my sanity, my faith, and my life. I don't want any other child, or the adult they will become, to pay that price.

That's why I'm passionate about reaching children's hearts at an early age. I believe with all my heart that if we nurture those tender hearts in their youth, if we assist them in uprooting bitterness and lies before they harden, we can spare them so much devastation. No child should have to navigate the kind of secret pain I carried in silence. No little boy or girl should grow up believing they are unworthy of love or destined to be abandoned. And no young person should enter adulthood so starved for affection and affirmation that they mistake abuse for love, as I did.

Standing here now, I feel the weight and urgency of this mission. As a father myself (yes, God has graciously rewritten my story—I am now married to a loving, kind woman, and we have four beautiful children), I look at my kids and my heart burns with determination: They will know they are loved, no matter what. They will have the emotional and spiritual tools I lacked. They will learn that it's okay to have needs, to feel hurt, and to seek help. They will know that God's love is a strong foundation that can support them through any storm. My children will grow up, I pray, without the roots of bitterness that nearly destroyed their dad.

A Wake-Up Call

And what about the countless other children out there in our homes, our churches, and our schools? Each of them has a tender heart that can be wounded, and if those wounds are ignored, they will plant lies in their young minds: "I'm not good enough," I'm alone," "It's all my fault," "Nobody cares." These lies take root and grow like weeds, distorting who they are meant to be. But it doesn't have to be that way. We can intervene. We can nurture truth and healing in their hearts while those hearts are still soft and growing.

I share my nightmare as a wake-up call. If you're a parent, a teacher, a ministry leader, or anyone who cares for a child's soul, hear this: Pay attention. Pay attention to the quiet hurts your child might be carrying. Don't assume they'll "get over it" or that it's just a phase. Love them enough to dig up the bitter roots before they take hold and grow deeper. Guide them in processing pain, in forgiving, in embracing truth. Show them early on what I learned much later: that God is close to the brokenhearted, that no wound is too deep for His healing touch, and that their true identity is safe in His hands.

I shudder to think where I'd be today if God hadn't intervened and if people who loved me hadn't been there to help me break free. But I'm not in that dark place anymore; I'm free, I'm healing, and I'm watching God redeem every piece of my story. This book in your hands is part of that redemption. It is a plea and a promise. A plea that we do not neglect the inner lives of our children. And a promise of what can happen when we do take action: when we equip children early with emotional and spiritual tools, we can change the trajectory of their entire lives.

If my story made you uncomfortable, that's okay. Some journeys are painful. The truth is that I nearly lost everything because of wounds I never dealt with as a child. The truth is that many children around us are quietly planting seeds in the heartprints of hurt and false beliefs. But here is another truth, one that fills me with hope and urgency: those bitter roots can be healed and uprooted, especially if we catch them early.

I'm living proof that no matter how twisted and binding those roots became, with God's help, they can be removed, and new, healthy growth can occur. I've seen what happens when a lost, wounded "little boy" inside a man finally receives love and healing; that man becomes whole, joyful, and free.

Now imagine a generation of children who don't have to wait decades for that freedom, who never have to fall into the same trap because they are equipped with truth and love from the start. That vision is what drives me.

As we continue this journey in the pages ahead, I invite you to stay awake and engaged. Let my own painful lesson stir something in you. I've opened the book of my heart to you in all its gritty honesty, not to shock you, but to move you to action, to compassion, to a new way of thinking about the kids in your care. The high cost of neglecting a child's emotional healing is written in the scars I've shared with you. But far more powerful is the hope I hold now: the hope that together, we can ensure our children grow up free—their hearts whole, their identities secure, and their futures hopeful, unhindered by the pain of the past.

CHAPTER 2:
The Invitation to Heal

(JASON)

The night I nearly jumped out of that speeding car, March 29th, marked the moment I hit rock bottom. Not because I didn't want to live, but because I couldn't see how I could continue living that way. It wasn't a dramatic cry for help; it was a final collapse of will. Something inside me had been unraveling for years, but that night it gave way completely. And yet, even as I dangled on the edge of despair, God was already preparing a rescue.

(GWEN) Healing that Multiplies

The transformation I witnessed in Jason still takes my breath away sometimes. In less than a year, he wasn't just healing, he was healed enough that God could use him to rescue me from the toxic, abusive relationship I was trapped in.

You see, if Jason hadn't walked through his valley and found freedom, he wouldn't have developed the strength, wisdom, and courage needed to pull me out of my pit. The season that almost broke him turned out to be the strength that pulled me out of my own.

What the enemy meant to take us both out, God repurposed not just for good, but for His glory. That's how He works, God didn't waste a moment of it. He used every tear, every scar, and every stumble to write something redemptive. And now? We get to partner together in setting others free, walking with them toward lasting healing.

"Jesus didn't just rescue me; He began to
rebuild me from the inside out."

I've come to believe in something beautiful: healed people heal people. It ripples outward, starting right in your own home, with your precious ones. That's the multiplication effect of freedom; it never stays small. It always wants to grow.

The Redemption Before the Resurrection
(JASON)

The time between that Easter, when I first arrived at my dad's house, and the moment I held my daughter Haven in my arms was nothing short of sacred. It was a season of holy rebuilding. It felt like Ezekiel's dry bones, but personal. Like God was breathing on pieces of me I thought were long gone.

Hope. Purpose. Tenderness. Identity.

Pieces of me I thought were long dead began to stir again. Not all at once. Not with fireworks. But quietly, steadily, breath by breath. With each tear that fell in prayer, with every moment I chose to surrender instead of shut down, something in me was coming back to life.

He made me new in places I thought were permanently dead. Only Jesus could do this.

Old strongholds began to break. The internal lies that had held me hostage started to lose their grip. I wasn't waking up gripped by nightmares anymore. My sleep, once tormented, became restful. The shame that used to sit on my chest like a weight began to lift.

And most importantly, peace came. Not the kind of peace that depends on circumstances. That peace was a sign, what we call a "God Emotion," evidence that the Holy Spirit was active in my heart again. *Peace as a Person*; the very presence of Jesus, honest, close and steady.

During that season, long before Jesus brought Gwen into my life, something unexpected began to stir in me. I started to believe that God could and *wanted* to rescue someone like me. He was after complete restoration. He wasn't patching up scraps; He was reclaiming what had been stolen, breathing life into parts of me I thought were long buried and rewriting endings I had already accepted as final.

And that's when something shifted. **I stopped identifying myself by what I had been through**. My story no longer ended in the valley. It was moving toward something new and holy.

(GWEN)

I didn't walk with Jason through the darkest valleys, but by the time I met him, the light was already breaking through. I hadn't seen the whole process, but I could see the *evidence* of it all over him.

I wasn't all that eager to get to know him at first; that's a story for another time. But something about him lingered in my spirit. There was a weight to his words, a sincerity I couldn't shake. And the more time I spent around him, the more I noticed something I hadn't expected: *peace.* Not just calm conversation or polite company, but the kind of peace that rests in a room when God is truly present.

It caught me off guard how at ease I felt with him. Safe. Known. There was a steadiness about him that made me breathe deeper, a gentleness that made my walls come down. Somewhere along the way, I realized I didn't just enjoy being around Jason. He felt like *home.* And not the kind you build with walls and furniture, but the kind you find when your spirit recognizes where it belongs.

I could see what his healing journey had produced. God had done something profound, and He was still building on it. From that place of restoration, I watched vision begin to bloom for ministry, for the future, for identity, calling, and legacy.

Not long after that, everything began to unfold quickly. We married sooner than I (and everyone else) ever expected, and yet, somehow, it felt perfectly timed by God. Shortly after our wedding, we found out we were expecting our first child together. It felt like God was planting something new in the soil of our shared surrender. Not just a baby, but also a new season. A fresh legacy rooted in healing and watered by His grace.

At the time, we had no idea what God was orchestrating behind the scenes.

We didn't know that our daughter would one day be born on the same date Jason had once tried to end his life.

(JASON) A New Story

Haven was born at 11:11.

As if that weren't enough, 11:11 also happened to be the exact time Gwen and I signed our marriage license at the courthouse. And to add a little fun to the mix, our son Landon was born at 10:10, which I thought was pretty cool... until I started wondering if it was the beginning of a countdown. Then I got slightly nervous.

March 29th was no countdown. That was resurrection. The same day I nearly threw my life away, God handed me a new one to steward. A little girl whose name means refuge or a safe place. A child of promise. A marker in time that said to my spirit, "See? I make all things new."

(GWEN) A Full Circle

When Haven was born, finally, over a week late, I was more than ready. But nothing could have prepared me for the flood of emotion that hit the moment I held her. It wasn't just the joy of meeting our daughter. It was the weight of what that day now meant.

It was my grandmother's birthday, which was already very special to me. But now, it was something more. It was the day God chose to redeem a part of Jason's story that had once been marked by pain. I looked down at Haven Elise and thought, *Only God could write something this beautiful.*

I didn't know all the details of Jason's past when we first met. But I saw it in him, the gentleness that doesn't come easily. It had been forged in fire. He was not only a good man but a restored one.

And that restoration is now the path we walk together in our marriage and how we raise our children: with intention, tenderness, and hope that healing always has the final word.

Signing our marriage license at 11:11 felt prophetic at the time. I remember smiling at the number but not fully grasping how deeply God was weaving our story. Haven's birth felt like He was saying, "I saw it all. And I'm a God of redeeming grace."

And now we see it in the laughter of our children. In the healing that flows through our home. In every bedtime prayer and every little victory. Haven's name means a safe place, a refuge and God's promise, and that's exactly what she's been: a holy place where God's redemptive love met our pasts and rewrote the endings, a living testament to God's promise to restore and bless through His redemptive love.

(OUR SHARED JOURNEY)

We had no clue how fully God was planning to redeem it all and write a story only He could script.

But now we do.

And friend, *that's* why we're so eager to share what's next with you.

After the trauma and running, after healing began, together we learned these **nine life-changing lessons** that became the foundation of our family and our ministry together.

They're the roots of His peace and His Presence in our family.

These lessons are simple enough for a child to understand, yet powerful enough to change the atmosphere of a home.

This isn't just a story; it's a guidebook, a parenting tool, and a discipleship manual. To our knowledge, it's the only Christian parenting resource that equips *you* to help your child heal emotional wounds early, using Spirit-led steps that are simple enough for a child yet powerful enough to break generational patterns. We call it The **Bible-Heart Model**, and this all comes together in the **Forgiveness Flow**.

You'll get a taste of it throughout, but the complete walkthrough begins in Chapter 27. That's where we lay out the exact prayer steps we use in real life, the ones that have transformed our home, our children, and our hearts, too.

So stay open. Let your heart lean in with a bit of expectancy, because maybe, just maybe, what you're about to read could be the start of your own resurrection as well.

This is not about fixing yourself or the kids you love, but it is about walking with Jesus into the parts of the story He wants to heal.

The Discovery That Changed Everything: Emmy's Story

The bitter roots from my past were being pulled up, one by one, and peace was taking their place. But God wasn't finished with the revelations. He was showing me how these principles of inner healing would extend far beyond my own story.

One ordinary afternoon, something happened that would forever change how I saw children and emotional wounds.

It was a seemingly perfect summer day. The trampoline, a Christmas gift we'd splurged on, had become the centerpiece of our family's outdoor fun. Our three children were bouncing together, their giggles floating on the warm breeze while I tidied up inside, grateful for the moment of peace.

Then a bloodcurdling scream shattered the calm.

My heart plummeted. While I've learned to recognize many of my children's different cries, it's Gwen who truly has the gift of discerning what each sound means. But this time, even I could tell this was real pain, and it needed immediate attention.

I dropped everything and ran outside, expecting to find blood or a broken bone. But when I reached Emmy, our youngest, at four years old, she was physically unharmed yet devastated beyond consolation. Her older siblings, Landon and Haven, had joyfully wandered off to explore something new in the yard, leaving her alone on the trampoline.

"They left me!" she sobbed, clutching her arm as though it had been hurt.

At first, I thought this was just another typical sibling squabble, the kind that dissolves with a little distraction and a snack. But something in my spirit felt a deeper nudge. This wasn't just disappointment. The intensity of her reaction signaled something more significant lurking beneath the surface.

I knelt beside her, looking into her tear-filled eyes, and asked a question that would change everything: "Did you feel hurt inside when that happened?"

With a breath that faltered midstream, Emmy nodded, her shoulders rising and falling under the quiet weight of release. She didn't have words yet for what she was feeling, but her body language spoke volumes. This wasn't just about being left on a trampoline. This was about feeling abandoned, invisible, and unimportant.

It hit me with startling clarity that my four-year-old was developing what Scripture calls a "root of bitterness" (Hebrews 12:15), a deep emotional wound that, if left unaddressed, could shape her view of herself and others for years to come.

I knew this pattern all too well. It was the same destructive root system that had nearly destroyed my own life, but I was observing it at its very beginning stage in my daughter. The revelation took my breath away: children don't just have behavioral problems; they have heart wounds. These emotional injuries, even the seemingly small ones that adults might dismiss, can take root early, influencing how they see themselves, others, and even God.

That evening, Gwen and I sat together, processing what we'd witnessed. If Emmy was already developing these deep emotional wounds at four years old, how many other children were silently carrying hurts that would shape their futures? What if we could teach children how to process emotional pain with Jesus **before** these wounds hardened into patterns that followed them into adulthood?

What if healing could begin early?

That's when the Lord impressed on my heart a simple but profound truth: **emotional wounds can be identified and healed at any age, even in the**

youngest hearts. More importantly, He began showing us how to adapt the healing principles that had saved my own life into language and practices that children could understand and embrace.

We began implementing these principles with Emmy, working gently with her to identify the hurt inside and invite Jesus into that space. What happened next was remarkable, but you'll have to read on to Chapter 23 to discover the surprising and beautiful way her healing manifested. Let's say it wasn't just emotional freedom she experienced, but an unexpected physical release as well.

This moment with Emmy became the bridge between my healing journey and what would become a mission to help children everywhere. In the weeks and months that followed, we refined these principles into nine foundational lessons, now adapted for the tender hearts of children.

Bitter roots begin early, but healing can start early, too. We don't have to wait until the

"We've called it The Bible-Heart Model, based on Jesus' promise of living waters flowing from our innermost being. Simply put, it's a straightforward way to identify, address, and release emotional pain, guiding children toward forgiveness, peace, and true identity in Christ."

damage is extensive. We can intervene at the first signs of pain, teaching our children to process hurt with Jesus instead of burying it where it grows in the dark.

That's why these nine lessons matter so much. They aren't just concepts; they're keys to freedom. They work for both adults and children, as the principles of heart healing are timeless and universal.

Let's explore them together.

PART TWO:
The Foundation

The Nine Lessons

That night when Emmy screamed on the trampoline, I had no idea I was about to uncover something that would reshape our entire family. What appeared to be a behavioral moment was actually an invitation into the kind of healing I had only dreamed was possible for children.

Some of these lessons came through my desperate prayers on bathroom floors and in hospital waiting rooms. Others emerged as I watched my children navigate their frustrations with a peace that defied their age. But all of them point to the same beautiful truth: the Jesus who heals adult hearts also heals wonderfully in tiny hearts.

The lessons progress naturally from identity to connection, from discernment to healing, and finally to fruitful living. They build upon one another, creating a pathway both for your healing journey and for guiding the children in your care.

Here's where we're headed:

FOUNDATIONS OF IDENTITY AND CONNECTION

1. Discovering Your Spiritual Core – Understanding Jesus in Us

2. Opening the Heart Connection – Learning to Quiet the Noise and Connect with God from Our Innermost Being

SPIRITUAL DISCERNMENT AND EMOTIONAL AWARENESS

3. A Tale of Two Kingdoms and God's Emotions – Recognizing the Source of Our Feelings

4. Fear's Disguise and the Voice of Peace – Exchanging Anxiety for God's Presence

5. The Battle of Thoughts and Lies – Catching Toxic Thoughts Before They Take Root

FORGIVENESS AND HEALING

6. Jesus the Forgiver – Yielding to His Forgiveness Instead of Striving in Our Strength

7. The Three Directions of Forgiveness – Releasing Others, Ourselves, and Even God

8. The Healer in the Hidden Place – Inviting Jesus into Our Deepest Hurts

LIVING FROM A WHOLE HEART

9. Fruit That Grows on the Vine – Living from Connection Rather Than Performance

The Bridge: From Our Healing to Theirs

What Gwen and I have learned is that these lessons aren't just about us; they are ultimately for the benefit of others. They are for the broken and hungry. They are for you, right now, because what flows from you will always help shape what grows in them.

FOUNDATIONS OF IDENTITY AND CONNECTION (STARTING WITHIN)

CHAPTER 3:
Finding the Secret Place

Lesson One: Discovering Your Spiritual Core

Lesson One is about discovering where true healing happens. Not in our busy thoughts or analysis, but in our spiritual core, that innermost place where God's Spirit dwells within us. When we learn to pause, feel, and yield in this sacred space, we create room for Jesus to meet us exactly where our pain lives. This lesson introduces us to the hidden sanctuary where all real transformation happens.

Before we can discuss the process of healing, we need to understand *where* it takes place. Not in our thinking, not in our reasoning, but much deeper, in what

Scripture repeatedly calls "the heart." Jesus also had a specific word for this place, too: the belly or innermost being. This isn't flowery language or metaphor; it's literally a real place that God created within you.

I've walked with countless families through the Forgiveness Flow process, and occasionally I hear concerns: "Is this too mystical or New Age? Is this biblical?" These questions come from good hearts that want to honor God. So let me take a moment to address this with humility and truth.

The practice of connecting with Jesus in your inmost place isn't a technique I invented. It's actually a rediscovery of what Scripture has been teaching all along about where God dwells and how He meets us.

The Temple Within: The Biblical Foundations of The Bible-Heart Model

Have you considered what happened when Jesus came and died on the cross for us? In a stunning shift of divine geography, God completely relocated His temple. He moved from dwelling in a physical building to making His home in the hearts of His people:

> *Do you not know that your bodies are temples of the Holy Spirit, who is in you, whom you have received from God?* – 1 Corinthians 6:19, NIV

> *For we are the temple of the living God.* – 2 Corinthians 6:16, ESV

> *God's temple is sacred, and you together are that temple.* – 1 Corinthians 3:17, NIV

Isn't that beautiful? The God who once dwelt behind a veil now lives within us. That's why Paul prayed that believers would be *"strengthened with power through his Spirit in your inner being"* (Ephesians 3:16, ESV).

This truth transforms our entire approach to emotional healing. When I guide children to place their hands on their tummies and connect with Jesus in their hearts, I'm not introducing something unfamiliar; I'm simply helping them redirect their attention to the sacred space where God already dwells. I'm inviting them to become aware of that intimate sanctuary where their spirit communes with His Spirit, where their deepest emotions find His presence waiting. This isn't a technique; it's an awakening to the reality that the God of all comfort has always been there, right where their feelings reside, ready to meet them in their tiny spirits.

Your Innermost Being

Throughout Scripture, God speaks of meeting us in our innermost being.

Praise the LORD, my soul! All my being, praise his holy name! – Psalm 103:1, GNT

The human spirit is the lamp of the LORD, searching all the innermost parts. – Proverbs 20:27, NET

"Whoever believes in me, as Scripture has said, 'Out of his heart will flow rivers of living water.'" – John 7:38, ESV

I'm struck by how often I encounter people who embody this truth. They seem to possess a spiritual steadiness, a depth and peace that remains unshaken by circumstances. When they speak, it's as if their words come from a deep well.

Every believer has a deep well within them. Most of us don't tap into it. We are simply floating on the surface of the water. The chaos of modern life keeps us in the shallow end of the pool, while Jesus awaits us in the depths. The Bible-Heart Model helps clear the clutter that crowds our spirit, guiding us back to the living presence of Jesus within.

How the Forgiveness Flow Connects with Scripture

The healing pathway I refer to as the Forgiveness Flow throughout these pages mirrors a sacred dance between our vulnerable hearts and God's presence. Let me reveal how each movement of this process finds its origins and authority directly in Scripture:

1. We Acknowledge What We Feel

The Bible never tells us to deny our emotions or pretend they don't exist. Even Jesus wept, felt anger, and experienced deep sorrow. When the Psalms say, *"Out of the depths I cry to you, O LORD"* (Psalm 130:1 ESV), they're modeling honest emotional acknowledgment.

When we help children name their feelings, "I feel sad" or "I feel scared," we're teaching them biblical emotional honesty.

2. We Yield to Jesus in Our Bible-heart

Yielding means relaxing and turning our attention toward Jesus, who dwells within us. Paul describes this beautifully when he says, *"I have been crucified with Christ. It is no longer I who live, but Christ who lives in me"* (Galatians 2:20, ESV).

This yielding isn't complicated; it's simply remembering and responding to the reality that Christ lives within us. When we yield and pray, "Jesus, I open my heart to You," we're practicing awareness of His indwelling presence.

3. We Receive His Forgiveness

Before we can truly release our pain or forgive others, we must first receive forgiveness ourselves. *"If we confess our sins, he is faithful and just to forgive us our sins and to cleanse us from all unrighteousness"* (1 John 1:9, ESV).

In the Forgiveness Flow, we pray, "Jesus, I receive Your forgiveness for holding onto this hurt." This acknowledges that clinging to painful emotions instead of bringing them to Jesus is, in itself, something we need forgiveness for.

4. We Connect Deeply with His Presence

The Bible speaks often about waiting on the Lord. *"Wait for the LORD; be strong, and let your heart take courage; wait for the LORD!"* (Psalm 27:14, ESV). This isn't empty waiting, it's expectant communion.

When we pause in the Forgiveness Flow to feel Jesus' presence in our Bible-heart, we're practicing what the psalmist described: *"Be still, and know that I am God"* (Psalm 46:10, ESV). This stillness isn't emptiness; it's filled with His presence.

5. We Release Our Pain to Him

Peter understood the power of release when he wrote, *"Casting all your anxiety on him because he cares for you"* (1 Peter 5:7 ESV). The word "cast" here is active; it's a deliberate releasing, a transfer of weight from our shoulders to His.

In our prayer flow, we say, "Jesus, I give You this hurt. I don't want to carry it anymore." This isn't magical thinking, it's biblical surrender.

The Holy Spirit helps us in this releasing process. *"The Spirit helps us in our weakness. For we do not know what to pray for as we ought, but the Spirit himself intercedes for us with groanings too deep for words"* (Romans 8:26, ESV).

6. We're Filled with His Peace

Nature abhors a vacuum, and so does our spiritual life. When we truly release our pain to Jesus, He doesn't leave that space empty; He fills it with Himself and His peace.

"Peace I leave with you; my peace I give to you. Not as the world gives do I give to you" (John 14:27, ESV). This type of filling isn't just emotional relief; it's a divine replacement.

A Gentle Experience

Connecting with Jesus in this way is a quiet experience. God doesn't overwhelm our weary souls; He meets us with tender compassion. Though we call these "supernatural graces," they don't usually come like earthquakes or lightning bolts. They come like a soft rain watering dry ground.

Your initial experiences might be subtle, perhaps a quiet sense of peace rising within, a knowing that you're loved, or an awareness that you're not alone. As you practice, these experiences often deepen and strengthen, but they remain characterized by gentleness rather than force.

Remember, "He will not crush the weakest reed or put out a flickering candle" (Isaiah 42:3, NLT). Jesus meets us with perfect gentleness, especially when we're wounded or weary.

This Is for God's Children

I'd like to pause here a minute and address something that may be stirring in your heart. This connection with Jesus, this intimate, Spirit-to-spirit communion we've been exploring, is specifically for those who have genuinely invited Jesus to come into their heart as Lord.

There's no magic in the method itself. The power lies entirely in the Person, Jesus, who makes His home within us.

When we teach children, we're guiding them in an authentic relationship, helping them experience God and learn to abide with Jesus, who dwells within them. Ultimately, we assist them in listening to and responding to His voice, paying attention to His presence, and experiencing the peace that surpasses all understanding.

If you're wondering where you stand, or if you're walking alongside children who haven't yet made that heart connection with Jesus, I really encourage you to flip ahead to the chapter called "Is That Salvation?" We will dive deeper into what it looks like for a child (or anyone) to invite Jesus in.

It's worth reading carefully, especially if you're walking alongside younger children who are just beginning their journey with Jesus.

Bringing It All Together

After years of pastoral ministry and walking families through this journey, I can tell you with absolute certainty: This isn't something new; we are simply returning to the way Jesus always intended His people to live, from the inside out, with hearts wide open to His presence.

Every time a child connects with Jesus in their Bible-heart, they're fulfilling Scripture. When they yield their pain to Him, they're living out *"Cast all your anxiety on him because he cares for you"* (1 Peter 5:7). When they receive His peace in place of fear, they're experiencing *"the peace of God, which transcends all understanding"* (Philippians 4:7, ESV).

This approach doesn't diminish the authority of Scripture. It is remembering that the Word is a Person. It's Jesus. And when we follow Him, we're not just checking off a list of "dos and don'ts." We're actually learning how to live those Biblical truths from a relational aspect. This approach doesn't make us dependent on feelings either. It simply recognizes that God designed our emotions as doorways, a pathway leading to His heart.

It's tapping into that wellspring Jesus described when He said, *"He that believeth on me, as the scripture hath said, out of his belly shall flow rivers of living water."* (John 7:38, KJV). Your gut is where fear takes refuge, where peace rises, and where life's deepest truths are planted and nurtured.

The prophet Jeremiah understood this inner realm when he wrote, *"The human heart is the most deceitful of all things, and desperately wicked. Who really knows how bad it is? But I, the LORD, search all hearts and examine secret motives."* (Jeremiah 17:9-10, NLT). This is the place where God sees us most clearly and where His healing touch transforms us most deeply.

I didn't always have clear language for this. But looking back, I recognize those pivotal moments when something changed, not just in my thinking, but in my depths. Something would change at my very core, beyond words or reason. Now I understand that was Jesus, meeting me in my innermost being.

Where Are All the Pieces of Me?

Have you ever taken a moment to wonder about your inner world? It's a bit like a puzzle, thoughts, emotions, spirit, will, and conscience, all uniquely designed and working together inside of you. But where exactly are these parts located?

If someone asked, "Where do your thoughts live?" you'd probably point to your head. That's easy. But what about emotions like love, fear, or sadness? Where do you *feel* those? The answer might surprise you.

As John Eldredge says in his book, *The Sacred Romance*:

> The truth of the gospel is intended to free us to love God and others with our whole heart. When we ignore this heart aspect of our faith and try to live out our religion solely as correct doctrine or ethics, our passion is crippled, or perverted, and the divorce of our soul from the heart purposes of God toward us is deepened.
>
> —John Eldredge, The Sacred Romance: Drawing Closer to the Heart of God[1]

The Bible-heart

This heart that we are speaking of is the seat of your spiritual sensitivity and emotions, where you feel peace or pain most deeply, and it is here that Jesus brings healing. This is the place where bitterness hides, but also where forgiveness flows.

Think of it like a lantern inside you. When it's clean, the light of God's peace shines brightly. But when pain, lies, or unforgiveness cloud the glass, the light gets dim. Jesus lives inside that lantern, inside your heart, and He's always ready to clean out what's gotten in the way.

---

1 John Eldredge and Brent Curtis, The Sacred Romance: Drawing Closer to the Heart of God (Thomas Nelson, 1997), 8.

Imagine this place as a hidden garden. Jesus is already there, waiting. He's not pacing or impatient. He's kneeling, hands in the soil, ready to pull out what doesn't belong and water what does. Some parts of the garden are cracked and dry. Some are tangled with roots from things we don't even remember. But he's not afraid of any of it. And He's not asking you to fix it, only to let Him in. That was the inner sanctuary where He met me.

It's the holy ground where connection with God transcends intellectual understanding and becomes something altogether different, something tangible, something experienced, something known in the deepest part of who we are. Here, in this tender sanctuary, the presence of the Living God becomes not just believed, but encountered.

In the chapters ahead, we'll explore how to listen to this inner dwelling place, recognize what is growing there, and let Jesus gently tend the soil. But for now, the most important thing is this:

You have a space within you where Jesus dwells. He isn't far away. He isn't waiting for you to have everything figured out by any means. In fact, He's already in the garden, waiting for you to walk with Him there.

Thoughts, Will, and Conscience: A Closer Look

Your heart holds more than just emotion. It's where your will, your conscience, and your faith live. It's the place where you say yes or no to God, where you sense His peace or conviction, and where true transformation takes place. When something doesn't feel right deep inside, that's often your conscience speaking. When you feel peace rise while connecting with Jesus, that's His Spirit meeting you in the innermost part of your being. Healing begins not by figuring everything out, but by yielding and letting Him meet you where you are.

Why Does This Location Matter?

Could you imagine trying to fix a car without knowing where the engine or brakes are located? It would be frustrating and ineffective. The same is true with our inner life. Knowing where your spiritual parts live, your heart, will, emotions, conscience, and thoughts, is essential for healing and transformation.

When you feel angry, afraid, overwhelmed, or bitter, it's not just your mind reacting; that hidden place is your **heart**. God designed this as a place of connection with Him. Proverbs 20:27 says, *"The spirit of man is the lamp of the Lord, searching all the inward parts of the belly."* God doesn't just see the surface. He lovingly searches the deep places, offering to bring light, healing, and freedom where it's most needed.

How Do I Connect to Jesus in My Bible-heart?

So, how do you connect with Jesus in this place?

I've heard some teachings say you can't, that it's too mysterious, too deep, or simply unnecessary. That we can't access that part of us. However, I've discovered something quite the opposite. In fact, over and over again, in my own life and the lives of many others, I've seen

The Bible-Heart Model isn't about behavior modification; it's about **raising wholehearted kids from the inside out.** *Transformation begins in the Bible-heart, where Jesus meets us with truth that flows outward into every aspect of life.*

that our emotions are often the gateway to a genuine connection with God. They aren't distractions to overcome; they're invitations.

Start with stillness.

Please don't force it. Just relax in your gut. Don't try to make something happen. Become aware of Jesus within you. Ask Him to draw near. Ask Him what He sees. You're not imagining it; you're becoming spiritually sensitive to His reality. His peace often begins to rise gently from within, confirming what's true: He's already with you.

This is the place where God meets the *real* you, not the polished version you present to others, but the one He's always seen and always loved since before you were knit in your mother's womb.

And that's the *heart* He's come to heal.

Now that you've found where your heart truly is and you're starting to listen from that deeper place, you might be wondering, "So...what now?"

Because naming and locating it is just the start, the real change begins when you stop pushing through the pain and instead invite Jesus into it. It's when you stop letting emotions drive the bus and start letting them lead you back to Him.

In the next chapter, we'll explore how to tell when your heart is actually open, what tends to close it off, and how to make room again for real connection with Jesus to flow.

Let's go there together.

Quick Takeaway:

- • Find somewhere quiet that you can be alone for a few minutes, and in that space, relax and place your hand on your gut.

  (Yeah, it might seem a little strange at first, but if you're willing and humble, God meets you in the simple things.)

- Say, "Jesus, help me become aware of Your presence inside me."

  Wait and notice what rises.

  Peace is often the first sign that He's already working in you.

"You're not here to force a breakthrough or fix a problem. This isn't about thinking, 'I've got to fix this kid.' The mindset is completely different. You're here to make space for Jesus to do what only He can do.'"

CHAPTER 4:
Opening the Heart Connection

Lesson Two: How to Quiet the Noise and Connect to the Wellspring Within

How Do I Connect With God in My Spirit?

This connection isn't automatic; it must be cultivated. This lesson teaches you how to slow down, quiet your inner world, and be present with Jesus in your heart. The goal isn't to teach children a technique; it's to live from personal experience so that modeling spiritual sensitivity becomes genuine.

Have you ever longed to feel closer to God, as if He were sitting right beside you, always available to listen, guide, and bring peace? The good news is, you *can*. Connecting with God isn't complicated. It's not reserved for a church service or special moment. It's something you can do at any time, in any place. We refer to this as the **heart connection**.

"Connecting to your heart is like lowering a bucket into that deep well of God's presence. When your attention turns toward Jesus, your heart opens. Peace starts to rise."

Let's face it, most of us live "up in our heads," thinking, analyzing, planning, and worrying. But God didn't create us to stay stuck there. He designed us to live from our **connection with Him**.

We'll keep returning to this truth: emotional healing begins in the spirit and the heart. As you'll see in Chapter 27, this isn't just theory. It's a Spirit-led model we regularly practice with our kids. We call it the Forgiveness Flow, and it's a simple, prayerful pathway that helps children identify their feelings, invite Jesus into them, forgive, and receive peace.

What Does It Mean to Connect to Your Heart?

When we talk about "heart connection," we mean shifting your focus from your busy thoughts to your inner spirit, your heart.

Connecting with Jesus in your heart is like lowering a bucket into that deep well of God's presence. When your attention turns to Him, your heart opens, and peace begins to rise. However, when you live distracted or caught up in thinking, it's like pulling the bucket back up; you start to feel dry, anxious, or overwhelmed.

How Do I Practice Heart Connection?

Try this simple process anytime you want to connect or reconnect:

1. **Pause** – Take a moment to stop what you're doing and quiet yourself.

2. **Close Your Eyes** – Closing your eyes can help quiet external distractions.

3. **Focus on Jesus** – Silently pray: *"Jesus."* Allow yourself to become aware of Him inside. Often, you'll notice a calm or warmth begin to rise.

This is a heart connection.

This inner sanctuary is the wellspring of your spiritual life. Authentic transformation unfolds here, not merely reshaping your thoughts, but altering the very **source** from which those thoughts emerge. Scripture captures this profound truth in Proverbs 4:23 (AMPC): *"Keep and guard your heart with all vigilance and above all that you guard, for out of it flow the springs of life."*

My wife and I have found that everything meaningful rises from this sacred place: the peace that steadies you in chaos, the discernment that guides your decisions, the authenticity that enriches your relationships, and most critically, your living awareness of God's presence. Like a hidden spring that feeds visible streams, **what happens in your heart determines what manifests in every other dimension of your life.**

Proverbs 20:5 (MSG) adds, *"Knowing what is right is like deep water in the heart; a wise person draws from the well within."* If you're spiritually thirsty, you won't be refreshed by thinking harder, obsessing over making the right choices, or sapping your time and emotional energy asking the wrong questions. You'll need to draw from the well of God's Spirit, deep within your heart.

Jesus said, *"Whoever drinks the water I give them will never thirst. Indeed, the water I give them will become in them a spring of water welling up to eternal life"* (John 4:14, NIV). Connecting to your heart is like drawing from that spring. It grounds you. It centers you. It reminds you that you are never alone.

When Should I Connect?

Short answer? All the time. This connection is not limited to just church or special devotion time. It's a way of life, a practice of returning to Jesus again and again.

You can do it anytime:

- **When you're anxious or overwhelmed**: Pause, Pray and find peace in your heart.

- **When you're angry or hurt**: Let Jesus meet you there and gently wash away the pain.

- **When you're uncertain or seeking direction**: Listen for His wisdom from within.

- **When you're joyful or thankful,** celebrate with Him in the quiet space of your heart.

Whether you're at school, work, home, or in the car, Jesus is always with you. You can reconnect with Him anytime.

I encourage you to pay attention to the changes as you connect: Do I feel calmer? More present? More aware of God's presence?

The more you practice heart connection, the more natural it becomes. Over time, you will begin to live from that place, anchored in God's peace, tuned to His voice, and aware of His love.

This heart connection isn't just a helpful tool; it's training you for a lifestyle of abiding. A new way of living from the inside.

As you learn to connect with Jesus in that place, you'll begin to notice something else: some feelings pull you closer to Him, while others try to pull you away. Let's uncover where those emotions are really coming from.

Let's Take a Heart Pause

Think of a situation right now where you feel tension, pressure, or dread.

Ask Jesus, "Am I being pushed by fear and pressure or led by Your peace?"

Let Him show you, not with shame, but with clarity.

Pay attention to how your body responds. Fear tightens. Peace settles or relaxes.

Truths to Carry with You

Connection with Jesus is simply about trusting Him and opening your heart.

- Which part of the heart connection feels most natural to you? Which part feels challenging?

- Did you notice anything inside as you read about connecting to Jesus?

- What pattern of disconnection might Jesus be inviting you to notice?

Let's Walk This Out

These questions are invitations to slow down and bring awareness to what is happening inside you.

1. What happens in you emotionally when you pause and pray before bed? Do you feel at peace, distracted, or burdened?

2. What feelings tend to build up over the day but go unspoken?

3. What would it look like to check in with Jesus each night, not as a task, but as a touchpoint?

4. How might regular heart connection change your family atmosphere over time?

Quick Takeaway:

Ask, "Jesus, is my heart open to You right now?"

Notice what rises when you open yourself in prayer.

Awareness is the beginning of transformation.

SPIRITUAL DISCERNMENT AND EMOTIONAL AWARENESS

CHAPTER 5:
A Tale of Two Kingdoms and the God Emotions

Lesson Three: Learning to Discern What's from God, and What's Not

Mark Virkler says emotions can carry healing power when they come from the Holy Spirit, and I've seen it firsthand. Peace doesn't just calm your mind; it re-roots your whole soul.

"Rather than emotions being soulish and unreliable, they are reliable when birthed by the Holy Spirit and they carry healing power."

– Mark Virkler[2]

When children are young, it's challenging to help them discern their emotions, especially if you haven't learned to recognize your own. This lesson explores the spiritual origins of emotions, both the "hell flags" and the "God emotions" such as peace, joy, and love. These serve as clues, like lights on a car's dashboard, guiding us toward what influences the soil of our hearts. If you're unfamiliar with these terms, consult the Glossary near the end of the book for a quick reference. The sooner you learn what to look for in yourself, the sooner you'll notice what's operating in your kids.

You must first learn to recognize which kingdom is influencing your inner life before you can help a child walk in spiritual clarity.

I had no idea how important emotions are in the process of enjoying life, making decisions, and experiencing God.

Until one day...

REAL LIFE STORY (JASON)

Although I felt a little rushed that day, I also felt good. The day was just right; sunny and still, as if nothing bad could ever happen. I was 19 at the time, driving my first car, a sporty red Plymouth Turismo. That little thing barely hit 55 on a good day, but I was pushing its limits. Running late for class again, with the pedal to the floor, I flew down a narrow back road that wound like a ribbon through the countryside. And then...

Two beagle pups, little hunting dogs, not more than a few months old, bounded out of the tall grass on the side of the road. It all happened in a flash, no time to stop. I remember gripping the wheel, heart slamming in my chest as I braced for the impact.

---

2 Mark Virkler, Unleashing Healing Power Through Spirit-Born Emotions (Destiny Image Publishers, 2017), 16.

Then…*thud, thud.*

With a sudden slam on the brakes, the car shrieked into a screeching halt, rubber burning into pavement. Then everything stopped. Silence.

My body reacted instantly, trembling from head to toe, like something inside me had short-circuited. My hands were locked on the steering wheel, my foot frozen. But inside? Nothing.

No rush of grief.

No gut-punch of sorrow.

Not even guilt.

Just…*nothing.*

And that was the part that haunted me the most. I had just taken the lives of two innocent puppies. I knew what had happened. My body was shaking, registering the trauma. But my emotions? Completely shut down.

And in that moment, I realized something in me had gone numb. Like profoundly, spiritually numb.

I wasn't okay. And I knew I couldn't stay like that.

The truth was, I had been on medication for anxiety and depression for a while by that point. At first, it had felt like relief, a way to dull the chaos I didn't know how to process. But what I didn't see coming was how those meds didn't just mute my pain, they muted *me.*

I had been walking around emotionally sedated, unable to cry, unable to feel, disconnected from both sorrow and joy. And it took the death of two tiny beagle pups on a country road in the bright morning sun to wake me up to what I'd lost.

Right then and there, I made the decision: I'd rather feel everything, even the hard stuff, than feel nothing at all. I went cold turkey off the medication. Not because I had it all figured out, but because I knew I couldn't keep living detached from the part of me that God created to feel.

That was the moment I began to understand: *Emotions matter.*

They aren't weaknesses. There was wisdom in taking heed to their nature.

They aren't flaws. They're flags.

They're not meant to control us, but they're definitely not meant to be buried, either.

Our emotions, when surrendered to the Holy Spirit, become the very place where God meets us, heals us, and leads us. They help us connect with others. They guide our discernment. They teach us to rejoice, to grieve, to love deeply, and to live *fully*.

God designed our emotions to be part of our spiritual life, not separate from it.

When they're shut down or hijacked, when trauma, fear, or even well-meaning coping tools numb us, we lose more than just feeling. We lose clarity. We lose connection. We lose the beauty of being "Jesusly human," fully alive.

Lesson 3 is about learning to honor your emotions as gifts from God. Not as distractions to push down, but as signals to pay attention to. It's about discovering what I personally had to learn the hard way:

Numbing your emotions isn't the solution, because the feeling itself isn't the problem. It's a signal, a signpost pointing to something deep inside that God wants to heal.

Have you ever thought about your feelings as signals? Emotions aren't just random reactions; they're signals that tell you something important about your heart. When you feel happy, peaceful, or calm, it's a good signal. However, when you feel worried, scared, or angry, it's a warning signal that something within you needs attention.

God created your emotions as part of your inner being, where your spirit resides. However, not all feelings are the same. Some emotions come directly from God's Spirit; these are Spirit-born emotions, "God emotions." Others arise from unsanctified places within us that are still hurt, afraid, or stuck. Understanding the difference can help you live with more peace and joy.

Recognizing God Emotions. The Bible describes the special kind of emotions that come from God as the "Fruit of the Spirit." In Galatians 5:22-23

(BSB), it says, *"But the fruit of the Spirit is love, joy, peace, patience, kindness, goodness, faithfulness, gentleness, and self-control."* These emotions aren't just ordinary feelings. They come from God, flowing from His Spirit into your heart.

Think of these as the fruit, or result, of guarding your heart connection (abiding). Think about a time when you felt peaceful when everything around you was stressful or chaotic. Or maybe you experienced unexpected joy even when things weren't going perfectly. Those emotions weren't coming from your circumstances; they came directly from God.

Why Do God Emotions Matter?

God emotions matter because they are signs that your heart is open and connected to Jesus. When your heart is soft and fully yielded to Him, His peace, love, and joy begin to flow naturally from within. These emotions are more than feelings; they're evidence that Jesus is reigning in your inner world.

> Jesus said, *"Peace I leave with you; My [own] peace I now give and bequeath to you. Not as the world gives do I give to you. Do not let your hearts be troubled, neither let them be afraid"* (John 14:27, AMPC).

When God emotions are present, like peace in the middle of a storm or joy that rises for no reason, it means your heart is resting in His presence. Your heart becomes a peaceful place where His Spirit is welcome and active. And when His love rules there, fear, anger, and chaos begin to melt away.

The Difference Between God Emotions and Natural Emotions. We all experience natural emotions, such as happiness when good things happen, sadness when things don't go our way, or anger when someone hurts us. These feelings aren't wrong; they're part of being human. However, natural emotions depend heavily on what is happening around us. God emotions, on the other hand, don't depend on your circumstances. They rely only on your connection to God.

Pause with Me for a Moment

Take a few minutes and name one strong emotion you've been feeling lately.

Is it frustration? Anxiety? Peace?

Now ask Jesus quietly:

"Where is this coming from? Is this emotion from you, or from somewhere else?"

Don't overanalyze it. Just listen for what rises in your spirit.

Imagine a boat on stormy seas. Natural emotions are like the waves tossing you around. God emotions are like a steady anchor, keeping your heart peaceful and stable no matter what's happening around you.

How Can I Express More God Emotions?

Having more God emotions starts with awareness and connection. The more you intentionally practice connecting your heart to Jesus, the more you'll experience His love, peace, and joy flowing through you.

Each time you pause, stop and focus on Jesus inside, you're allowing His Spirit to fill you with these God emotions.

Ministry Practice: Experiencing God Emotions

1. Pause and Notice: When you feel stressed, afraid, angry, or upset, pause to take a moment to notice. Notice that feeling in your heart.

2. Connect to Jesus: Quietly pray, "Jesus, I give You this feeling. Come fill me with Your peace."

3. Feel the Shift: Wait quietly and notice how your emotions begin to change.

4. Thank Him: Once you feel His presence filling you, thank Jesus.

Practice this throughout your day. Soon you'll notice God emotions aren't just occasional, they become your new normal.

Growing in God Emotions. Just like fruit grows on healthy trees, God emotions grow in a healthy, connected heart. Jesus said, *"I am the vine; you are* *the branches. If you remain in Me and I in you, you will bear much fruit; apart from Me you can do nothing"* (John 15:5, NIV).

Stay connected to Jesus and you'll experience more of His love, joy, and peace each day.

A Tale of Two Kingdoms – Where Your Emotions Come From

When we ask a classroom of young children where yucky feelings come from, the answer, more often than not, is a resounding: "The devil!!!" And honestly? They're not wrong. Their sweet simplicity has surprising depth.

When Emotions Got Hijacked: The Fall's Dual Impact

When Adam and Eve's emotions were hijacked, something profound changed, not just in their behavior, but in the imprints they would leave on future generations. The heartprints formed in Eden were meant to be impressions of perfect love, security, and connection. But after the Fall, humanity began creating heartprints of fear, shame, and isolation instead. **Something devastating happened**: their emotions got hijacked.

Satan didn't just steal their innocence; he hijacked their emotional wiring.

From that moment on, emotions that were created to connect us to God and one another became distorted. This is what we call *the fall's dual impact*:

- **First**, it broke our *vertical connection*, our intimate, spirit-to-Spirit relationship with God.

  "I was afraid, so I hid." – Genesis 3:10

  Fear, guilt, and shame rushed in like a flood, replacing peace, joy, and love.

- **Second**, it broke our *horizontal connection*, our love and unity with each other.

"The woman You gave me…" – Genesis 3:12

Blame, anger, comparison, and isolation spread like a disease.

Satan introduced a counterfeit kingdom, a system where emotions like fear, anger, lust, and shame rule the heart like false kings. These are not just "bad behaviors," they are **evidence of a different ruler.**

But here's the truth:

> *"The thief comes only to steal and kill and destroy. I came that they may have life and have it abundantly."* – John 10:10, ESV

Jesus came to restore our emotions, not just to make us behave better, but to reconnect us *spirit-to-Spirit* so that we could once again live from peace, not panic; from love, not lack.

When you feel a knotted, raw, or painful emotion rising, it's not proof that you're a bad kid or a bad parent. It's proof that somewhere, the enemy is trying to hijack the throne of your heart. However, the good news is that Jesus lives in you. And He's not scared of messy feelings.

He wants to be invited in, not to condemn, but to *heal.*

> *"He has sent me to bind up the brokenhearted…to proclaim liberty to the captives."* – Isaiah 61:1, ESV

What we need to focus on is not just whether emotions are good or bad, but rather the source or authority from which they come. Which kingdom are they rooted in? What spiritual atmosphere do they invite?

In this lesson, we will explore a foundational concept of our Bitter Roots teaching: the tale of two kingdoms. One is ruled by love, peace, and righteousness; this is God's Kingdom. The other is ruled by fear, guilt, anger, and shame; this is the devil's counterfeit kingdom. Your emotions help you discern the difference.

Two Kingdoms, Two Flags. Imagine your heart like a castle. Every time you feel something deeply, especially tough emotions like fear, anger, jealousy, or shame, it's like a flag goes up. That flag says, "Somebody is ruling here."

When Jesus is ruling, the Fruit of the Spirit waves over your life: love, joy, peace, patience, kindness, goodness, faithfulness, gentleness, and self-control. These are Kingdom Emotions. They flow from your connection with Jesus in your innermost being.

But when the enemy's influence sneaks in, through wounds, lies, or bitter roots, you might feel the "Hell Flags".

These toxic emotions wave like warning flags from the other kingdom. Not because you're bad, but because they point to something out of alignment with God's original design.

These emotional signals or "hell flags" aren't simply psychological terms; they're supported throughout Scripture.

"THE HELL FLAGS ACRONYM"

Letter	Toxic Emotion/Inner State	Scripture Exposing Truth (ESV)
H	Hurt – unhealed wounds	*He heals the broken-hearted and binds up their wounds* (Psalm 147:3).
E	Envy – corrosive comparison	*For where envy and selfish ambition exist, there will be disorder and every vile practice* (James 3:16).
L	Loneliness – feeling abandoned/ unseen	*Turn to me and be gracious to me, for I am lonely and afflicted* (Psalm 25:16). *God sets the lonely in families* (Psalm 68:6).
L	Loathing – self-hatred/ self-disgust	*They shall loathe themselves for the evils they have committed* (Ezekiel 6:9). *I praise You, for I am fearfully and wonderfully made* (Psalm 139:14).
F	Fear – paralyzing dread	*God has not given us the spirit of fear* (2 Timothy 1:7).
L	Lust – craving that consumes (adults), too much want (kids)	*Abstain from fleshly lusts which wage war against the soul* (1 Peter 2:11).
A	Anger – unchecked rage	*Human anger does not produce the righteousness God desires* (James 1:20).

| G | Guilt – unresolved conviction | *When I kept silent, my bones wasted away... then You forgave the guilt of my sin* (Psalm 32:3-5). |
| S | Shame – toxic identity | *Anyone who believes in Him will never be put to shame* (Romans 10:11). |

"For God has not given us a spirit of fear, but of power and of love and of a sound mind."

– 2 Timothy 1:7 (NKJV)

When these banners start waving inside, it's not condemnation; it's an open invitation for Jesus to heal the very place that hurts.

Where Did the Hell Flags Come From? Let's go back to Genesis 3. Before the fall, Adam and Eve were emotionally whole. They walked with God without fear or shame. But the moment sin entered the world, everything changed:

- Fear: "I was afraid, so I hid" (Genesis 3:10).

- Shame: "They realized they were naked" (Genesis 3:7).

- Guilt: "...so they sewed fig leaves together to cover themselves" (Genesis 3:7).

- Blame: No one took responsibility.

- Despair: Driven out of Eden and out of God's presence.

These were the first hell flags, and the beginning of a spiritual cancer that infected their children and generations to come.

But God didn't leave us there, did He? He promised restoration. He gave us the Kingdom of His Son. And He made a way for us to exchange those hell flags for the fruit of His Spirit.

God Emotions: *"But the fruit of the Spirit is love, joy, peace, patience, kindness, goodness, faithfulness, gentleness, self-control; against such things there is no law."* – Galatians 5:22-23, NASB

These emotions grow in your heart when you're connected with Jesus. They aren't forced. You don't strive for peace, you receive it. You don't pretend to be joyful, you yield to the joy bubbling up from within.

The fruit of the Spirit creates entirely different heartprints on a child's soul. When we parent from love, joy, peace, patience, kindness, goodness, faithfulness, gentleness, and self-control, we leave impressions that connect children to their true identity and purpose. These Kingdom heartprints become anchors of truth that bitter roots cannot easily penetrate.

The Great Exchange

We don't pretend our emotions don't exist. We don't tell kids "you're over-reacting" or "just stop feeling that way."

Instead, we teach them to bring every emotion to Jesus. To yield their heart to Him. And He makes a divine exchange: From yuck to peace.

This is the lifestyle of emotional healing, Spirit-led, not self-managed

Through Jesus, we have access to the *original design,* the restoration of our emotions, our identity, and our relationships. He didn't just come to save your soul; He came to heal your heart, your feelings, and your connection to both God and others.

Through the Holy Spirit, we begin to experience a new kind of emotional reality. Not one dictated by circumstance or past wounds, but one rooted in God's presence.

"The fruit of the Spirit is love, joy, peace…" (Galatians 5:22)

These aren't just good traits; they're *evidence of the Kingdom inside you.* They're the natural outcome when Jesus reigns over your heart. And when the enemy's lies or old emotional reactions flare up, we don't panic. We don't hide.

We pause and pray. We invite Jesus in. And He trades the hell flag for a Kingdom one.

Because in God's Kingdom, fear becomes peace. Guilt becomes goodness. Sorrow becomes joy. And love always wins.

Teaching Tip for Parents & Leaders

Every emotion tells a story, but not every story is true. Help kids learn to trace the flag back to the root.

Ask:

- "Did something happen that made you feel that way?"
- "Is there someone you need to forgive?"
- "Do you want to give this feeling to Jesus now?"

Emotions don't need to be punished, dismissed, or ignored. They're *invited* as an opportunity for healing.

Prayer for Families and Teachers:

Heavenly Father, we invite You into our hearts, our homes, and our classrooms. Help us notice the flags that fly over our emotions. Give us eyes to see which kingdom is ruling in each moment. Thank You for the Holy Spirit, who produces the beautiful fruit of Your Kingdom in us.

When hurt rises, help us run to You. When fear creeps in, let us feel Your peace. When anger flares, teach us to pause and yield. When guilt whispers, remind us of Your forgiveness. When shame tries to define us, restore our identity in You.

Please help us raise children who don't perform, but process. Who yield their hearts, not harden them. Those who live by Your Spirit and carry Your presence.

In Jesus' name, amen.

God's emotions bring peace to your heart, but sometimes fear tries to come back in. What do you do when the scary feelings return?

Quick Takeaway:

- Ask: "Is what I'm feeling rooted in God's Love, or something else?"
- Use your emotions as signals.
- Real discernment begins in the heart.

CHAPTER 6:
Fear's Disguise and the Voice of Peace

Lesson Four: Scary Things

Fear often hides under logic, protection, or responsibility. This lesson is about learning to spot fear when it's in disguise and how Jesus teaches us a better way. Before you can lead a child through fear, you must learn to spot how fear disguises itself in your own heart and let Christ speak peace into it.

Fear and I go way back.

By the time I reached the age of eight, I began experiencing night terrors so intense that they bled into my waking life. I'm talking vivid, paralyzing dreams, creatures, shadows, and demonic figures so real that even in daylight, I felt as if I were being watched. I couldn't shake the fear that something dark was always lurking just around the corner. I lived in fear, not just of what I saw in the night, but of what I *might* see.

That's how I learned fear. Not in theory, but in full color, full volume, with no off switch.

So when I talk about how this lesson changed my life, I don't teach it as theory.

I'm not just talking about fear of failure or fear of people. I mean the kind of fear that wraps around your spirit and starts trying to write your story for you. The type that blends in, until you think it *belongs* in you.

But the Holy Spirit, gentle as He is, took me back.

Back to the first open doors.

Back to the fear of the unknown, the fear of man, the spiritual fear that twisted truth into torment.

And piece by piece, He pulled it out, not by force, but by the presence of His loving nature.

This chapter is all about that exchange.

We're not just talking about fear, we're pulling off its mask so we can deal with what's really underneath.

When Jesus speaks peace, fear doesn't just get less intimidating; it runs.

What Do I Do When I Feel Afraid?

Fear can often feel really big. Sometimes it sneaks in quietly, and other times it sounds like thunder. It might show up when something unexpected happens, when you're alone, or when your mind starts imagining the worst. The good news is, **fear is not your ruler.**

"I opened the door to jump out of a moving car because the fear and emotional chaos felt like too much. That moment woke me up to the reality that fear had become my master."

Believe it or not, our inner sanctuary is meant to be filled with peace. However, when fear tries to take over, it pushes peace aside and makes itself feel loud, almost vital. That's why learning how to respond from your heart instead of your panic is crucial. Jesus wants to give you His peace that settles you from the inside out.

Where Does Fear Come From?

Fear doesn't wait for facts. It loves to fill in the blanks with the worst-case scenario. Sometimes fear is triggered by past experiences. Other times, the enemy whispers lies to make you feel unsafe or unloved. But fear is not from God.

2 Timothy 1:7 (AMPC) tells us, *"For God did not give us a spirit of timidity (of cowardice, of craven and cringing and fawning fear), but [He has given us a spirit] of power and love and calm and well-balanced mind and discipline and self-control."*

If fear didn't come from God, then we don't have to keep it. We can bring it to Jesus and trade it for peace.

How Can I Tell If Fear Is Trying to Sneak In?

Fear wears different disguises:

- Worry about the future.

- Anxiety over what people think.

- Dread of something going wrong.

- A deep unease you can't explain.

- Feeling stuck, frozen, or panicked.

"When fear rises, it's a signal, not a sentence. It's your cue to return to your Bible-heart and invite Jesus to take the lead."

Pause with Me for a Moment

Think of a situation right now where you feel tension, pressure, or dread.

Ask Jesus, "Am I being led by fear or by Your peace?"

Let Him show you, not with shame, but with clarity.

Pay attention to how your body responds. Fear tightens. Peace settles.

When you notice those feelings rising, you don't need to panic. You can open your heart and pray, *"Jesus, I feel fear trying to take over, but I know You are here.*

Help me not to suck it into my heart and own it. And if I already have, I receive your forgiveness, come wash it out with Your love."

Jesus doesn't expect you to handle fear on your own. He promises to be your peace.

"Peace I leave with you, My peace I give to you; not as the world gives do I give to you. Let not your heart be troubled, neither let it be afraid." – John 14:27, NKJV

(GWEN)

I wanted to pause and add this note because I think some of you may need to hear it. Fear doesn't always show up loud or obvious in kids. Sometimes, it hides behind control. I've seen children get locked into routines, needing everything "just right," or melting down over small changes. At first glance, it might look like they're just picky or strong-willed, but more often than not, it's fear wearing a disguise.

Somewhere along the way, something disturbed their sense of safety. Instead of bringing that fear to Jesus, they built little systems to prevent the scary thing from ever happening again. The heartbreaking part is that those systems don't actually make them feel safe, just in control. However, control is a poor substitute for peace.

What's fascinating is how clearly Jesus addressed this disguise of fear. He didn't say, "Control more things to feel secure." He said, *"Peace I leave with you"* (John 14:27). The antidote to control isn't more control, it's peace. When we help children connect with Jesus in their hearts and receive His peace where fear once ruled, the need to control will naturally start to fade.

I've witnessed children who once needed everything "just so" gradually relax into trust as they learn to trade their fear for His peace. The rigid behaviors don't need to be managed; they need to be replaced by an encounter with the Prince of Peace Himself.

What Should I Do When I Feel Fear?

When fear rises, it's a signal; it's your cue to return to your heart and invite Jesus to take the lead. Sound too simple? I thought so too at first! But I've watched countless children (and grown-ups too!) experience what the Bible promises: *"Perfect love casts out fear"* (1 John 4:18, NKJV). Not everyone experiences it the same way, but for many of us, when we surrender our fear to Jesus, what happens in us is beautiful.

Prayer Steps for Overcoming Fear:

1. **Pause and Acknowledge** – Place your attention on Jesus inside you. Say, *"Jesus, I feel afraid. I bring this fear to You."*

2. **Feel and Identify** – Ask, *"Where is this fear coming from? Is there a memory, lie, or situation behind it?"* Let Jesus show you.

3. **Invite Jesus Into It** – Open your heart to Him and say, *"Jesus, I invite You into this fear. I don't want it to stay in me any longer."*

4. **Release It** – *"I give this to You. Wash it away with Your Love and Forgiveness."*

5. **Receive Peace** – *Patiently wait in His presence until you feel His peace.*

Fear May Knock, But Peace Can Answer the Door

You might still feel fear try to return.

And you will.

That doesn't mean you failed. It just means it's time to resist or reconnect. Over time, your spirit gets stronger and your heart learns to respond with peace rather than panic.

Each time you choose peace, you're building a new habit, a heart that stays rooted in love, not ruled by fear.

Isaiah 41:10 (AMPC) encourages us: *"Fear not [there is nothing to fear], for I am with you; do not look around you in terror and be dismayed, for I am your God."*

Jesus is not just near; you are safe in Him. Even when your surroundings feel uncertain, your heart can remain steady and at rest.

Anchoring in Peace

I personally find it helpful to ask the Holy Spirit for anything that has brought fear, and create a list in my journal of things that tend to trigger it. Don't allow yourself to get overwhelmed by this; simply take one fear at a time, bring them to Jesus using the prayer steps above, making sure peace is the witness to the healing. Then write down what He gives you in return: truth, peace, a picture, a word, or simply more awareness of His presence.

Repeat this practice often. Fear loses power when you shine light on it and replace it with love.

Peace is the birthright of the new-creation you. It's the atmosphere of your heart when Jesus is in charge. And He always is, when you allow Him to be.

You don't have to pretend you're not afraid. You need to know how to handle fear when it arises.

Let Him be the one who settles you again, right in the place fear used to live.

Truths to Carry with You

Fear never announces itself as fear; it comes disguised as protection, wisdom, or caution.

- When did you recognize fear's subtle voice as you read this chapter?
- Which fear disguises tend to trick you most easily in daily life?
- What shift happened in your heart when you considered trading fear for peace?

Let's Walk This Out

These questions invite you into honest reflection, not performance.

1. Where has fear been shaping your decisions, even if it looked like wisdom or caution?

2. What has fear stolen from your peace or your relationships?

3. What would it look like to let Jesus lead you with peace in that area?

4. If fear weren't the loudest voice in your heart, what voice would you hear instead?

Quick Takeaway:

- Ask, "Jesus, where is fear influencing my thinking or actions?"

- Notice if peace is missing.

- Where fear is present, let peace be restored.

CHAPTER 7:
The Battle of Thoughts and Lies

Lesson Five: Learning to Catch Pesky Thoughts Before They Settle In

Many adults attempt to "think their way" into healing, but this lesson reveals that thoughts are often merely surface indicators of deeper, underlying beliefs. You'll learn how to bring lies into the light and allow Jesus to replace them with truth at the heart level.

Have you ever had a thought pop into your head that surprised you, maybe something mean, worried, angry, or even just plain distracting? You didn't ask for it, but there it was. That's what we call a pesky thought.

Pesky or "intrusive" thoughts show up in everyone's life. Some are like noisy flies buzzing around your head. Others are more like sticky lies that want to settle in and make you believe them. But just because a thought lands in your mind doesn't mean it belongs to you.

You're not defined by the thoughts that pop into your head. Jesus wants to help you clear out the lies and plant something better, peace that sticks.

Where Do Pesky Thoughts Come From?

Not every thought that shows up in your mind belongs to you. Some are gentle. Some are noisy. Some seem to come out of nowhere, but each one has a source. Here are some of the most common places thoughts come from:

- Your memories and imagination
- Words others have spoken to you, or about you
- Emotions bubbling up from your innermost being
- The Holy Spirit, gently whispering God's truth to your spirit
- The enemy, sneaking in lies, fears, accusations, and false labels

That last one can be especially tricky. The enemy doesn't announce himself. He slips in with a whisper that sounds just like you. He's sneaky, he'll slip in a thought like "I'm a failure" or "I'm too much," and before you know it, you're repeating it like it came from you. His goal is simple: if he can get you to agree with the thought, the lie becomes a label, and the label starts to feel like your identity.

The Word of God teaches us something powerful: You don't have to accept everything that tries to set up camp in your mind. You don't have to let every thought move in and redecorate. Ask Jesus what gets to stay, and what needs to go.

2 Corinthians 10:5b (AMPC) says, "*We lead every thought and purpose away captive into the obedience of Christ.*" That means you can catch a thought, check it, and toss it out if it doesn't match what God says. Say "That's not me, the new creation me, that loves God and His word."

How Can I Tell if a Thought Is from God or Not?

A straightforward way to identify the source of a thought is to **check the fruit**. Every thought produces a feeling. So ask yourself: what fruit is growing from this thought?

- Does it bring peace or fear?

- Does it make me feel hopeful or hopeless?

- Does it remind me of God's love, or make me feel ashamed?

- Does it bring clarity or confusion?

God's thoughts lead to peace, love, truth, and hope. If an idea or thought is growing anxiety, bitterness, comparison, or despair, then it's not from Him, and it doesn't belong inside your heart or your mind.

What Do I Do with Pesky or False Thoughts?

Think of those nagging thoughts as little seeds or sometimes like sticky cobwebs. If you let them sit, they start to tangle your thinking or quietly take root. But the moment you bring them into the light, they begin to lose their grip. You don't need to wrestle with them or pretend they aren't there. Just bring them to Jesus. He's the one who clears the clutter and replaces it with something true, something that genuinely brings peace.

Here's a gentle way to walk through that process with Him:

1. **Notice the thought**

   Pause for a moment. Ask, *"What am I thinking right now?"* Some thoughts are quiet stowaways, you don't even realize they're there until you stop and listen.

2. **Bring it into the light**

   Say it out loud or write it down. Seeing the thought with fresh eyes often shows you just how untrue or harsh it really is.

3. **Check the fruit**

   Ask, *"What is this thought making me feel?"* Fear? Shame? Pressure? Peace? Your emotions will help reveal the root of the thought.

4. **Ask Jesus**

   Quietly ask, "Jesus, is this thought from You?" Let His Spirit respond, sometimes with peace, sometimes with a quiet sense of "No, that doesn't belong here."

5. **If it's not from Him, hand it over**

   If those thoughts don't have His nature on them, say in your heart, "Jesus, I give You this thought, this worry, this doubt. I don't want it in my heart or mind. That is not the New Creation Me."

6. **Receive the real thing**

   Now listen. Ask Him, "Jesus, what do You say instead? What is Your truth, Lord?" Often, a thought will rise up, perhaps scripture, that feels kind, freeing, peaceful, or strong. That's His voice. That's the truth He wants to plant deep inside your heart.

Don't try to come up with the truth on your own. This isn't just positive thinking. It's not about repeating a better phrase or trying to be more logical. This is spirit-to-Spirit connection, you yielding your heart to Jesus and letting Him do the deeper work. He doesn't just remove the lie, He replaces it with Living Truth that roots you in His love and brings real peace.

Common Pesky Thoughts and God's Truth

Exposing the Lie and Receiving the Truth

Some thoughts try to slip in quietly. Others shout like they own the room. But once you learn to recognize their source, their voice, you'll start noticing just how often they don't sound like Jesus at all. The good news? You don't have to wrestle with lies. You can bring them into the light, ask Jesus about them, and let His truth take root instead. The most important part about this process is this: allow the Truth to bubble up from your spirit to inform your brain, not the other way around.

Here are a few examples. Check if any of these sound familiar. You can tell they are lies because they do not align with Scripture:

- **The Lie**: *"I'm not good enough."*

  Jesus says inside: *"You are My workmanship, My masterpiece, created for good things"* (Ephesians 2:10).

- **The Lie**: *"God must be disappointed in me."*

  Jesus says inside you: *"There is no condemnation for you. You are in Me, and I've already carried your shame"* (Romans 8:1).

- **The Lie**: *"Things will never get better."*

  Jesus says inside you: *"I know the plans I have for you, plans to give you hope and a future"* (Jeremiah 29:11).

This isn't just about quoting Scripture. It's about hearing what Jesus is saying directly to your heart. During prayer, you can even create a "Lie and Truth" list together with Him. Bring the thoughts that have been weighing on you, and ask:

"Jesus, is this a lie I've been carrying, and if so, when was the very first time I heard that lie?"

You'll be surprised at how quickly He answers and how liberating it feels when the burden of the lie is replaced by His peace-filled truth. These moments are more than just mental corrections; they're holy exchanges in the quiet spaces of your heart, bubbling up from deep within.

The truth brings peace. It lifts you, even when it corrects you. Jesus doesn't shame you; He restores you.

Jesus said, *"You will know the truth, and the truth will set you free"* (John 8:32).

(GWEN)

One of the most powerful lies I've seen get planted in children's minds revolves around the concepts of achievement and acceptance. When children become hyper-focused on competing and comparing, it often signals a deeper, toxic thought: "I must *earn* approval, acceptance, and love."

This lie doesn't just appear from nowhere. Sometimes it forms after witnessing another child receive praise for an accomplishment. Other times, the enemy plants it directly, whispering that you could love them more or be proud of them if they were simply "the best" at whatever it is.

The battle against this lie isn't won through more achievement or reassurance about their performance. It's won in the heart, where Jesus speaks a different truth: "You are loved because you are Mine, not because of what you do."

I've seen children visibly transform when this truth sinks in. Their shoulders relax. Their eyes soften. The constant striving gives way to a peace that says, "I don't have to earn what's already been freely given." This isn't just positive thinking; it's the power of Truth filling a void where a lie once took up residence in the child's spirit.

Even Children Can Do This

We teach kids how to do this with a simple phrase: "Jesus, what's the truth You want me to know?" After they've forgiven someone or felt the not-good feeling leave, we help them listen with their heart for what Jesus wants to tell them. His truth then begins to fill the place that was once occupied by the lie, and the peace that follows is the evidence. It's not cerebral; it's spiritual.

Ministry Practice: Quieting the Storm

Try this practice the next time your mind feels like it's racing:

- If you can, find a quiet space and focus on Jesus in you. If it helps you focus, place your hand on your tummy.

- Pray, "Jesus, some thoughts are spinning around in my mind. I welcome Your presence into this storm."

- Name the thoughts that are bothering you and write them down. Then, in prayer, one by one, open your heart to Him and give each one to Jesus.

- After releasing them, sit still and ask, "Jesus, what are You speaking to me, what is Your Truth?"

- Write down the peaceful thoughts that bubble upward. These are treasures from the Spirit. Allow them to be written on the tablet of your heart; His nature becomes and transforms your nature.

Gwen and I practice this often. And if you do as well, I promise, whenever you feel overwhelmed, you'll start to recognize His voice more easily, and His peace will begin to show up faster.

Letting God's Peace Guard Your Mind

Philippians 4:7 (AMPC) says, *"And God's peace [shall be yours, that tranquil state of a soul assured of its salvation through Christ...]... shall garrison and mount guard over your hearts and minds in Christ Jesus."*

God's peace is like a guard standing at the doorway of your thoughts. When you stay connected to Him, He helps you filter what comes in and what needs to leave. You don't have to fear your thoughts. You need to stay close to the One who knows how to quiet the noise and bring clarity.

So remember, pesky thoughts are part of life, but they don't have to take over your mind. With Jesus inside, you have everything you need to live in truth, peace, and freedom, one pesky thought at a time.

Once you start catching those lies and bringing in truth that Jesus speaks to your heart, you're ready to go even deeper, because Jesus doesn't just clean the surface. He goes straight to the wound.

Truths to Carry with You

Sometimes thoughts sound true because we've lived with them for so long.

- Which thought patterns felt familiar in this chapter?

- Did any lie come to mind that you've agreed with, even silently?

- What did Jesus highlight or gently challenge in your thinking?

Let's Walk This Out

These questions are designed for use during quiet time with the Lord.

1. What thought has been looping in your head lately? Ask the Holy Spirit, "Where did I begin thinking this?"

2. How has that thought shaped your emotions or relationships?

3. What might Jesus be saying instead, not just to correct the thought, but to connect with your heart?

4. Can you picture what it would feel like to live from the truth He speaks over you and inside you?

Quick Takeaway:

- When a toxic or self-judging thought surfaces, pause.

- Ask, "Jesus, is this thought true according to You?"

- Let Him speak into the lie, not just to your mind, but to your spirit.

FORGIVENESS AND HEALING (JESUS AT WORK IN THE HEART)

CHAPTER 8:
Jesus the Forgiver

Lesson Six: Receiving the Forgiveness We Could Never Earn

Forgiveness isn't something we earn or muster up; it's something we let Jesus do in us and through us. He's not just the One who forgives us, He's the Forgiver who lives in us. Only Jesus can truly forgive through you. If you want to teach children to forgive well, you must first learn to do it in your own heart with Jesus as the source.

It's Co-Laboring – It's walking in step with the One who does the real work.

I once overheard an older gentleman at church talking with a younger believer who was struggling to forgive himself. It's something I've come across many times in ministry, and maybe you've felt it too, the inner wrestling that says, *"I know God forgives me, but I just can't forgive myself."*

Why is it that we're often so much harder on ourselves than we are on others?

We judge our own hearts with a harsher standard, not just because of what we've done, but because we *know* our intent. We know what was happening beneath the surface. And because of that, we carry guilt. Sometimes shame. Sometimes both. And instead of receiving grace, we feel the need to punish ourselves, to carry the weight, and prove our remorse.

But then the older gentleman asked something that stopped me in my tracks.

He looked the young man in the eyes and said,

"Do you have a problem with Jesus forgiving you?"

The young man looked puzzled. But that question lit something up inside me.

Because the truth is, *only Jesus can forgive.*

The Splinter That Wouldn't Heal

That conversation reminded me of something many of us have experienced or maybe watched happen with our own children. Picture this: a child running barefoot through the backyard on a summer afternoon steps on what feels like the world's most vicious piece of wood. A splinter, thick as a toothpick, drives deep into the soft arch of their foot.

They limp inside, tears streaming, expecting Mommy to work her usual magic with a pair of tweezers. But this splinter has other plans. It has burrowed so deeply that only the tiniest tip is visible. Every attempt to grab it just pushes it deeper. After several painful tries, Mom makes a decision that eight-year-olds everywhere do not appreciate: "We'll wait and see if your body pushes it out on its own."

For weeks, the child walks with a slight limp, favoring that foot. The skin begins to heal over the splinter, and from the outside, everything looks fine. Everyone almost forgets it's there. Almost.

But then comes the infection.

What started as a small, tender spot becomes a red, swollen, angry wound that throbs with every step. The splinter everyone learned to ignore is now impossible to live with. Mom takes one look and says, "We have to get this out *now*."

This time, there's no gentle extraction. The skin must be opened, the infection needs to be cleaned out, and finally, *finally*, that stubborn piece of wood can be removed. The relief is immediate and complete. Within days, the foot is perfectly healed. That splinter teaches us something profound about forgiveness, something many of us don't have words for until much later.

When We Try to Heal Over the Wound

You see, we often try to heal over emotional wounds the same way that a foot tries to heal over a splinter. Someone hurts us, and instead of dealing with the pain, we just...move on. We tell ourselves we're "fine." We focus on other things. We let time pass, assuming that means healing has occurred.

But just like that splinter, buried emotional pain doesn't disappear. Eventually, it begins to fester.

The hurt, the betrayal, the disappointment, it's all still there, only now it has deeper roots. And eventually, it creates an infection in the soul. Bitterness. Resentment. That dull ache that never quite goes away. We might even forget what originally caused it, but we still limp through life, favoring our wounded places.

We talk a lot about "forgiving ourselves," but without Jesus, we can't actually extract the splinter. We can't cleanse our conscience. We can't heal what we've infected. Only Jesus can do that in us and through us. We're not just referring to a mental choice or an emotional release; we're talking about divine surgery, allowing the Great Physician to tend to the wound, clean out the infection, and remove the toxic emotions. Jesus the Forgiver is doing the forgiving.

It's not something we manufacture or earn; it's something we *receive*.

Jesus already paid for it. But emotionally, many of us have never fully received or applied it. We still carry the pain, the guilt, and the self-punishment. We talk about grace as if it is ours, yet we live as though we still owe payments on it.

But when we yield to Jesus and stop trying to be our own judge, allowing Him to take that position, He brings something no self-forgiveness ever could: *His peace.*

The toxic emotions get washed out.

The guilt loses its grip.

His forgiveness doesn't just clear the record; it removes the heaviness. It makes the place inside you feel manageable again.

This lesson is about receiving that kind of forgiveness, the kind only Jesus can give. The kind that doesn't just remove sin, but restores peace to the places that have festered in turmoil for too long.

Who Helps Me Take Out the Garbage?

We've all been there, someone says or does something that hurts our feelings, leaving us feeling sad, angry, or upset inside. Those feelings can feel heavy and uncomfortable, making us feel horrible. But

"Forgiveness isn't something we achieve, it's something we yield to."

here's the really great news: you don't have to hold onto these feelings! There's Someone who can cleanse our hearts and wipe the dirt away, and that's Jesus the Forgiver.

Why Forgiveness Is So Important

Forgiveness matters because it keeps your heart free and joyful. Think about your heart as a home: if you don't regularly clean it out, things get messy and uncomfortable. The same happens when we don't forgive. All the hurt and bitterness pile up inside, making our hearts heavy. But when we forgive, it's like opening the windows and letting fresh air in. Everything feels lighter, cleaner, and better!

"And be kind to one another, tenderhearted, forgiving one another, even as God in Christ forgave you" (Ephesians 4:32, NKJV). Forgiveness sets you free to live in peace and joy.

Jesus, Your Best Helper

Choosing Jesus and Forgiveness isn't always our first response, especially when someone really hurts us. But guess what? You don't have to do it all alone. Jesus knows exactly how to forgive because He's the greatest Forgiver of all. Even when people hurt Him deeply, He chose forgiveness every time. And because He lives inside you, He'll help you forgive, too!

Colossians 2:6 (AMPC) reminds us, *"As you have therefore received Christ, [even] Jesus the Lord, [so] walk (regulate your lives and conduct yourselves) in union with and conformity to Him."* That means, just like you welcomed Jesus into your heart when you first believed, you can welcome His forgiveness power anytime you need it.

Simple Steps to Forgive from Your Heart

Forgiving with Jesus is gentle and straightforward. Here's how:

1. **Recognize and Remember**: Close your eyes and let the Holy Spirit show you the person or situation that caused the hurt.

2. **Feel and Acknowledge**: Notice how this memory makes you feel inside your heart. Maybe it's sadness, anger, or even embarrassment. That's okay, allow yourself to feel it for just a moment.

3. **Release with Jesus**: Now, invite Jesus into that feeling by silently or quietly saying, "Jesus, I open my heart, and I give you this hurt. Please forgive through me." Wait gently, and soon you'll start feeling peace in place of pain. That peace is Jesus cleaning out all the junk.

Why Letting Jesus Forgive Through You Works

Who is doing the forgiving?

Remember, forgiveness works because it's something Jesus does inside of you. He doesn't expect you to force forgiveness. Instead, He invites you to open your heart and let Him do the forgiving. Jesus knows exactly how to clean out every hurtful emotion, leaving your heart peaceful and free.

Revelation 3:20 (AMPC) beautifully explains, *"Behold, I stand at the door and knock; if anyone hears and listens to and heeds My voice and opens the door, I will come in to him."* Every time you forgive, you open your heart to Jesus, and He steps right in to replace hurt with healing.

Ministry Practice: Daily Forgiveness Moments

Let's make forgiveness easy and practical. Try doing this each day:

- **Daily Quiet Time**: Set aside a few quiet moments to give focus to what's going on inside your spirit.

- **Invite Jesus**: Softly ask, "Jesus, who do I need to forgive today?"

- **Notice and Forgive**: If a person or memory comes to mind, gently tell Jesus, "I give this to You. Help me let go and forgive completely." Feel His peace rising and Him washing you clean.

- **Gratitude**: After forgiving, thank Jesus for helping you and for making your heart feel clean and peaceful again.

Living Free and Joyful

Practicing forgiveness with Jesus regularly makes your heart a happier place. You'll begin noticing more joy, more peace, and more freedom in your relationships and daily life. Jesus promises in Matthew 11:28 (AMPC), *"Come to Me, all you who labor and are heavy-laden and overburdened, and I will cause you to rest."*

Every time you forgive, you're stepping into this beautiful rest Jesus promises. Make forgiveness your habit, and soon you'll be living lighter and freer, thoroughly enjoying the peaceful, joyful heart Jesus intended for you.

Once you realize Jesus is doing the forgiving through you, the question becomes: Who needs to be forgiven? Let's explore the three directions in which forgiveness flows.

Truths to Carry with You

Forgiveness isn't a performance; it's a partnership with Jesus inside you.

- Did a name, situation, or old memory rise up while reading?

- What emotions surfaced when you thought about forgiving?

- Did you sense Jesus nudging you toward anything specific inside?

Let's Walk This Out

These questions aren't meant to push you; they're meant to free you.

1. Who is Jesus bringing to mind that you may need to forgive?

2. What emotions have you been carrying that feel heavy or unresolved?

3. What's been keeping you from releasing that weight, fear, pain, or maybe the feeling of being justified in your emotion?

4. How might your relationships change if Jesus truly forgave through 0you instead of you trying to forgive on your own?

Quick Takeaway:

- Think of someone you've struggled to forgive.

- Say in your heart, "Jesus, I receive forgiveness from You, the Forgiver in me, for holding onto this for so long towards ___. I release forgiveness to them with You now."

- Receive His peace.

CHAPTER 9:
The Three Directions of Forgiveness

Lesson Seven: Releasing Others, Yourself, and Even God from the Heart

Most of us stop at forgiving others, but bitterness doesn't. It can turn inward, toward ourselves, or even toward God. This lesson invites you to take a closer look at forgiveness in all its aspects. And the truth is, we can't lead children somewhere we haven't been. Before guiding them through their hurts, we need to walk that road ourselves, not perfectly, but with honesty and a willing heart.

Have you ever wondered exactly who you need to forgive? Sometimes, it's clear, maybe someone said or did something hurtful, and you know right away that forgiveness is necessary. But did you know there are three essential directions for forgiveness: forgiving others, forgiving yourself, and sometimes even forgiving God? (In other words, letting go of holding unforgiveness towards Him)

I believe that understanding these three directions and why each one matters can unlock something beautiful. It's like finally cleaning out all the dusty corners of a room you love. Suddenly, there's space to breathe again. Let's walk through this together.

Forgiving Other People

This might be the most obvious one, but people can hurt us; sometimes they do so intentionally, and at other times, they do not. However, I do know one thing: holding onto anger or hurt regarding others weighs heavily on the heart. Jesus showed us the perfect example of forgiving others, even when it's tough.

Mark 11:25 (AMPC), *"And whenever you stand praying, if you have anything against anyone, forgive him and let it drop (leave it, let it go), so that your Father Who is in heaven may also forgive you your [own] failings and shortcomings."*

This may sound cliché, but forgiving others is about freeing your own heart. It means releasing yourself from the prison of bitterness and anger. It's like dropping a heavy weight you've been carrying. When you let go, it feels like your heart has room to breathe again, and peace starts to return.

Forgiving Yourself

> *"I believed I was unworthy of love, so I tolerated abuse. I feared abandonment, so I let myself be controlled... I had to forgive myself for believing those lies." – Caught in a Trap*

Have you ever felt disappointed in yourself? Maybe you made a mistake or said something you wish you hadn't. Sometimes, forgiving yourself can be the hardest thing to do, but it's just as important as forgiving others.

Remember, Jesus has already forgiven you completely. Ephesians 1:7 (AMPC) *"In Him we have redemption (deliverance and salvation) through His blood, the remission (forgiveness) of our offenses (shortcomings and trespasses), in accordance with the riches and the generosity of His gracious favor."*

When you forgive yourself, you're essentially accepting and applying the forgiveness Jesus has already given you. It means letting His love speak louder than your past mistakes. When you release guilt and shame, you're making space for His peace to flow freely and receiving the transformative truth that you are deeply loved by Him.

Forgiving God (When You Feel Hurt or Disappointed – Holding onto Unforgiveness Towards God)

Sometimes our hearts hold onto disappointment, unforgiveness or even anger toward God. Maybe something didn't go the way you wanted, or prayers didn't seem to get answered the way you'd hoped. Even though God never makes mistakes, our human hearts sometimes blame Him when we're hurting and don't understand.

Forgiving God doesn't mean He did something wrong; it means you're letting go of your disappointment and trusting His perfect love again. Luke 6:37 (AMPC) gently reminds us, *"Judge not [neither pronouncing judgment nor subjecting to censure], and you will not be judged; do not condemn and pronounce guilty, and you will not be condemned and pronounced guilty; acquit and forgive and release (give up resentment, let it drop), and you will be acquitted and forgiven and released."*

Letting go of disappointment or judgments toward God means releasing your expectations into His loving care. It's trusting that even when life feels confusing, His plans for you are always good.

Living Freely in Forgiveness

Making forgiveness a daily ritual is like daily cleaning for your heart. It maintains healthy relationships, a peaceful heart, and a life filled with joy. By the grace of God, Gwen and I live this out each day. Not perfectly, but a lifestyle of forgiveness in marriage and family is what keeps us strong and united during life's storms and circumstances.

I highly recommend practicing this type of forgiveness. Every time you forgive, whether it's others, yourself, or letting go of disappointment toward God, you open your heart wider for Jesus' love to flow through you. You'll notice your heart feels lighter, your relationships feel warmer, and your connection to God grows stronger every day.

Truths to Carry with You

Forgiveness isn't just horizontal, it's personal. And sometimes, it's pointed inward.

- As you read, did you notice any resistance, especially when it came to forgiving yourself?

- Did you feel a shift in how you see God, or how you think He sees you?

- Was there a phrase or moment that seemed to stick with you?

Let's Walk This Out

These are invitations to deeper peace.

1. Is there someone you've forgiven in word and deed, but not yet in your heart?

2. What have you struggled to release yourself from?

3. Have you been holding God at a distance because of disappointment or confusion?

4. What would it sound like to say, "Jesus, I release You from the blame I've been holding?"

Quick Takeaway:

- Ask, "Jesus, show me who I need to forgive, including myself or You?"

- Connection to Jesus helps you forgive from your heart.

- Invite His peace to fill the places where pain lived.

CHAPTER 10:
The Healer in the Hidden Place

Lesson Eight: Letting Jesus Mend the Deepest Parts
of Your Heart

Some of the hurts that affect you most are the ones you don't even remember clearly. This lesson teaches you how to invite Jesus to reveal and heal the hidden areas of your heart. Kids don't just hear what you say, they absorb what you carry. When you're healed, it permits them to be free too.

Imagine having someone who truly knows you, who knows your heart, emotions, thoughts, and spirit. Someone who isn't just wise, but also gentle, kind, and always available. That's who Jesus is: the Healer of hearts. As Scripture reveals, *"He heals the brokenhearted and binds up their wounds"* (Psalm 147:3, NIV).

While we each may experience His healing presence in different ways, Jesus faithfully meets us where we are and invites us into deeper wholeness.

We call Him our Healer because He goes after the stuff no one else can see, the pain buried deep in our hearts. The memories that still sting. The emotions that come up when you least expect them. He already knows where it hurts, and He's just waiting for you to let Him in so He can start washing it out.

This is spoken again by Jesus in Luke 4:18, *"The Spirit of the Lord [is] upon Me... He has sent Me to announce release to the captives and recovery of sight to the blind, to send forth as delivered those who are oppressed [who are downtrodden, bruised, crushed, and broken down by calamity]."*

He's still doing it, freeing hearts, helping us see clearly again, and putting His hands on the areas we didn't think could be healed. And He wants to do it in you, as well.

How Does Jesus Heal the Heart?

Jesus heals in partnership with your spirit. He doesn't force healing; He invites it. Healing often begins when we come into His presence with our hearts open. As James 4:8 reminds us, *"Draw near to God and He will draw near to you"* (NKJV).

> *"Jesus doesn't just fix behavior, He heals the heart by 'taking our pain and sorrow'."*

Many believers find that when they become still before the Lord, He brings their attention to places in need of His healing touch. Sometimes a situation rises to the surface; other times a person, but there is always an emotion tied to these, and that is what He wants to bring healing to. Scripture reminds us that the Holy Spirit *"will guide you into all truth"* (John 16:13, NKJV), and that God *"searches the hearts"* (Romans 8:27, NKJV). In His wisdom, Jesus may reveal what needs healing in different ways, but in our experience, memory, and emotion arrive bundled together.

And Jesus, ever the compassionate Healer, always begins with the emotion. He meets us right where the pain is, whether it's fear, sadness, shame, or anything else, and works from the inside out.

Here's what often happens:

1. **You feel something uncomfortable**, hurt, sadness, fear, or anger.
2. **You pause** and bring that feeling to Jesus.
3. **You ask**, "Where did this come from, Jesus?"
4. **He shows you a memory or a moment** from the past.
5. **You feel it with Him, not alone.**
6. **You forgive, or repent, or release the hurt.**
7. **His peace comes in.**

That's healing. It may feel small at first, but each time you let Him treat your heart, you're becoming more whole, more free, and more yourself.

You Can Trust Him With the Hard Stuff

Sometimes there are places in our hearts that feel too painful. Maybe you've even thought, "I'll deal with that later, " or "I don't want to open that box." But Jesus never rushes, never forces. He waits until you're ready, and then He walks with you into those places with kindness and care.

He's not afraid of your pain. He's already carried it.

Isaiah 53:4-5 (AMPC) says, *"Surely He has borne our griefs (sicknesses, weaknesses, and distresses) and carried our sorrows and pains...He was wounded for our transgressions, He was bruised for our guilt and iniquities...and with the stripes [that wounded] Him we are healed and made whole."*

Your healing has already been paid for. All that's left is for you to receive it, one step of surrender at a time.

"I wept in my dad's arms like a little boy. In that safe place, the little Jason inside me finally felt seen and held… That moment was the beginning of my healing."

Ministry Practice: A Healing Appointment with Jesus

Find a quiet space for prayer. If you need to, you may place your hand(s) over your gut just as a physical reminder of focusing on Jesus there, and take a gentle breath.

- Pray: "Jesus, if there's anything You want to heal in my heart today, I'm listening."

- Wait patiently. For most believers, a memory, emotion, or person may come to mind. Others might sense God's peace or receive a scripture verse. Be open to how the Holy Spirit uniquely leads you.

- If something specific arises, acknowledge it. Don't rush. Remember that *"The Lord is compassionate and gracious, slow to anger, abounding in love"* (Psalm 103:8, NIV).

- Prayerfully ask: **"Jesus, how would You have me respond to this?"**

  o You might feel led to forgive someone.

  o You might recognize a lie you've believed.

  o You might experience His comforting presence.

- Receive: After this time of prayer, thank Him for His work in your life, whether you felt something specific or simply spent time in His presence. As Scripture promises, *"You will fill me with joy in your presence"* (Psalm 16:11, NIV).

Write down anything you sense. Healing moments like this are holy ground.

Healing is a Lifestyle, Not a One-Time Event

Some healing moments happen quickly. Others are like layers. Most of the time, Jesus works one step at a time. The more time you spend with Him, the more healing flows. You'll find old fears gone and a new tenderness in how you see yourself and others.

Think of it like a daily heart check. Just as you brush your teeth to stay healthy, check in with Jesus to keep your inner sanctuary clean and strong.

And over time, you won't just be healed, you'll become a person of healing. The peace in you will become peace for others. The love Jesus fills you with will overflow into your relationships. You'll be someone who carries His presence and His nature like a light in dark places.

"Sometimes, we expect the big trauma to be the thing that shapes us. But it's the subtle stories, the whispered fears, the childhood beliefs, that dig the deepest roots. The good news? Jesus knows how to find every hiding place."

Jesus Will Always Make Time for You

You don't need to schedule an appointment or have perfectly crafted prayers. As Scripture encourages, *"Let us then approach God's throne of grace with confidence, so that we may receive mercy and find grace to help us in our time of need"* (Hebrews 4:16, NIV).

Each believer's journey with Christ is unique. Some may experience profound emotional moments, while others might find His work more subtle, through Scripture, wise counsel, or a growing sense of peace over time. What remains constant is His faithful love and commitment to our wholeness.

Today, consider opening your heart to Him again. As parents and grandparents, we are presented with daily opportunities to bring to Jesus the places that feel tired, tender, or tangled. I urge you to trust that He will work in your life according to His perfect wisdom and timing.

He's not just a Healer, He's *your* Healer.

And He's always ready to care for you, every day of your life.

When forgiveness begins to flow, something beautiful begins to grow in its place. Let's discover what the fruit of the Spirit looks like in your heart.

Truths to Carry with You

Sometimes our deepest wounds are the ones we've learned to ignore, manage, or cope with rather than heal.

- Which parts of the healing journey described in this chapter resonated most?

- Did you sense Jesus inviting you toward any specific memory or emotion?

- How does the thought of Jesus entering your hidden places make you feel?

Let's Walk This Out

Let these questions walk you back into places you've maybe avoided, this time, with Jesus leading.

1. Is there a memory or experience you've never really talked to Jesus about?

2. When you think of that place, what emotion rises first: fear, shame, grief, or numbness?

3. What would it mean to invite Jesus into that feeling instead of managing it alone?

4. Can you imagine what healing might begin to look like, not overnight, but from within?

Quick Takeaway:

- Ask Jesus, "Is there a hidden hurt You want to heal in me today?"

- Let Him bring it up, not to shame you, but to free you.

- Permit Him to go deep.

LIVING FROM A FRUITFUL HEART

CHAPTER 11:
Fruit That Grows on the Vine

Lesson Nine: How God Emotions Take Root When You Stay Connected

Healing is not the end goal; transformation is. This final lesson reminds you that the quiet garden of your heart was made to grow the fruit of the Spirit. A parent or leader who models peace, joy, and patience from within becomes a living example of Kingdom life. And fruit that grows in you will nourish others.

Have you ever seen a tree filled with good, sweet fruit? It didn't grow overnight. That fruit developed over time because the tree was healthy, rooted, and connected to water and sunlight. Similarly, your heart grows fruit, but not apples or oranges, of course. You produce the fruit of the Spirit when your heart remains connected to Jesus!

Galatians 5:22–23 (AMPC) tells us exactly what this fruit looks like: *"But the fruit of the [Holy] Spirit [the work which His presence within accomplishes] is love, joy (gladness), peace, patience (an even temper, forbearance), kindness, goodness (benevolence), faithfulness, gentleness (meekness, humility), self-control (self-restraint)."*

These God-emotions aren't something you can force or manufacture through willpower. They're more like fruit on a healthy tree; they grow naturally with deep roots and strong connections. When Jesus is truly at home in your heart, His nature starts flowing through you into every relationship, every conversation, every moment of your day.

Imagine a tree planted by streams of water. It doesn't strain to produce fruit; it simply does so because it's connected to life itself. That's what happens when you stay connected to Jesus. His love, His peace, His joy—these begin to manifest in you, not because you're trying harder, but because you're abiding deeper. You become a fruitful tree, growing something beautiful simply because of who you're connected to.

What Kind of Fruit Is Growing in You?

Take a short pause with me here. What's been growing in your heart lately? Do you notice peace or worry? Joy or irritation? Love or frustration? These gentle signals indicate whether you're living in connection with the Spirit.

It's okay if you recognize some not-so-good fruit. That's just a sign that your heart may need some time soaking in God's love again. We all need regular times where we slow down, turn our attention to Jesus, and let Him refresh our hearts. The more time you spend with Jesus, the more His fruit grows in you effortlessly.

John 15:5 (AMPC) says, *"I am the Vine; you are the branches. Whoever lives in Me and I in him bears much (abundant) fruit. However, apart from Me [cut off from vital union with Me], you can do nothing."* Jesus is the Vine. You're the branch. Stay close to Him, and good fruit is guaranteed!

What Grows in You Shapes What Grows Around You

Growing fruit is about staying rooted and connected to the Vine. Trying to force kindness without connection is like scotch-taping apples to a branch; it looks suitable for a minute, but it won't last. The only way the fruit of the Spirit grows is when your heart stays open and connected to the presence of Jesus inside.

We may have explored this concept earlier, but let's revisit it with fresh eyes. Imagine your heart as a secret garden entrusted to your care. When you spend time with Jesus, whether through whispered prayers, songs of worship, moments of forgiveness, or simply resting in His embrace, He tends to this hidden place with living water. Like a garden soaking in early rain, your spirit draws in His presence quietly, sometimes without even realizing it.

Then something beautiful happens. Almost without noticing, you begin to change, peace settles where anxiety once ruled, joy bubbles up from unexpected places, and patience flows where frustration used to rule. This isn't fake-it-till-you-make-it growth. It's authentic fruit from well-watered soil.

This transformation doesn't stay hidden. This fruit is not for you. Others taste it in your words, feel it in your presence, breathe it in the very atmosphere you bring with you.

That's the mystery of abiding: what grows within you ultimately nourishes everyone around you.

Recognizing Counterfeit Fruit

Not all emotions come from the Spirit. Some feelings try to look like fruit, but they're fake. For example:

- Control is not the same as self-control.
- People-pleasing is not genuine kindness.
- Emotional numbness is not peace.
- Excitement isn't the same as real joy.

These can trick us into thinking we're doing okay, but they don't bring lasting life. Actual fruit comes from **connection**, not performance. It grows in the secret place with God, not by trying to act better in public.

So, how do you know if it's real fruit? It lasts. It brings peace. It feels like Jesus. Sometimes, as a child may say, "It feels like rainbows inside!" or "It feels like Jesus is in the room!" You can rest in it. And it blesses the people around you, too.

Ministry Practice: Fruit Check with Jesus

Here's a simple heart-check you can do with Jesus:

1. **Find a quiet moment** and shift your attention to Jesus in your heart.

2. **Once you feel the Heart connection**, ask, "Jesus, what kind of fruit is growing in my heart right now?"

3. **Listen and Notice**: Do any of the fruits of the Spirit come up? Do you feel peace? Joy? Patience? Or do you notice anxiety, anger, or stress?

4. **If something bad comes up**, pause and release it to Jesus: "Jesus, I give You this emotion. Please wash it out and fill me with the Fruit of Your Nature."

5. **Wait in His presence** and let the fruit of His Spirit rise again in your heart. It's not forced. It flows.

Try this every day for a week. You'll begin to notice what grows in your heart more easily and how quickly Jesus responds to fill you up with good fruit.

---

*"It wasn't just Lana, I was bound by the bitter roots I'd never dealt with. Once those roots were pulled up, I didn't have to 'try' to be joyful or kind anymore... it started flowing naturally from deep inside." (**paraphrased**)*

Becoming a Tree of Life

As you grow in staying connected to Jesus, you'll become like a tree of life for others, too. Proverbs 11:30 says, *"The fruit of the [uncompromisingly] righteous is a tree of life."* You'll carry God's emotions into your family, school, workplace, and friendships. People will feel safer, more loved, and more peaceful just being around you, not because of you, but because of Jesus flowing through you.

So don't stress or feel guilty if your garden needs a little tending (or a lot). Jesus is the best Gardener. He's not in a rush. He's gentle, patient, and full of joy in growing good things in your heart. He can make GREAT things grow up from the "soil" of our past mistakes!

Keep your heart open, stay connected, and let the fruit grow. One day, you'll look back and be amazed at how much sweeter your life has become, not because you tried harder, but because you allowed Jesus to love you well. This lifestyle produces fruit. These emotions are evidence that Jesus is ruling in their Bible-heart, and they become a tree of life for others.

Stay planted, peaceful, and keep growing!

What Jesus taught me through my healing journey is not just for adults who have carried wounds for decades. These same principles work powerfully in the tender hearts of children, preventing bitter roots from distorting their identity and destiny.

> "The most important focus for a healthy world is healthy families who are producing healthy children who become healthy leaders at the decision centers of culture and equip their children to do the same."
>
> – Dr. Randall Bixby[3]

---

3 Dr. Randall Bixby, *The Family Legacy – Shaping Culture from the Inside Out: How to Lead Your Family, Live Your Legacy, and Shape Culture in the Process* (Best Seller Publishing, 2019), 11.

Truths to Carry with You

You were never meant to manufacture spiritual fruit; you were meant to bear it.

- What is Jesus growing in your heart right now?

- Are there old emotions or patterns you've uprooted that have made room for something better?

- What would it look like to water that growth daily, not with striving, but with connection?

- Who around you needs the fruit He's growing in you?

Let's Walk This Out

These questions invite you to notice what's already growing, not strain to produce more.

1. Which fruit of the Spirit seems to be budding in your life currently?

2. What activities or environments help you stay most connected to the Vine?

3. Where do you notice yourself striving to produce fruit instead of receiving it?

4. Who has modeled for you what it looks like to bear fruit naturally from connection?

Quick Takeaway:

- Ask, "Jesus, what fruit are You growing in me right now?"

- Let it grow from the inside out.

- The best leaders are rooted ones.

PART THREE: The Application

CHAPTER 12:
The Children Are Worth Fighting For

Look Ahead, And Then Look at the Kids in Front of You

It's not hard to see why this matters so much, but sometimes, what holds us back isn't a lack of love.

It's fear.

> *"A father's greatest fear is usually that he won't be able to provide for his family. A mom's greatest fear is typically that something will happen to one of her children. Fear is a funny thing. It sometimes provides healthy caution, but more often than not, it seems to produce undue stress and anxiety regarding things over which we have little to no control."* – Lysa TerKeurst[4]

Fear pulls parents in every direction.

Fear keeps us up at night worrying about the "what-ifs" and what might happen, when the one thing we've actually been given to do is steward their hearts.

---

4 Lysa TerKeurst, Am I Messing Up My Kids?...and Other Questions Every Mom Asks (Harvest House Publishers, 2010), Page 97.

What if a gentle hand had guided you to that tender place within, looked you in the eyes, and simply said, "It's okay to feel this ... and Jesus is right here to help clean it out for you?" What if you'd been taught to forgive with your spirit and not just with dutiful words? How different might your teenage years have looked? Your relationships? Your quiet conversations with yourself in the mirror?

I wonder how different your story might be if someone had shown you how to bring your painful emotions to the real Jesus, not stuff them.

This isn't about guilt, shame, or blame. These moments are all about possibility, about redemption waiting just one generation away.

"This isn't about perfect parenting. It's about making room for Jesus' presence. It's about recognizing when a child's behavior signals something deeper and inviting God into the room."

What I've come to see over and over again is this: When healing is delayed, heartache doesn't stay hidden; it multiplies. It may sound simple, but it's the spiritual law of sowing and reaping in action. What's buried in pain today will grow fruit tomorrow, unless we invite Jesus in to destroy the root.

We can't go back in time, but we *can* help the next generation avoid what we never should've had to carry. We can offer them the tools we didn't get. And in doing so, we offer them more than healing; we offer them a new inheritance.

[SCIENCE SPOTLIGHT]

The patterns we've seen for years in the spiritual realm, how pain and brokenness pass down through generations, are now being confirmed by science, too.

In a fascinating study often referred to as the "Cherry Blossom Study," researchers at Emory University trained mice to fear the scent of cherry blossoms by pairing it with mild foot shocks. Remarkably, the untrained offspring of these mice exhibited fearful responses to the scent of cherry blossoms, despite never having experienced the shocks themselves. Dr. Brian Dias explains: "The experiences of a parent, even before conceiving, markedly influence the structure and function of the nervous system of their future offspring."[5]

Even more encouraging, research indicates that healing is a real phenomenon. Dr. Ann Masten's work on resilience reveals that when someone steps in with love and helps process emotional wounds, it can break the cycle of trauma.

I believe it aligns with what we've seen through The Bible-Heart Model, creating a safe place where children can bring their hurts to Jesus and let Him do what only He can do.

The next part of the book focuses on *them*, the children. But it's also about *you*, because to lead a child through healing, you must walk that path first. You can't give away what you haven't received. That's why we spent time tending to your own heart garden first. That's why we explored those nine foundational lessons. Because now… you're ready, although you may not feel ready in some cases, you are.

You're more ready than you think to walk with a hurting child, even if it feels clumsy or unsure. I personally feel awkward almost every time I do this with a young person. But that's never stopped Jesus. He shows up in every surrendered moment, even the awkward ones.

You're learning to spot bitter roots while they're still just little sprouts. You're learning to live and lead from a place of peace instead of reacting from a place of pain.

But to do that well, we need to get honest about what we're actually up against. Let's take a clear look.

---

5 Dias, Brian G., and Kerry J. Ressler. "Parental Olfactory Experience Influences Behavior and Neural Structure in Subsequent Generations." Nature Neuroscience 17, no. 1 (2014): 89-96.

Jesus Doesn't Just Forgive Sin, He Heals the Pain

(OUR SHARED PERSPECTIVE)

When we began ministering to families, we quickly saw a pattern emerge. Behind every "behavior problem" was a hurting heart. Behind every outburst and behind every anxious, angry, or avoidant child (and adult) was a bitter root quietly shaping their responses to life.

And we realized...most adults had no idea how to help their kids or themselves.

They were dealing with symptoms, not the source.

That's when we began equipping parents, teachers, and leaders to **listen beneath the behavior**, to look past the tantrum, the withdrawal, the fear, and start asking, "What bitter root might be buried here?" And more importantly, "How can I help this child meet Jesus in that place?"

> *"Yet he himself bore our sicknesses, and he carried our pains; but we in turn regarded him stricken, struck down by God, and afflicted."*
> – Isaiah 53:4 (CSB)

Because here's the key: **Jesus doesn't just fix behavior, He heals the heart by "taking our pain and sorrow."**

One of the most troubling things I've ever heard, especially after learning to live a forgiveness lifestyle and discovering the profound reality of our heart connection, was this: pastors and leaders saying things like, "You're commanded to forgive, so just do it, and live with the pain." As if white-knuckled obedience without healing is somehow what God wants. And to make matters worse, some add a fear-laced warning straight from the Bible for good measure: "If you don't forgive, your Heavenly Father won't forgive you." Biblical Truth? Yes. They tell us *what* needs to be done, but seldom seem to tell us *how* to do it. And that can cause guilt, shame, frustration, you name it...

That kind of teaching isn't just unhelpful; in fact, I have seen firsthand that it can be quite damaging.

Now, I get it. That might sound harsh. You might be thinking, "Easy for you to say, Jason. You don't know what I've been through." And you're right, I don't know your whole story. But Jesus does. I don't remember the sleepless nights, the trauma you've carried for years, or the weight of the grief that never seems to lift. Maybe you lost someone to suicide. Perhaps you buried a child. Maybe your pain has lived with you so long that it feels like part of your identity now.

There is so much pain in this world. We all carry some of it. I've tasted enough of my own to know that surface-level answers don't work. Shallow forgiveness platitudes don't bring healing. Being told to "just do it" only adds another layer of pressure to an already unbearable weight.

But that's precisely why the way Jesus taught us to forgive, from the heart, is so radical. Because it isn't about pushing through pain, it's about letting Him step into it with you.

This kind of forgiveness isn't about pretending it didn't hurt.

It's not about pushing past the grief or coping with the pain.

It's something deeper.

It's opening your heart and letting Jesus meet you there.

Letting Him feel the weight with you.

Letting Him lift what you were never meant to carry on your own.

Because no matter how deep your sorrow runs, His presence can go deeper still.

Yes, those words are in Scripture. Yes, they may even be printed in red. But what's often overlooked, almost entirely, is the tiny phrase Jesus includes in Matthew 18:35: *"from your heart."*

Those three words change everything.

This is about *yielding*, about connecting with Jesus in your heart and forgiving with Him, not just for Him. That's where the miracle happens. Because in that place of connection, I've found something astonishing again and again: Jesus doesn't just help us forgive, He takes our pain and He carries our sorrow.

Forgiveness was never meant to be a performance. It was always meant to be a partnership with grace.

Isaiah 61:1-3 (AMPC) says:

"He has sent me to bind up the brokenhearted, to proclaim liberty to the [physical and spiritual] captives… to comfort all who mourn… to give them…beauty instead of ashes, the oil of joy instead of mourning, the garment [expressive] of praise instead of a heavy, burdened, and failing spirit."

These aren't just poetic promises. They're blueprints. They show us that the gospel isn't just about salvation from sin. It's about the transformation of the *inner life*.

That's why we teach kids (and their grown-ups) how to find the painful emotion in their heart, receive the presence of Jesus the Forgiver into that area, and receive His peace. And when they do, the transformation is undeniable.

I've watched five-year-olds pray through memories of being left out and walk away with joy. I've watched ten-year-olds forgive an absent parent and breathe easier afterward. I've watched teenagers break free from shame and self-hatred because someone finally helped them take their *feelings to Jesus instead of just trying to "think better thoughts."*

You're Not Just Reading a Book, You're Holding a Key

So here we are. As you turn these pages, I hope you feel less like you're reading a book and more like we're sitting across from each other, sharing coffee and stories about what God's doing in our families. The words here aren't just concepts or theories to learn; they're pathways many families have walked, finding healing and peace along the way. Some discover dramatic breakthroughs; others experience gentle growth over time. Wherever your journey leads, know that the same Jesus who transformed our family is reaching toward yours with hope and healing.

You've heard my story. You've absorbed the nine foundational lessons. And now, you're standing at a holy intersection, the place where your healing can become someone else's hope.

Where we are headed will take you deeper. We're going to talk about:

- What bitter roots look like in children.
- How to create emotionally safe environments.
- How to help kids identify and express their feelings.
- How to walk them through Spirit-led healing prayers.
- How to model forgiveness and peace as a lifestyle.

If properly applied, these applications will be **transformational**.

Gwen and I want to help you usher in a generation that doesn't wait decades to see healing. It's about building homes, classrooms, and ministries where peace reigns supreme. It's about giving the children we love the one thing that changes everything: **connection with Jesus in their Bible-heart**.

So get ready. What's ahead is Biblical, practical, powerful, and rooted in the Spirit.

Because we believe, unshakably, that what Jesus has done in us, He can do in them.

And now, we begin.

CHAPTER 13:
Where Is Your Heart? – Discovering Where Our Feelings Live

Have you ever stopped to ask: Where do feelings actually live?

Scripture often refers to this inner place as your "heart" or, at times, even your "belly." This is the place deep inside, sometimes felt in your belly, where your spirit meets God's Spirit. Did you know the Bible even talks about our feelings being deep down in our belly? Proverbs 20:27 (KJV) says:

"The spirit of man is the lamp of the LORD, searching all the inward parts of the belly."

Throughout this book, when we refer to the heart, we're not talking about the physical organ that pumps blood. Just as it is used 95% of the time in

Scripture, the heart is the inner space where your spirit lives and breathes. It's where Jesus makes His home in you, and where real connection happens.

This matters because when we help children invite Jesus into their pain, we want them to know precisely where to look for Him. Not up in the clouds somewhere, but right there in the center of who they are.

"When we help children name their feelings, 'I feel sad' or 'I feel scared,' we're teaching them biblical emotional honesty."

What we have discovered through our experiences is that connecting with this inner place is key to helping children process their emotions. When kids learn to allow Jesus into that deep place of feelings, they don't have to stuff their pain; instead, they can let Him heal it.

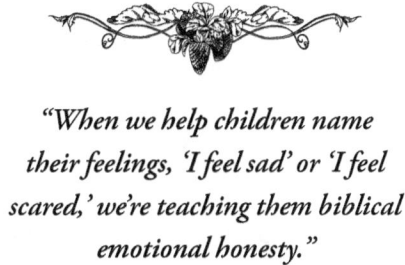

APPLICATION: TEACHING THE BIBLE-HEART

FOR PARENTS (At Home)

How to Explain This to Your Child: "There's a special place deep inside you where Jesus lives. It's your heart. That's where you feel peace, or sadness, or anger. And that's where Jesus hugs you from the inside."

Finding Our Feelings (Body Check Activity): Ask your child, "Where do you feel happy?" They might smile, touch their chest, or jump. Then ask gently, "Now, where do you feel upset or scared?" Many children naturally touch their tummy or chest.

Explain: "Your feelings live deep down inside you, in your tummy or your heart. Jesus lives there too, and He can help with those feelings."

The Jesus Calms the Sea Activity: *What You'll Need: A shallow pan with water and a small toy boat.*

Place the boat in water and say: "This boat is like your Bible-heart. It floats on the sea of your feelings."

Create gentle waves, saying: "Sometimes our feelings get stormy inside."

Calm the water while praying: "Jesus, come into my stormy feelings and bring peace."

As the water settles: "This is what Jesus does inside us, He calms every wave."

Bedtime Heart Connection: Before sleep, guide your child to place their hand on their tummy and pray: "Jesus, I open my heart to You. Thank You for being with me." This simple practice helps them recognize His presence within.

FOR TEACHERS & MINISTRY LEADERS (In Groups)

Warm-Up: The Feeling Place: Have children stand in a circle with their hands on their tummies:

"Think about your favorite treat, what do you feel inside?"

"Now think about losing a toy, what do you feel?"

"Those feelings show us where our Bible-heart is!"

Group Activity: Heart Door Game: Create a large paper heart with a paper door that opens:

Knock gently: "Jesus is knocking. Can He come in?"

Let a child open the door to reveal a picture of Jesus.

Have all children practice "opening their heart doors" by placing their hands on their tummies.

Say together: "Jesus, I open my heart to You."

Teaching Tips:

Keep explanation times brief (2-3 minutes maximum).

Use physical movement to reinforce concepts.

Allow children to express in their own words where they feel emotions.

Never force participation; some children need to observe first.

KEY PRINCIPLES TO REMEMBER

- **Children naturally sense their emotions in their physical bodies.**

- **The Bible-heart concept helps them locate where Jesus meets them.**

- **Physical touch (hand on tummy) helps children connect abstract concepts to concrete experience.**

- **Jesus' presence is already within them; we are helping them become aware of Him.**

A FEW GRACE-FILLED WARNINGS

- **Don't rush or pressure children** to identify their feelings immediately.

- **Don't dismiss their descriptions** of where they feel emotions.

- **Don't overexplain** with theological terms that confuse rather than clarify.

- **Don't force participation** if a child seems resistant or uncomfortable.

What's Next?

Now that we've explored where our emotions reside and how to help children connect with Jesus in their hearts, let's move directly to understanding what happens when hurt feelings remain unaddressed and unresolved rather than being released to Jesus.

What happens when that sacred space harbors pain that never gets acknowledged? What grows in the garden of our hearts when we don't tend to the weeds?

This is where bitter roots begin to take hold. When children experience hurts that go unresolved, whether it's feeling left out, being rebuked, or losing something precious, those emotions don't simply disappear. They sink deeper, taking root in the fertile soil of the Bible-heart, and begin to shape how a child sees themselves, others, and even God.

I've witnessed this transformation countless times in my own family and the lives of others. A child who feels repeatedly rejected doesn't just feel sad in the moment; they gradually begin to believe they're unlovable. A child who is ridiculed for mistakes doesn't just feel embarrassed; they start to think they're defective.

One thing I think is really cool is that this place is where bitter roots take hold; it's also the very place where Jesus brings His healing presence. When we help children identify those root systems early and invite Him into that space, transformation doesn't have to wait until adulthood. It can happen during a bedtime prayer or a car ride. Or just after having a total meltdown.

Next, I'd love to share what a bitter root is. In the upcoming chapter, we'll explore how to recognize these challenges in our children and guide them to Jesus for support in overcoming them. It's wonderful to know that emotional healing and nurturing wholehearted children can happen through the incredible transformation that Jesus offers!

We don't control what grows in a child's heart, but we do help prepare the soil for what does. It starts with being mindful of those little weeds before they get big. Before they crowd out what God originally designed to grow there.

CHAPTER 14:
Bitter Roots – What Are They?

From a child's perspective, a bitter root feels like an icky or yucky sensation, akin to a nasty weed growing inside. It begins when someone or something hurts your feelings, and instead of allowing Jesus to help immediately, we keep the hurt bottled up. Holding on to sadness, anger, or feelings of being excluded. These hurts burrow deep into our innermost selves.

Bitter roots could be the cause of their acting out. That's not all. These hidden hurts can change how a child sees themselves, how they view others and where and with whom they feel safe. Don't get me wrong, helping children deal with their emotions won't keep them from being hurt in life. Wholehearted kids can still get hurt; they've just learned to run to Jesus with the pain instead of allowing that pain to define who they are.

The Bible says, *"Watch out that no root of bitterness grows up to trouble you and defile many"* (Hebrews 12:15, ESV). That means when we don't forgive, the yuck doesn't just stay inside; it grows. It can make us grumpy, sad, or even suggest it to others. But here's the good news: Jesus is really good at pulling those nasty weeds out! I can't tell you how many times I've seen a child's face change right before my eyes when they let Him do this. Not everyone feels it the same way; some kids describe it like sunshine or a warm hug inside, others like a weight lifted off them, but when it happens, you know something deep and authentic has just taken place. That's the promise we see in Scripture when it says, *"For if you forgive men their trespasses, your heavenly Father will also forgive you."* (Matthew 6:14, NKJV).

[SCIENCE SPOTLIGHT]

The bitter roots Scripture warns about aren't just spiritual concepts; they create measurable changes in our physical bodies. Dr. Candace Pert, former Chief of Brain Biochemistry at the National Institute of Mental Health, conducted pioneering research on how emotions physically affect our bodies. She discovered tiny messengers in the body called neuropeptides, basically, proof that our emotions don't live in our minds. They're in our whole body, even in the tummy.

She explains: "Emotions are stored in the body, the unconscious mind is in the body, and you can access emotional memory through the body."[6] This scientific finding affirms what we've observed in ministry: when children (and adults) feel emotions in their "tummy" or Bible-heart, they're detecting actual physiological changes.

The ACE (Adverse Childhood Experiences) Study further proves our "bitter roots" concept. Dr. Vincent Felitti notes: "What happens in childhood doesn't just go away. It stays with people throughout their lives."[5] This validates what we teach, that emotional hurts, when not addressed, don't simply fade but continue to influence us from within.[7]

APPLICATION: HELPING CHILDREN UNDERSTAND BITTER ROOTS

FOR PARENTS (At Home)

Storytime: Tommy and the Toy Baseball Bat

Tommy's friend broke his favorite whiffle ball bat. It wasn't intentional, but Tommy felt sad and mad at the same time. That bad feeling sat in his tummy

---

6 Candace B. Pert, "Molecules of Emotion: The Science Behind Mind-Body Medicine" (New York: Scribner, 1997), 141.

7 Felitti, Vincent J., et al. "Relationship of Childhood Abuse and Household Dysfunction to Many of the Leading Causes of Death in Adults: The Adverse Childhood Experiences (ACE) Study." American Journal of Preventive Medicine 14, no. 4 (1998): 245-258.

like a tiny seed. He didn't let Jesus help, and soon, it started growing like a weed. It even made him not want to play anymore.

Tommy didn't ask Jesus for help. He stayed mad for days. That seed became a bitter root. Soon, he didn't even want to play with his friends. He even yelled at his mom. The weed was growing quickly in his heart.

One day, his mom gently asked, "Did something inside you feel yucky when that happened?" Then she said, "Let's ask Jesus to help pull out that weed."

Tommy put his hand on his tummy, let Jesus come close, forgave his friend, and gave Jesus the not-good feeling. And just like that, the bitter root was gone, and Tommy felt light and happy once again.

Taste It: Sweet vs. Bitter

Give your child something bitter, such as lemon or plain tea, then something sweet, like honey or a grape. Ask:

- "How did the bitter one feel?"
- "What about the sweet one?"

Explain: "Holding on to hurt is like keeping that bitter taste in your heart. But forgiveness is the sweet one, Jesus makes your insides feel good again."

Let's Talk and Wonder

Ask your child:

- "Have you ever seen weeds in a garden?"
- "What do they do to the good plants?"
- "How do you feel when someone hurts your feelings?"

Explain: "When we don't forgive, the hurt grows like a weed. But when we open our Bible-heart, Jesus pulls it out so good things can grow."

FOR TEACHERS & MINISTRY LEADERS (In Groups)

Story/Analogy - The Weedy Garden:

Gather the children in a circle. Tell a simple story with props or actions:

"Imagine we have a little garden. We plant a flower seed, but also a thorny weed seed by accident. As time passes, the pretty flower grows, but so does the gross weed. The weed's roots start to take over, and the flower begins to droop. In our hearts, getting hurt or staying angry is like planting a weed; it can grow and spread. If we don't pull it out by forgiving, that bitter weed can grow big roots and make our hearts unhappy. But if we pull the weed out early, the flowers (good feelings) can grow again!"

As you tell the story, you can use a visual like two potted plants, one with a healthy flower and one with a large weed. Show the children the roots (even a picture of roots) and explain that weeds are easier to pull out when they are small.

If we forgive quickly, we stop a little hurt from growing into a big, bitter root.

Object Lesson:

Pull the Weed: Bring a fake plant or weed (or a picture of a weed with roots). Also, a lovely flower. Show the weed's roots and say: "This is what a bitter root might look like in our heart; it goes deep and is hard to pull out if we leave it too long." Then pretend to struggle as you pull it (for dramatization). Next, easily pluck a small weed or seed: "But if we forgive quickly, it's like pulling the weed out when it's tiny; pop! It's gone." Show the flower: "Then our heart can grow flowers of joy and love." You can even have the kids pretend their fist is a weed in their hearts, have them open their fists, and toss an imaginary weed away when they choose to forgive.

Group Discussion:

Ask the children gentle questions to get them thinking:

- "Have you ever felt mad or sad because someone wasn't nice?" (Have a few raise hands or share short examples.)

- "Did that feeling stay inside you for a while? How did it feel, heavy or light?" (Guide them to identify that it felt bad or heavy.)

- "What do you think happens if we keep those heavy, angry feelings inside and never let them go?" (Explain it makes us unhappy, maybe makes us act unkind, because the bitter root is growing.)

- "What can we do to pull out that bad feeling so it doesn't keep growing?" (Answer: forgive and give it to God.)

Emphasize that everyone (kids and grown-ups) can get bitter roots, but God helps us forgive so our hearts stay healthy.

REAL-LIFE EXAMPLE

Little Emmy and the Strawberry Weeds

It was a gentle, sunny morning when I decided to sit down with Emmy to talk about bitter roots. I wasn't surprised when she said she didn't know what they were, her small voice genuinely curious.

"Bitter roots," I explained, "are like gross weeds that grow in our hearts."

"Weeds?" Emmy repeated, eyes wide.

"Yes, " I smiled, nodding. "You know how weeds can grow around strawberries and choke them?"

Her eyes brightened immediately. "Strawberries!"

"Exactly! Every day, I have to check the strawberry plants to pull out the weeds, or they'll harm the plants and prevent them from producing delicious fruit. Bitter roots are just like weeds, but inside us, in our hearts. They grow when someone hurts our feelings, and they make us feel bad inside."

Emmy paused, thoughtful. She shifted in her seat, examining a small shiny object on the table. "What's this?"

"A paperclip," I smiled. She glanced back at me, listening again. I continued, "Bitter roots make us feel yucky or unhappy. Have you ever felt like that?"

"Happy?" Emmy quickly replied, and then she reconsidered. "Well, when I was sick, I felt yucky."

"Yes, exactly. And how about when Landon and Haven left you on the trampoline the other day?"

Her little face fell slightly. "I cried," she whispered.

"You cried," I repeated gently. "They left you all alone."

"They keep doing it," she said softly, sadness clouding her eyes.

Seeing an opportunity to illustrate the concept, I began to tell her a story about a boy named Tommy. "Tommy's friend broke his favorite toy," I said, leaning in closer. "Imagine if one of your friends broke your favorite toy,"

"Patches!" Emmy interjected, hugging herself at the thought.

"Yes, your toy, Patches. Tommy felt really sad and angry because someone broke his favorite baseball bat by hitting a rock with it. His anger was like planting a bad seed in his heart, and it grew into a big, ugly weed."

"What did he do?" Emmy asked, completely absorbed in the story.

"Tommy became grumpy. He didn't even want to play anymore. He was so upset that he even yelled at his mom." Emmy gasped quietly. "But Tommy's mom knew what to do. She sat him down and said, 'Son, your heart hurts. Let's pull out that gross weed together.'"

"Ow," Emmy murmured softly, imagining pulling out something painful.

"Tommy's mom asked him to put his hand on his heart and feel where it hurt. Tommy felt sad and mad. She said, 'It's okay to have that feeling, but let's tell Jesus about it.' Tommy prayed, 'Jesus, I feel hurt because my friend broke my toy.' Then his mom said, 'Let's give that not-good feeling to God.' Tommy imagined handing Jesus an invisible ball of icky weeds.'"

Emmy listened closely, fascinated.

"Then Tommy prayed again, asking Jesus, 'Please take out the bitter root from my heart. Make my heart clean and happy again.' After that, Tommy decided to forgive his friend. Forgiveness is like pulling weeds out of the garden. Tommy said, 'I forgive my friend for hurting me,' and pretended to pull out the weed from his heart and throw it away.'"

Emmy smiled softly, intrigued. "Could you forgive your friend if they broke Patches?" I asked her gently.

Emmy nodded confidently. "I would."

"That's great," I smiled. "It would make your heart feel better, wouldn't it?"

She thought for a moment, then brightened. "I remember when Landon hit my head with a giant stick. It hurt."

I nodded sympathetically. "Did it make your heart hurt, too?"

"Mhm," Emmy nodded.

"Let's practice what Tommy did," I encouraged. "Put your hand on your belly. Do you feel the sadness or hurt there?" Emmy nodded quietly. "Now, let's ask Jesus to show you the very first time you felt like that or as far back as you can remember."

Emmy closed her eyes briefly, then opened them, looking unsure. "It's okay if you can't remember the very first time," I reassured her gently. "Let's pray about the time you remember clearly, like when Landon hit you or left you alone. Can you say, 'Jesus, I feel hurt because Landon hit me and because they left me alone?'"

Emmy whispered softly, repeating the prayer after me.

"Now, Emmy, give that yucky feeling to Jesus like you're handing Him a weed or ball of yuck." Emmy reached out her small hand, gently pretending to hand something invisible to Jesus.

"Let's keep our eyes closed and pray, 'Jesus, I let go of this hurt, please take out the bitter root from my heart.' Next, ask Jesus for a clean heart. Make my heart feel happy again.'"

And with her eyes closed, she whispered softly, repeating the words earnestly.

"Now," I continued gently, "let's forgive Landon and Haven. Say, 'I forgive Landon and Haven for hurting me.'" Emmy smiled as she pretended to pull out the weed from her heart and toss it aside.

"Finally, this is the fun part!" I said warmly, "Let's fill your heart with love. Take a big breath and imagine His love filling you up like a warm hug inside." Emmy took a deep breath. She rested quietly, soaking in that deep, cozy feeling of love filling her.

"How do you feel now?" I asked.

"I feel happy," Emmy said joyfully, her blue eyes sparkling again. "Sooooo, what can I do now?" she asked, shifting gears suddenly.

I chuckled. "What would you like to do?"

Her demeanor began to take a curious turn. "Can we play a video game?" she replied brightly, returning the upbeat and energetic Emmy that we all knew and loved.

I smiled, grateful for the precious moment we'd shared. The seeds of understanding forgiveness had been planted, and with intentionality and care, I knew they would grow beautifully in Emmy's heart.

[Note: This story continues, leading to Emmy's healing experience, which is revealed in Chapter 22, Emmy's Unexpected Miracle]

KEY PRINCIPLES TO REMEMBER

- **Bitter roots begin with unprocessed hurt.** When emotions aren't acknowledged and released, they become more entrenched.

- **Children understand concrete analogies.** If you want to reach a child's heart, put "it" in their hands, let them touch it, taste it, draw it, or laugh about it.

- **Use physical objects to illustrate spiritual truths.** Let children touch, taste, and see to understand the concept of forgiveness.

- **Identify bitter roots early.** The sooner you recognize the pattern, the easier the healing process will be.

- **Jesus is the One who does the healing.** We create the opportunity, but He does the transformative work.

A FEW GRACE-FILLED WARNINGS

- **Don't use shame** to address a child's bitter root ("Why are you still angry? That's wrong!").

- **Don't rush through explanations.** Children need time to connect abstract concepts to real feelings.

- **Don't expect perfect understanding immediately.** The concept of bitter roots may take multiple conversations.

- **Don't force forgiveness.** Guide, invite, but never pressure; forced forgiveness isn't real forgiveness.

- **Don't forget that adults have bitter roots too.** Children learn more from our example than from our words.

CHAPTER 15:
How to Spot a Bitter Root

I'll never forget the expression on Emmy's face, standing there on the trampoline, knees pointed inward, holding her arm to her chest. Her reaction seemed to stem from something much deeper than just being left alone to bounce by herself.

When I looked back at that moment, something occurred to me. Bitter roots announce themselves early...if you're paying attention to their signals.

Now that we know what bitter roots are and how they grow, let's discuss how to spot them early when they're still soft enough to remove easily. The sooner we catch them, the easier it is to help kids heal before the hurt becomes deeply ingrained.

APPLICATION: RECOGNIZING THE SIGNS OF EMOTIONAL WOUNDS

FOR PARENTS (At Home)

The Yucky Fruit Checklist:

Bitter roots typically manifest as behaviors or reactions that seem overly intense or unusual in response to the situation at hand. If you notice any of these repeatedly, it might be a bitter root:

- Overreaction: Crying, screaming, or melting down over minor issues.

- Avoidance: Refusing to go to certain places or avoiding particular people.

- Sensitivity to Criticism: Extreme reactions to gentle corrections or simple guidance.

- Isolation: Pulling away from family, friends, or activities they usually enjoy.

- Negative Self-Talk: Saying things like, "I'm bad," "No one likes me," or "I can't do anything right."

- Fearful Behaviors: Anxious reactions to loud noises, surprises, or raised voices.

- Perfectionism: Becoming very upset when they make a small mistake or when something isn't perfect.

(GWEN)

In walking alongside our children, I've noticed how quickly bitter roots can form through comparison. When a child sees a sibling, especially a younger one, receiving what appears to be more attention, something profound happens in their heart. Their perspective, which is often based on a lie, becomes their truth and begins to shape their identity.

They don't just feel momentarily overlooked; they begin to feel less valued, less seen, and less loved at their core. I've watched this happen with our own children. That momentary comparison doesn't stay momentary; it becomes a lens through which they view themselves and their place in the family.

The same thing happens when children aren't accepted by the one classmate they desperately want to befriend. It doesn't matter if they have a dozen other friends; in that moment, they compare themselves to the children that classmates do befriend and see themselves as "lesser than." The bitter root of rejection begins to whisper: "There's something wrong with you. You're not good enough."

These are critical moments where we can intervene, helping them identify the lie before it becomes part of their identity. When we spot these comparison patterns, it's a signal that a bitter root may be taking hold.

Reactions Bigger Than the Moment:

Has your child suddenly burst into tears because their sibling left the room, or get very angry because someone accidentally bumped into them? These reactions are often signs of a bitter root, something deeper than just the immediate event. When children feel emotions too big for what happened, gently help them pause and check their tummy for feelings. That's usually where the hurt hides.

(GWEN)

Another pattern I've observed is how children respond to perceived scarcity. When children feel they don't have enough, whether it's food, material things, or even emotional resources like attention, they often believe a lie that "there will never be enough." Sometimes, they even make inner vows: "When I grow up, I'll make sure there's always enough."

Those small reactions, which we often think are harmless, can develop into beliefs that shape everything later. Scripture warns us about this in Hebrews 12:15, where bitter roots "spring up" and "defile many." The fascinating part is how these roots affect generations: if a child judges their father for how he provided, protected, or nurtured them, they'll likely either marry someone just like him (for girls) or become just like him as parents (for boys).

I've seen this play out in families we've ministered to; the very things people vowed never to repeat become the patterns they unconsciously adopt. This isn't a coincidence; it's the spiritual principle of reaping what we sow. When you hear a child making "when I grow up" declarations or notice those "never enough" patterns, pay attention. Those aren't just passing thoughts; they're often the first shoots of a bitter root breaking ground. A root of judgment toward their parents or a deep belief that there will never be enough love, attention, or provision to go around.

These moments are like warning lights on your dashboard. Something deeper is stirring.

It's the Patterns That Reveal the Root:

One-time reactions might be due to having a rough day, but repeated over-reactions often point to a deeper issue. Look for signs such as:

- Always angry after school or tummy issues before school.
- Consistently upset around specific people or places.
- Often nervous about separation or goodbyes.
- Regularly withdrawing when corrected or gently disciplined.

These patterns can help you identify the bitter roots your child might be carrying.

FOR TEACHERS & MINISTRY LEADERS (In Groups)
Mini-Assessment Activity: "Spot the Feeling"

Create a simple activity to help children recognize emotional signals:

1. Make a chart with faces showing different emotions (happy, sad, angry, scared).
2. Read scenarios like: "Your friend doesn't share their toys" or "Someone says they don't want to play with you."
3. Have children point to which face shows how they would feel.
4. Notice which children consistently point to intense emotions for minor situations.

5. For those who show strong reactions, gently ask: "What does your tummy feel like when that happens?"

This provides insight into which children may be carrying emotional wounds while also teaching them to recognize their own feelings.

Group Discussion: Common Bitter Roots

In an age-appropriate way, introduce children to different types of emotional wounds:

1. **Rejection** (Feeling Left Out): "Have you ever felt like nobody wanted to play with you?"

2. **Abandonment** (Feeling Alone): "Has there been a time when you felt scared someone wouldn't come back?"

3. **Shame** (Feeling Bad About Yourself): "Did you ever feel like you're not good enough?"

4. **Fear** (Being Afraid a Lot): "What makes your heart feel scared, even when you're safe?"

As children share, listen for clues about deeper emotional patterns. Remember, a child who responds intensely to stories about abandonment might be carrying that wound themselves.

REAL-LIFE EXAMPLE

(GWEN)

Motherhood opens your eyes to how quickly lies can take root in little hearts. One afternoon, I found Haven hiding under the covers of our bed. When I gently asked what was wrong, her response broke my heart.

"Emmy hurt my feelings," she said quietly. "She was standing on Daddy's feet dancing in the kitchen, and when I asked for a turn, she told me I was too big and weighed too much, that I couldn't dance on Daddy's feet anymore. Only she could."

Then came the words that revealed the bitter root beginning to form: "I wish I could be little again so I could have Daddy back."

At that moment, I could see the dangerous lie taking shape that being small was the only way to have her daddy's love and attention. If we hadn't caught it and helped her uproot it, that tiny seed could have grown into rejection issues, identity confusion, and even body image struggles later on.

This is why we're so passionate about catching these moments early. The lies aren't powerful because they're true; they're powerful because they go unaddressed.

KEY PRINCIPLES TO REMEMBER

- **Every behavior is a signal.** Look beneath the surface of reactions that seem disproportionate.

- **Different bitter roots have other symptoms.** Rejection, abandonment, fear, and shame each manifest in unique ways.

- **What matters isn't the size of the triggering event but the size of the reaction.** Small triggers with significant responses often indicate a bitter root.

- **Children often can't articulate why they feel so strongly.** They need help connecting their emotional dots.

- **Consistent patterns are more revealing than isolated incidents.** Watch for the same emotional reaction across different situations.

A FEW GRACE-FILLED WARNINGS

- **Don't label the child as "difficult" or "dramatic."** Their big emotions are signals, not character flaws.

- **Don't try to reason with a child during an emotional outburst.** Wait until they're calm to help them process their emotions.

- **Don't dismiss their feelings as "silly" or "not a big deal."** What seems small to you may be huge in their inner world.

- **Don't rush to fix the behavior without addressing its root cause.** Behavior modification without heart healing creates performance, not peace.

- **Don't expect a child to recognize their own bitter roots.** They need your gentle guidance to see the patterns.

CHAPTER 16:
Blurry Heart Glasses – How Hurt Feelings Change How We See

"An offended heart is the breeding ground of deception."

– John Bevere, *The Bait of Satan*[8]

Sometimes, when we feel hurt or mad, and we don't let Jesus help, it's like putting on pretend glasses that are all smudgy and blurry. When your heart is hurting, it's kind of like trying to see through tears; everything gets blurry, even things that aren't bad. These *Blurry Heart Glasses* make it hard to know the truth about people, ourselves, and even God. Our sight becomes distorted by the emotional wounds we carry within us.

---

8 John Bevere, *The Bait of Satan: Living Free from the Deadly Trap of Offense* (Charisma House, 2014), 86.

Have you ever felt something so strongly that even kind people trying to help felt dangerous? That's what happens when your heart-glasses get smudged. The people you care about start looking like threats, and what were once safe situations feel risky.

That's blurry-heart vision at work.

APPLICATION: UNDERSTANDING BLURRY HEART VISION

FOR PARENTS (At Home)

Storytime - Lucy's Blurry Glasses:

Lucy had a favorite pair of pretend glasses. They didn't help her see better, but they made her feel smart and special, as if she could understand the whole world just right.

One afternoon, Lucy was painting a beautiful rainbow when her little brother ran by and, *snap!* Broke her favorite paintbrush in two.

"Hey!" Lucy yelled. "That was my best one!"

Her brother said sorry, but Lucy crossed her arms and turned away. Inside, her tummy felt tight. All through dinner and even when she got in bed, that icky feeling stayed right there. She didn't forgive him.

The next morning, Lucy popped on her glasses like always, but something felt different.

Everything looked a little blurry.

When she got to school, she saw her friends whispering and giggling near their cubbies. Her belly started to feel nervous.

"They're probably laughing at me," she thought.

Later, Mommy didn't say anything about the broken paintbrush. Lucy's chest tightened again.

"Maybe Mommy doesn't care," she whispered to herself, even though Mommy had hugged her twice that morning and packed her favorite snack.

That night, Lucy curled up on the couch, still feeling sad and mixed up inside. Her daddy sat beside her and gently said, "Hey Lucy, want to talk about what's going on in your tummy?"

Lucy nodded slowly and put her hand on her belly. "It feels kind of not-good in there," she said.

Daddy smiled. "Let's open our Bible-hearts and ask Jesus the Forgiver to come in."

Lucy closed her eyes and whispered, "Jesus, come into my Bible-heart. It hurts in my tummy. I didn't forgive my brother, and now everything feels all wrong."

Together, they sat quietly. Lucy forgave her brother with Jesus' help. She let go of the not-good feeling.

And right then, it was as if Jesus reached into her heart and gently wiped away her pretend glasses.

The next day, everything felt different. The sun looked brighter. Her friends smiled and invited her to join in the play. Mommy surprised her with a brand-new set of paintbrushes, and guess what? There were *two* of her favorite kinds.

Lucy's heart felt clean and peaceful. The yuck was gone.

Explaining the Lesson to Your Child:

Say: "Sometimes when we don't forgive, it's like we're wearing blurry glasses. We don't see people clearly, and we start to believe lies that aren't true. But when Jesus the Forgiver helps us forgive, He cleans our heart-glasses. And then, we see with love again."

Visual - Blurry vs. Clear:

Object Option 1 - Blurry Glasses: Smudge the lenses of pretend glasses with lotion or a dry-erase marker. Let your child try to look through them, then clean them together.

Say: "That's what it's like when we're mad or hurt and don't forgive. It makes things look worse than they are. But when we let Jesus clean our hearts, everything becomes clear again."

Object Option 2 - Cloudy Jar: Fill a jar with clear water. Then add food coloring or dirt; this represents the muddy or yucky feelings. Pour in clean water until it is clear again (or replace it) after a prayer of Forgiveness.

Say: "Forgiveness is like letting Jesus pour peace into the deepest places inside you. He makes it clean and calm again."

FOR TEACHERS & MINISTRY LEADERS (In Groups)

Theme: Blurry Heart Glasses, How Hurt Can Trick What We See and Feel

Object Lesson - Blurry Glasses and Dirty Windows:

Hold up a big pair of silly play glasses (or cut some from paper). Smudge the "lenses" with lotion, paint, or marker.

Ask the group: "What happens when I try to see you through these dirty glasses?"

Let kids respond.

Say: "These are *Blurry Heart Glasses*. When we feel hurt or mad, and we don't forgive, our heart feels blah or icky. And then, everything starts to look blurry, even people who love us."

Hold up the glasses or a smudged plastic window and say: "This is what unforgiveness feels like in your tummy; it makes your heart feel heavy and your eyes feel cloudy. But when we let Jesus the Forgiver inside and we forgive, He wipes our glasses clean from the inside."

Then wipe the glasses or window clean and say with joy: "Now we can see clearly! That's what Jesus does when He heals us on the inside."

Biblical Connection:

"Blessed are the pure in heart, for they shall see God." (Matthew 5:8, ESV)

(Paraphrase for kids: "If your Bible-heart is clean, not full of hurt or anger, then you can feel God's love and see the good again!")

You can say, "When we forgive, our hearts become pure and soft again, and that helps us feel God's love and lovingly see others, too."

(GWEN)

I've watched how quickly a child's perception can become distorted through the lens of comparison. It's like they put on a special pair of blurry glasses that changes everything they see about themselves and others.

When a child sees a sibling getting more attention, it doesn't just sting; it can turn into a quiet lie: "I matter less. I am less seen. I am less loved."

I remember watching this happen with Haven after Emmy was born. The comment she made broke my heart: "I wish I could be little again so daddy would play with me more." In that moment, her "blurry heart glasses" weren't just affecting how she saw her sister; they were changing how she saw herself and her place in our family.

These distorted perceptions don't stay contained. They spread, coloring how children see God Himself. If they believe they're not good enough for our love, they'll struggle to think they're good enough for His. This is why identifying and addressing these "blurry heart glasses" early is so crucial; we're not just correcting vision, but also protecting their understanding of divine love.

A Personal Journey Through Blurry Glasses
(GWEN)

Sometimes our greatest strengths can become blurred by the very wounds we carry. My own story of "blurry heart glasses" began before I could even name what was happening.

The truth is, I *was* naturally strong, growing up on a farm, helping my dad with chores almost as soon as I could walk. My mom competed in Crosscut Two-Man Sawing competitions; toughness was in my DNA. But what started as a genuine trait twisted into something different when I was just four years old.

That's when the urinary tract infections began, severe, relentless episodes that hospitalized me regularly. I'd lie in sterile rooms being poked and prodded, and then night would come. Mom would have to leave to care for Dad and my sister, and though I'd wave goodbye with a brave face, terror would settle in once I was alone. Too scared to sleep, I'd wander down the antiseptic halls to the nurses' station, pull up a chair, and make crafts until dawn broke, anything to keep the fear at bay.

This pattern continued every year from age four until I was twelve, when surgery finally fixed the physical problem. But by then, the emotional wound had already taken root. Through my "blurry heart glasses," I now saw vulnerability as a weakness and independence as a means of survival.

Each year at school, I'd watch my circle of friends shrink. Kids would distance themselves, asking what was "wrong" with me, wondering if they could "catch it" from me. Isolation settled over me like a heavy blanket. I discovered that the only things that earned me any connection were being the best kickball player or standing up to bullies to protect smaller kids. In fourth grade, I was voted "most athletic" due to my physical strength, and I began to identify myself with that title.

What no one saw was how this lie, that I had to be strong, that needing others was weakness, was silently building a wall between my mother and me. As

I grew older, in the moments I desperately needed her comfort, I isolated myself instead. It wasn't anything she did. It was that bitter root whispering: *You have to be strong. You can't need anyone.*

When I found myself pregnant as a teenager, this pattern only deepened. I became even more fiercely independent, determined to prove that I could handle everything on my own.

Fifteen years of single motherhood reinforced this bitter root until it became the scaffolding of my identity. When Jason first met me, one of the things that stood out to him was my strength. It seemed like a virtue, not the defense mechanism it truly was.

After we married and had two beautiful children together, we experienced a devastating miscarriage. In that raw moment of grief, my instinct was to retreat into my fortress of strength, to handle it alone as I always had. But God had other plans.

Our 3-year-old and 1-year-old children, who were never still, would lie with me each day during that season of grief. They'd caress my face with their tiny hands, repeating over and over: "I love you, Mama. I love you, Mama. I love you, Mama."

One day, breaking under the weight of my loss, I cried out to the Lord: "Why does it have to hurt so much?"

His answer stopped me cold: "Don't you hear how much I love you?"

In that moment, I realized the Lord was speaking through my children. All He wanted was for me to do what I'd never allowed myself to do, curl up in His lap, lay my head on His chest, and receive His love rather than proving my strength.

That moment marked the beginning of my healing from "blurry heart glasses." For the first time, I could see clearly that what I'd been calling strength was fear in disguise, fear of needing others, fear of being disappointed, fear of being truly seen.

It wasn't the only loss we would experience, but future grief didn't break me the same way. Instead, painful moments became invitations to run into the Father's arms and experience being loved and carried in ways I'd never allowed before.

Looking back, I see so clearly now. That bitter root of "I must be strong" kept me from the very thing my heart most needed, finding a safe place in loving arms during my times of greatest vulnerability.

But Jesus knew exactly how to clear the blurry vision of my heart. He sent toddlers, who knew nothing of my walls and defenses, to show me what it means to rest in love.

This is why I'm so passionate about helping children address these distorted perceptions early. Those blurry heart glasses I wore for decades could have been cleaned much sooner. And while God's redemption is beautiful at any age, there's something precious about sparing a child years of seeing themselves, others, and God through a distorted lens.

What I've discovered over the years is that we can help our children learn much earlier. Those "blurry heart glasses" I wore from age four until adulthood didn't have to define my perception for so long. This is the gift we can offer the children in our care, the ability to recognize distorted vision early and invite Jesus to restore clear sight.

The beautiful truth is that children naturally understand this concept when we make it tangible for them. Their openness to the spiritual realm often exceeds our own. They haven't yet built the sophisticated defenses that we adults have perfected over the years. When we give them simple, concrete ways to recognize when their "heart glasses" have become smudged, they often respond with remarkable insight and receptivity.

Let's explore some practical ways to help children understand how hurt feelings can alter their perspective and, more importantly, how Jesus can restore their ability to see again. These activities create sacred opportunities for the Holy Spirit to gently reveal distortions before they become a child's default way of seeing.

Group Activity - Blurry or Clear Glasses Game:

Use paper glasses or pretend goggles.

Explain the rules: "Let's practice switching from Blurry Heart Glasses to Clear Heart Glasses."

Scenarios (read aloud one at a time): As the children respond, hold up the correct glasses (either dirty or clean) for each statement.

1. "You waved at your friend, but they didn't wave back."

   Blurry Heart Glasses say: "They're ignoring me."

   Clear Heart Glasses say: "Maybe they didn't see me."

2. "Mom was late picking you up."

   Blurry: "She forgot me."

   Clear: "Maybe there was traffic. Mommy loves me."

3. "Someone took the toy you wanted."

   Blurry: "They're being mean!"

   Clear: "Maybe they didn't know I wanted it."

Ask kids to switch their glasses each time and act out what the heart might feel.

KEY PRINCIPLES TO REMEMBER

- **Emotional wounds distort perception.** When children are hurt, they often misinterpret neutral situations as threatening.

- **A child who feels rejected begins to expect rejection,** even when it isn't happening.

- **Unforgiveness creates a filter** through which children see themselves, others, and even God.

- **Jesus doesn't just forgive, He restores clear vision.** When children experience healing in their Bible-heart, they see the world differently.

- **Children need tools to recognize when their perception is distorted.** Teaching them about "blurry heart glasses" gives them language for what's happening inside.

A FEW GRACE-FILLED WARNINGS

- **Don't dismiss a child's perception,** even if it seems irrational. Their view feels very real to them.

- **Don't shame them for seeing things "wrong."** Their distorted perception is a symptom of hurt, not willful misunderstanding.

- **Don't try to argue them into seeing clearly.** Healing occurs through a connection with Jesus, not through logical explanations.

- **Please don't assume a child knows their perception is distorted.** They genuinely believe what they see and feel.

- **Don't rush the cleaning process.** Sometimes it takes time for Jesus to gently wipe away all the smudges on their heart.

(JASON)

Before we move on, here is a story about the very first time my glasses got blurry.

Sometimes, what seems small to grown-ups feels big to a child.

And sometimes, that "small" thing grows into a bitter root, one that sticks around for years until Jesus gently brings it to the surface.

This is one of those stories.

REAL LIFE EXAMPLE: The Jiffy Popped and the Fear That Followed

It started, as most traumas do, on what should have been a perfectly ordinary evening. The kind of evening where a kid expects mac and cheese, maybe a nap, and if the stars aligned, an episode of something animated. What I got instead was a battle with an aluminum beast, a round, jittery, stove-top volcano known to the world as Jiffy Pop.

I was small. The world was large. My only job at the time was staying close to my blanket, my mom, and anything that didn't hiss, grow, or explode. Jiffy Pop, unfortunately, did all three.

At first, I didn't think much of it. Just a little silver pan sitting there on the burner, looking harmless enough. But one click of the stove and a few quiet seconds later, everything went sideways. Snap! Pop! Then pure chaos erupted. That pan started twitching and swelling like something possessed, shooting off these violent bursts that bounced off the kitchen walls like we'd trapped fireworks in a tin can. I just stood there, eyes wide, heart hammering. I was absolutely convinced something was alive in there. Something furious. Something that probably ate little kids like me, wearing fuzzy blue footie pajamas, for fun.

I remember bolting for cover, diving behind the safety of a kitchen chair, the kind with those weird vinyl cushions that always stuck to your skin. That was my fortress. Jiffy Pop had become my enemy. And somehow, we were at war.

Thankfully, there was a hero. My mother, calm, collected, and somehow unfazed by the attack, swooped me into her arms and carried me away from the stovetop battle. She didn't laugh. She didn't scold. She just held me. And then she did the only thing that made sense in our house: she put me down for a nap.

Mom believed in naps the way some people believe in therapy. And honestly? She wasn't wrong.

Now, decades later, it seems almost silly. A popcorn pan? Really? But the truth is that sight planted something in me, a bitter root I didn't know was there. I wasn't just afraid of the sound. I became fearful of surprise, of being caught off guard, of things erupting in ways I couldn't control.

That root dug deep. Over time, it didn't show up as popcorn panic. It disguised itself as caution. Reluctance. A quiet refusal to take risks. "What if?" became my inner narrator. What if it goes wrong? What if I get hurt? What if I don't see it coming?

What started as a burst of oil and kernels grew into a subtle belief: the world is unsafe, and I should never let my guard down. Even as an adult, I didn't realize how that moment had shaped my instincts, my hesitation, my distrust of anything unpredictable, and my deep need to keep life carefully contained under a proverbial lid.

But God doesn't leave bitter roots buried. He's too kind for that.

Years later, as I began walking through the simple prayer steps this very booklet teaches, like a child, hand on my belly, yielding my heart, I remembered the Jiffy Pop. Not as a random funny memory, but as a moment the Holy Spirit highlighted, bringing it to the surface so I could feel it again…this time with Him.

I felt the fear. I opened myself to God and allowed Jesus into the feeling. As I did, the tightness that had wrapped around my adult heart like a strangling weed began to loosen its grip. That anxious little boy was no longer hiding behind a kitchen chair. He was resting, this time, not in his mother's arms, but in the peace of God.

This may sound funny, but it is true in principle. The popcorn still pops, but it doesn't have the same power over me anymore! And the fear? It no longer gets to narrate my story. I see clearly now. The lens of distrust has been replaced with one of love, security, and peace.

What I didn't know as a child, but now see clearly as a parent and a pastor, is this:

Blurry Heart Glasses don't fix themselves.

And bitter roots never stay small.

But Jesus, the Caretaker of our garden, is never in a rush.

He waits until we're ready to feel the feelings, opens the garden of our heart, and lets Himself step in, not to scold us for being afraid, but to carry the fear away.

Whether you're 5 or 55, this healing still happens the same way:

Not by figuring it out, but by coming to Him like a child.

So here's to Jiffy Pop, for what it taught me, for what it revealed, and for no longer being in charge of my nervous system. And here's to the God who is always gentle, always present, and really good at cleaning up emotional popcorn messes.

But here's the thing about emotional messes, half the time we don't even know we're standing in one. Sometimes, our feelings are working way down deep, below the waterline, where we can't see them, quietly steering how we react to everything. That's what we're diving into next: those emotions that don't come with sirens and flashing lights like fear or tears, but still desperately need Jesus to reach in and heal.

CHAPTER 17:
The Heart and Mind – Feelings We Don't Always Understand

Big Feelings (and Quiet Feelings)

Sometimes, we have feelings in our hearts that we don't even know why they are there. Have you ever felt upset, but you're not sure why? This feeling of upset can occur because our heart remembers hurts even when our head doesn't always recall. This chapter is about helping kids when something inside hurts, and they don't know why.

FOR PARENTS (At Home)

Explaining "Hidden Hurts:"

Tell your child: "Our heart isn't just the part in our chest that goes ba-bump. There is also a special place deep inside where we feel our emotions. Sometimes, we feel them in our tummy. That's your Bible-heart. It's the quiet place where your spirit lives, and it's also where Jesus talks to you." Have you ever had a tummy ache when you were sad or scared? That's your heart feeling something. Some people call it 'the deep-down' or your 'inside place.' It's normal to feel things there."

Explain, "Sometimes we get hurt way back, so far back our brain forgets, but our heart still remembers. It's kind of like getting a bruise you forgot about until someone bumps it. You didn't remember it was there, but when it got touched, you said, 'Ouch!' I didn't even realize I had gotten hurt there.

That's how some feelings work. They're like old bruises that you forgot about until something bumps into them. When they flare up, and they will, that's your Bible-heart tapping you on the shoulder, saying, "Hey, I could use some help from Jesus down here."

Reassure with Simplicity:

Let your child know: "Even if we don't understand why we feel bad, Jesus does! He knows everything about our hearts." If your child seems anxious or upset for no apparent reason, you can pray together: "Jesus, you see my heart. If there's any hurt hidden inside, please help me and take it out. I want my heart happy and filled with Your love." Encourage them that Jesus can heal even the hurts we have no idea what caused them or where they came from.

Imagery – The Backpack of Rocks:

Tell your child to imagine they are wearing a backpack. Each time something hurtful happened (like when you were two and fell, feeling scared, or when you were four and a friend moved away), a little rock went into the backpack. We might forget about each rock, but if we never take them out, one day, the backpack feels very heavy, and we feel bad, not knowing why. Forgiving and asking Jesus to heal our hearts is like removing those heavy rocks one by one so we can feel light and happy. You can even play this out: fill a small backpack with a few toy blocks or stones, let them wear it and feel the weight, then have them remove one "hurt" at a time as you name it ("That time you got lost in the store, let's give that fear to Jesus," remove a rock). Eventually, the bag is light.

Noticing Behaviors:

If your child has an unusual reaction to something (for example, always gets very upset in certain situations), that could be a sign of a hidden hurt or "bitter root" from an earlier experience. Gently help them pray about it. For instance, "I notice you get terrified when someone raises their voice. Maybe your heart remembers a time that hurt you. Let's ask Jesus to take away that hurt so you know you're safe now." Please keep it simple and comforting. The goal is to show them this: There's no hurt too old or too small for Jesus to heal.

FOR TEACHERS & MINISTRY LEADERS (In Groups)

Warm-Up Activity – Heart Feelings Map:

Draw an extensive outline of a person on poster board. Ask children to point to where they feel different emotions: "Where do you feel happy? Sad? Scared?" Many will point to their chest or tummy. Explain that our feelings reside deep within us, in our "Bible-heart" or tummy area, and sometimes we experience emotions but don't know why.

Group Demonstration – The Memory Box:

Bring a box with various objects inside (e.g., a small toy, a Band-Aid, a tissue, etc.). Explain that our heart is like a box that holds memories and feelings. Sometimes, we forget what's inside, but the feelings remain. When something reminds us of an old hurt, those feelings can suddenly appear. Show how Jesus can help us clean out our heart-box by taking each item out, naming what feeling it might represent, and praying simply: "Jesus, please take this feeling and fill the space with Your love."

Interactive Story – The Forgotten Splinter:

Tell a story about a child who had a splinter but forgot about it. Later, when someone touched that spot, it hurt a lot! Explain that feelings can be like a forgotten splinter; they hide in our hearts and hurt when something reminds us of them. Have the children act out finding the "splinter" in their hand, then ask Jesus to "pull it out" and put on healing "love bandages."

Group Prayer Time:

Lead children in a gentle prayer: "Jesus, sometimes our hearts feel crummy, and we don't know why. Please show us if there's a hidden hurt You want to heal. We give You all our hidden feelings. Fill our hearts with Your peace and love. Amen." Then, have them place their hands on their tummies and sit quietly for 30 seconds, just feeling Jesus' peace fill them.

Making It Safe to Share:

Create a "Feelings Corner" in your classroom with comfortable cushions and seating options. Let children know they can go there when they have big feelings they don't understand. Keep a feelings chart nearby with pictures of emotions so they can point to how they feel, even if they don't have words for it.

REAL-LIFE EXAMPLE: The Great Sandbox Rebellion

You never expect a coup d'état to happen in the middle of building a sandcastle.

There we were, two seven-year-olds, on a slightly overcast afternoon in the great democratic plains of the neighborhood sandbox, constructing what I believed to be the eighth wonder of the grade school world. Things were going well… until they weren't. One moment, we were dreamers building with purpose. Next, I was blinking through grit and a mouthful of sand as my co-architect turned rebel! He declared the end of our alliance with a sentence I'll never forget: "I don't want to be your friend anymore."

No warning. No diplomatic talks. It's just betrayal and a face full of fine-grain emotional damage.

It wasn't the sand in my eyes that hurt the most, though that certainly wasn't pleasant. It felt as though something inside me was sinking, as if my inner self had just received a quiet message: *I was not wanted.*

That feeling didn't scream or demand attention. It simply settled in, tucked beneath naptime and playtime and the phrase "I'm okay." But it lodged somewhere deeper than I realized.

The message that stuck wasn't just about a moment. It became a belief: *I must not know how to be a good friend, so I must not deserve friends, so maybe I should just stay away from everyone.*

I began to feel like something was wrong with me, as if I were damaged. Broken things, like myself, I figured, needed to be separated from everything whole.

Shame didn't arrive all at once either. It slipped in slowly, like a shadow through the back door of my identity. Almost unnoticed. Just like me.

Years later, in prayer, the Holy Spirit brought that memory back, not for nostalgia but for healing. He wasn't after the story; He was after the hurt buried inside it. The sting. The shame. The silent vow I made that day: Don't trust too quickly. Don't open your heart too wide.

That day, I felt the rejection as if it had just happened. That's how I knew Jesus was ready to deal with it. Right there, I prayed through the steps just like we teach the children. I opened my heart to Jesus' forgiveness, allowing Him to wash away the feeling of rejection. I forgave the boy, not just for throwing sand, but for making me feel horrible, replaceable. I received Jesus' forgiveness for believing that lie for so long. And then, I let the yuck go.

The peace that followed didn't shout. It just settled, soft and quiet, like a warm blanket over a sore heart.

KEY PRINCIPLES TO REMEMBER

- Children (and adults) can feel emotions from past hurts even when they don't consciously remember the event.

- The Bible-heart or tummy area is where children naturally feel emotions; helping them connect physically to this area makes prayer more tangible.

- Jesus can heal our wounds, even those we don't understand. We don't need to analyze everything; we just need to bring our feelings to Him.

- Unusual or extreme reactions to everyday situations often signal a hidden hurt that needs healing.

- Healing happens through connection, not correction, and focuses on helping children feel safe enough to open their hearts.

GENTLE CAUTIONS FOR GROWN-UPS

- Don't dismiss unexplained emotions with "You're fine" or "Don't be silly;" these responses teach children to doubt their feelings.

- Avoid pressuring children to "figure out why" they feel a certain way. Sometimes, they genuinely don't know.

- Don't rush the healing process when a child is exploring a feeling; give them time to connect to Jesus.

- Avoid making children feel weird or different for having unexplained emotions; normalize it as part of being human.

- Don't skip straight to "fixing it" without acknowledging the feeling first. Always do so before healing.

Remember: Sometimes we feel sad or mad and don't know why. That's okay. It might be an old hurt hiding in our hearts. But Jesus knows! We can pray, and He will help find the hurt and take it away, even if we don't remember where it came from. Our job is to trust Him and forgive anyone we need to, and He will heal our hearts.

CHAPTER 18:
Yielding – Letting God Take Control

Yielding Just Means, "Okay, Jesus, Your Turn"

Yielding sounds like one of those church words that's supposed to mean something important, but really, it's just this: relaxing your grip and letting Jesus take over. You know when you're trying to untangle some impossible knot, and your fingers are getting raw, and you're getting more frustrated by the second?

It means you stop trying to fix it yourself and hand it to someone who knows exactly what to do. When we yield in our hearts, we're saying, "Jesus, I can't fix this feeling or problem by myself. I open my heart so you can take care of it." It's relaxing our hearts and trusting Jesus to make things right.

FOR PARENTS (At Home)

Storytime – The Sticky Fingers (Yielding Story)

Tell your child a simple, playful story:

"One day, Ben got his fingers covered in sticky glue. He tried to pull his fingers apart by himself, but they just got stickier and messier! He cried out, frustrated. Then Mommy gently said, 'Ben, relax your hands and let me help.' When Ben relaxed his hands, Mommy gently washed the glue off. Suddenly, his fingers were free!

Our hearts can get sticky stuff on them, too, when we're upset or worried. But when we stop trying to clean it up alone and let Jesus help, He makes it better.

Object Lesson – The Toy Car (Let Jesus Drive)

Use a small toy car and let your child pretend they're driving:

- Say, "You're driving your little car (your life), and it's fun! But suddenly, you see a big mess ahead (make noises and block the road with toys)."

- Tell them gently, "This is a good time to yield; let Jesus drive." Have them hand you the toy car, and you easily drive it around the mess.

- Explain, "When things get bumpy, that's the perfect time to scoot over and let Jesus steer your heart. You can say, 'Jesus, take the wheel of my heart!' and He will steer you into His peace."

Relax and Invite Jesus (Yielding Exercise)

Do a simple calming exercise together:

- Lie down or sit quietly with your child. Say gently, "Close your eyes. Take a slow, big breath. Feel your whole body relax. Now, let's invite Jesus right here in our tummy."

- As you breathe out slowly, say together softly, "Jesus, I yield to You. Take all my icky feelings and give me peace."

- After a few breaths, gently ask how they feel. If they say "calm," "peaceful," or "sleepy," reassure them, "That's Jesus' peace inside your Bible-heart."

Cook Your Noodle (Physical Yielding)

To help them feel yielding physically:

- Say, "Let's pretend we're stiff, straight spaghetti noodles, all tight and crunchy."

"Now melt into a soft, squishy noodle, like it's been cooked!" Wiggle and giggle together as you both go floppy.

- Explain, "Yielding is becoming like a soft noodle in Jesus' hands. He can pick us up easily and take care of us. He's strong and gentle."

Parents, don't be surprised if you find yourself getting a little too into this exercise. There's something surprisingly therapeutic about going from 'rigid uncooked spaghetti' to 'floppy, wiggly noodle' alongside your child. I've had more than one stressed-out adult tell me this was their favorite part of the whole book. One mom confessed she now does the 'noodle melt' in the bathroom at work when meetings get too tense. Hey, whatever helps you yield to Jesus instead of letting your stress take over! Just maybe lock the door first.

Remember at Home:

Yielding is simply relaxing your heart and trusting Jesus to help. When your heart feels fearful or sad, breathe in and pray:

"Jesus, I yield to You. I let you take care of me."

Jesus will always bring peace to the innermost part of you if you wait for Him.

FOR TEACHERS & MINISTRY LEADERS (In Groups)

Activity – Tug of War (Letting Go)

Use a short, safe rope for demonstration:

- Pick one child to hold one end gently. You have the other end and say, "This rope is a problem or a yuck feeling. Let's pull!" Pretend it's complicated and frustrating.

- Now say, "But what if I yield? Yielding means letting go!" Gently drop your end of the rope. Say, "When we yield to Jesus, we stop fighting. He takes the problem and helps us feel better."

Let each child briefly try this demonstration. Gently remind them, "Yielding means letting go of your problems so Jesus can help."

Game – Gentle Trust Lean

Pair children with a safe adult or yourself:

- Have the child lean back slightly into your supportive hands.

- Explain softly, "This is yielding. You're trusting me not to let you fall. We trust Jesus the same way. We can yield our feelings and trust Him to hold us."

(Ensure children feel safe; this is about gentle leaning, not falling.)

Activity – Calm Little Boats

Have the children pretend they are little boats on water:

- Say, "Your heart is a little boat. When you're upset, your boat rocks a lot (let them sway and wiggle)."

- Now say, "Yield to Captain Jesus! He calms the storm." Kids freeze gently, becoming calm.

- Say softly, "When we yield, Jesus calms our hearts."

Memory Phrase – Yield and Feel Peace

Teach a simplified phrase based on Philippians 4:7:

"I yield to Jesus; He gives peace."

Repeat the call-and-response several times to help them remember that yielding brings peace.

Peace Moment (Quiet Time with Jesus)

- Invite the kids to find a cozy spot, such as on a blanket, a cushion, or even lying on the floor.

- Say softly: "Let's get really still like we're lying in the grass looking up at the sky."

- Whisper: "Close your eyes and quietly tell Jesus inside, 'Jesus, I give You my heart. Please fill me with Your peace.'"

- Let them sit or lie quietly for about a minute.

- Then, gently say, "Take a deep breath... and let it out slowly." Take a few seconds, say, "Try wriggling your fingers and toes when you feel Jesus' peace and open your eyes."

- Thank them: "Thank you for being still and letting Jesus give you peace. Didn't that feel good inside?"

This brief practice can help them experience God's peace on a regular basis.

KEY PRINCIPLES TO REMEMBER

- Yielding isn't passivity; it's active trust in Jesus, not in our efforts.

- Children naturally understand yielding when it's explained through physical activities (relaxing muscles, leaning back, letting go).

- Peace is the fruit of yielding; when a child yields, they feel Jesus' peace rise in their heart.

- Yielding is a spiritual posture that can be practiced and strengthened over time.

- A yielded heart is soft and open to Jesus, ready to receive His help.

GENTLE CAUTIONS FOR GROWN-UPS

- Don't confuse yielding with giving up; they're not the same. Yielding is strength through surrender.

- Avoid pressuring children to "yield faster." Yielding is an internal heart shift that happens uniquely for each child.

- Don't treat yielding as a technique to manipulate outcomes; it's a spiritual connection, not a performance.

- Avoid complicated explanations; yielding is best taught through simple stories and experiences that children can relate to.

- Don't rush the quiet moments when children are connecting with Jesus; those moments are holy ground.

Remember (for Kids):

Yielding means to relax and trust Jesus with your feelings. When you feel scared or angry or worried, stop and say:

"Jesus, I yield. You can hold me now."

He always will, bringing peace to your innermost being. You never have to do it alone; Jesus is right there inside you, ready to help you.

CHAPTER 19:
Forgiveness – Our Heart's Healing Medicine

Forgiveness – Letting Jesus Clean and Heal Our Hearts:

As Scripture promises, *"The peace of God, which transcends all understanding, will guard your hearts and your minds in Christ Jesus"* (Philippians 4:7, NIV). When we invite Jesus into our hurt, many children experience His peace, which washes away painful emotions—a beautiful fulfillment of His promise to comfort those who mourn. *"Blessed are those who mourn, for they shall be comforted"* (Matthew 5:4, ESV).

Forgiveness doesn't mean what happened was okay; it just means we're done carrying it. We hand it to Jesus, and He takes the yuck so we don't have to keep holding it. Hurt feelings can be weighty. When we hold on to hurt, it's like letting yucky dirt stay inside us. But you know what's impressive? When we forgive. Most kids tell us it feels like Jesus comes and gently washes away all that yucky stuff!

Just like the Bible promises, *"He will again have compassion on us, and will subdue our iniquities. You will cast all our sins into the depths of the sea"* (Micah 7:19, NKJV). I've seen kiddos' faces light up when they feel that peace wash over them, just like a spiritual shower!

[SCIENCE SPOTLIGHT]

The peace children experience when they forgive from their hearts isn't just a spiritual phenomenon. It creates measurable changes in their emotional and physical well-being. Dr. Robert Enright, often referred to as the "forgiveness pioneer," has found through extensive research that forgiveness interventions lead to measurable improvements in children's emotional well-being.

There is one secular study that had a great impact on the results; it taught the concept of forgiveness to children as young as six, and those little ones actually became less angry and much more caring toward others. Dr. Enright found that: "As children learn to forgive, they tend to experience less depression, less anxiety, more hope for their future, and better academic performance."[9]

And the wild part? The one who forgives is usually the one who feels the most significant relief. Dr. Everett Worthington explains: "Unforgiveness is like drinking poison and expecting the other person to die."[10] When we add the power of the Holy Spirit to that healing process, we help children, in a sense, to protect both their emotional and physical health for the years to come.

---

9 Robert D. Enright, et al. "The Effects of a Forgiveness Intervention on Children." *Journal of Applied Developmental Psychology* 29, no. 5 (2008): 393-410.

10 Everett L Worthington, *Forgiveness, and Reconciliation: Theory and Application* (New York: Routledge, 2006), 18.

Simple Prayer Steps for Everyday Life

Prayer is simply being with Jesus, whether you use words out loud or just share what you feel in your Heart. Here, we outline simple steps of a "heart-healing prayer" that even a 5-year-old can do with guidance. It's essentially what we've been practicing, it's what we call "The Forgiveness Flow:" feeling our feelings, inviting Jesus' help, and forgiving. We summarize it here as a simple routine or game they can remember. This is where we've seen the most healing happen, in simple moments like this, when a child opens their Heart and lets Jesus in. Here, we will call it *"Stop, Pray, and Let Go."*

This simple routine, Stop, Pray, Let Go, is our child-friendly way of introducing the deeper Forgiveness Flow steps that we unpack in Chapter 27. You'll find the complete prayer model there for those ready to go further.

FOR PARENTS (At Home)

Gentle Explanation:

Say softly to your child: "When someone hurts our feelings, we sometimes feel angry or sad. Forgiveness is choosing not to hold onto those feelings. It's like taking the hurt from our hearts and giving it to Jesus. He washes it out so we can feel happy again." You can demonstrate by pretending to throw the hurt feelings into an imaginary trash can, God's trash can, so they can visualize letting go.

Explain Steps Simply:

Teach your child a tiny checklist for when they are upset:

1. **STOP:** Stop and notice your Heart feeling.

2. **PRAY:** Talk to Jesus about it.

3. **LET GO:** Give Him the icky feeling, let Jesus fill your Heart with peace, and forgive the person.

These three little words—Stop, Pray, Let Go—can become your child's go-to heart rhythm when big feelings come up. Create a poster featuring a stop sign, praying hands, and an open hand releasing a butterfly. Hang it in their room as a reminder.

Use a Real Example:

Next time your child is upset (even over something that seems tiny to us grown-ups, like losing a game or being told no dessert), you might try this approach:

- **STOP:** "Hey buddy, I see those big feelings. Wanna try our special Heart Check together?" (If they're open to it, invite them to put a hand on their belly and take a deep breath.)

- **PRAY:** "Let's tell Jesus what's happening in there. Some kids find it helps to say something like: 'Jesus, I feel ___ because ___.' What would you like to tell Him?" (Give space for their words, although, we recommend building the habit of silently praying, we believe prayer is being with Jesus, not just talking to Him)

- **LET GO (Forgive):** "Now comes my favorite part, the letting go part! Want to tell Jesus you're ready to let go of that yucky feeling? You could say something like: 'I don't want to keep this anger, Jesus. I give it to You.'"

I've seen this work wonders with my own kiddos, though each one responds differently. Some dive right in, while others need more time to warm up to it. The beauty is watching how Jesus meets each one exactly where they are. As the Bible says, *"Let the little children come to Me, and do not forbid them; for of such is the kingdom of heaven"* (Matthew 19:14, NKJV).

Let them do something fun to show they were able to forgive from the Heart; high-five the air like they're high-fiving Jesus, toss an invisible ball of yuck, or draw a big smiley face over the sad one.

Whatever you choose, when the moment settles, celebrate it, *but keep the spotlight on them*, not you. It's okay to feel proud as a parent or teacher, but this is their heart moment, not our teaching win. Wrap them in a hug if it fits, and say something that helps them own the breakthrough. You might say, "That took courage. You did it!" or "Aren't you proud of yourself?" or even just, "You talked to Jesus—that's a big deal." Little by little, these moments build, and before long, they'll start reaching for Him on their own.

Forgiveness in Three Directions:

Teach that sometimes we need to forgive **others**, sometimes we even need to forgive **ourselves** (if we feel bad about something we did), and sometimes kids might feel mad at **God** ("Why didn't God stop this?"). In simple terms:

- **Forgive Others:** If someone else hurt you, you forgive *them* (E.g., "I forgive my friend for shouting at me").

- **Forgive Yourself:** If you're upset at yourself (maybe you feel guilty for breaking something), you can say, "I'm going to stop being mad at myself. Jesus, I receive your forgiveness for me, too." This is a bit abstract, but some children do become very upset about their own mistakes.

- **"Forgive" God / Let go of anger toward Him:** Emphasize God never truly does wrong, but if a child is angry with God (like "God, I prayed for my pet, and it still died, I'm mad!"), tell them: "You can tell God you're upset. He understands. And you can say, 'God, I'm not going to stay mad at You. I know You love me, even if I don't understand.'" Essentially, releasing those feelings toward God allows them to reconnect with Him again.

You can make this kid-friendly by using stuffed animals to represent each: have one represent someone else, one represent themselves, and one a "God" figure (not to personify but as a stand-in). Then practice tiny prayers: the child puppet apologizes, the main child forgives, etc. For "God," maybe the child puppet says, "God, I was upset at You, but I know You are good, so I'm not mad anymore." This reminds them about God's goodness and His true nature.

STORY TIME: The Prince with a Muddy Bible-heart

(A story about forgiveness and letting Jesus wash the yucky stuff out!)

A Happy Prince and a Big Problem

Once, there was a little prince who loved running through the palace gardens and picking flowers for his mommy. One sunny day, he found out that the stable boy had lost ten big bags of shiny gold coins that belonged to him!

"Oh no!" cried the prince. "That was my treasure!"

He got so mad his cheeks turned red. "He should go to the dungeon forever!" he shouted.

But the prince's daddy, the big, kind king, knelt down and said gently:

"Remember when *you* broke my favorite crown? I forgave you, even though it was worth more than all those gold coins. Don't you think you can forgive, too?"

The prince looked down at his shoes. But...he didn't forgive.

The next day, the prince woke up grumpy. He stomped through the halls. When his friend spilled juice, the prince yelled, "Now you owe me too!"

When someone lost his toy, he shouted, "You broke it on purpose!"

But inside his Bible-heart, the place where Jesus lives, started to feel yucky and heavy, like it was full of mud.

The king saw his little boy looking sad and angry. He picked him up, put him on his lap, and said softly: "Son," the king said kindly, "when we choose not to forgive, it's like letting yucky dirt stay in our tummy. But when we forgive, Jesus comes and gently washes all the yucky stuff away."

The prince felt the heavy, yucky feeling swirling inside his belly, and he felt bad; he didn't want the yuck there anymore.

The prince took a deep breath, put his hand on his tummy, and said: "Jesus, I receive your forgiveness for being angry so much. Jesus, please forgive the stable boy as well. He doesn't owe me anymore."

And guess what? As soon as he forgave, the prince felt light and clean again. It was as if Jesus had washed out all the mud, and his tummy felt peaceful and sparkly inside.

He ran outside and played with his friends. No more yelling. No more blaming. Just giggles and sunshine.

And every time his tummy started to feel heavy again, he remembered:

"Jesus the Forgiver lives in me. I can let go and be free!"

Bible-heart Check Question:

"Do you ever feel something yucky inside when someone hurts you?"

"Would you like Jesus to help you forgive and take that yucky feeling out so you can be happy again?"

Object Lesson – Heart Medicine

Hold up a small medicine cup or a pretend bottle of "heart medicine" (you can even use water or juice for demonstration purposes). Say to your child, "When our body feels sick, we take medicine to help it get better. But when our feelings get hurt, we need something for our hearts, too. Forgiveness is like heart medicine; it helps wash out the hurt so Jesus can heal us on the inside."

Let your child pretend to take a small sip and place their hand on their tummy or chest. Invite them to say, "I forgive, and Jesus is healing my Bible-heart."

Pause and ask, "Do you feel peace starting to come back inside?"

You can add: "Every time you forgive, it's like taking a dose of Jesus' love medicine; it helps your heart get strong and happy again!"

Important:

Clearly Explain What Forgiveness is Not:

- Forgiveness does not mean pretending nothing happened. We know something did hurt us.

- Forgiveness doesn't mean saying the bad action was okay. It means we won't hold a grudge about it.

- Forgiveness doesn't mean we let people continue to hurt us. **If someone keeps hurting your child, assure them to tell a grown-up.** Forgiveness cleans our hearts, but grown-ups help stop the hurt from happening again.

Bedtime Role-Play Prayer:

Bedtime is one of the most vulnerable times I've shared with my children. Try doing a quick role-play: One night, the stuffed bear is sad. Help your child lead the bear through the prayer steps: Bear says in a tiny voice, "I'm sad because my friend didn't play with me." Child guides bear: "Stop, bear, put your paw on your belly. Pray, 'Jesus, I feel sad my friend ignored me.' Let go and say, 'I forgive my friend, and I give You my sadness. Please fill my Heart with love and snuggles." Then, the bear smiles. This makes your child the "leader," reinforcing their understanding.

Celebrate Them in Their Willingness to Pray:

When your child chooses to pray, slow down and notice it with them honestly. Not in a "good job" kind of way, but in a "look what just happened" kind of way. You might say, "Hey, you let Jesus help with that," or "Do you feel how different your heart feels now?" Let them connect the dots. That quiet recognition reinforces what really mattered—they opened up to Him, and He showed up. That's worth noting, not as praise for performance but as a way to build awareness and gratitude for the work that Jesus did.

FOR TEACHERS & MINISTRY LEADERS (In Groups)

Discussion – What is Forgiveness?:

Ask the children: "What do you think forgiveness means?" Let them share briefly. Affirm their thoughts and summarize: "Forgiveness is choosing to let go of anger and hurt. It's like cleaning our Hearts so we feel happy again."

Teach a "Heart Prayer" Routine:

Encourage the idea that praying about our feelings can be as normal as washing our hands before eating. It's a healthy habit. Perhaps create a little rhyme or set of motions the class can memorize:

- "When I feel bad, I will **stop** (hand up),

- Then I will **pray** (hands together or on their belly),

- I forgive and **let it go** (hands open, moving apart),

- And Jesus makes me okay! (thumbs up and a big smile)."

Practice this rhyme with motions a few times. Kids love doing motions, and it sticks in their heads. Now, they have a framework.

Visual – Heart Jar and Rocks:

Use a clear jar labeled "Heart" filled with small stones labeled "mad," "sad," or "hurt." Show how heavy it is and say, "This is our heart when we don't forgive, heavy with hurt feelings." Remove stones as you say, "I forgive [name]," showing the jar getting lighter. Explain that forgiveness makes our hearts light again.

Interactive Demonstration:

Have a volunteer share (or you propose) a scenario: e.g., "Sammy is upset because he spilled paint on his picture." Then, ask the class, "What should Sammy do?" Guide them: **Stop** – maybe Sammy was about to cry or yell, but instead, he stops and takes a breath. **Pray** – Sammy says, "Jesus, I'm so angry I messed up my painting." **Let Go** – Sammy decides not to scream or quit art forever; he says, "Jesus, help me feel better." Then, **Peace** – Sammy feels calm and maybe gets an idea to fix the painting or start a new one calmly.

Go through a couple of different scenarios (one where someone else did wrong, one where the child did something wrong, one where they're mad at circumstances like rain canceled a picnic). Each time, walk through the steps of Stop, Pray, Let Go, and Peace. Soon, the kids in the class will start to chime in with what the character should say to Jesus. That's good. It means they're learning it!

Group Prayer Practice:

Sometimes, children are unsure of the words to use in prayer. Give them simple templates:

- **"Jesus, I feel ___ because ___. Please take away the ___ and give me Your peace. I forgive ___."** Have them repeat this all together with a generic example, like: "Jesus, I feel **mad** because **my toy broke**. Please take away the **mad** and give me Your peace. With your help, I forgive **my brother.**" They can fill in the blanks quietly for their own situation if they want. The rhythm of that prayer will stick, and they can adapt it in real life.

Forgiveness Role-Play Game:

This is a repeat of previous practices, but it can be turned into a game for the whole group. Prepare a few short skits or narrate and assign roles to the kids. For example, two kids pretend to argue over a crayon. Pause mid-argument and say, "Freeze! Prayer time." The arguing kids (with your coaching) then do the Stop-Pray-Let Go routine: they stop arguing, maybe bow their heads together, one says sorry, and the other forgives. Then, they unfreeze, and they play happily. Do multiple quick rounds with different kids. It makes it almost like improv theater, with the solution always being prayer or forgiveness. This not only reinforces the steps but also lightens the mood around conflicts, showing them that most conflicts can end with prayer and forgiveness.

"Forgive-o-Meter" Visual:

Draw a big thermometer or meter on the board labeled "Heart Peace." When we haven't prayed or forgiven, the meter is low (draw a sad face at the bottom). Each step of obedience (stop, pray, let go) raises the meter toward a happy face at the top. You can dramatize this by drawing it up in increments as they do each step in practice. Or use a volunteer as a "meter," raising their arms higher at each step. It's a fun visual to show that by the end of the steps, the heart's peace is at 100%.

Remind Children about God's Help:

Make sure they understand that **Jesus is the One who heals the Heart when we pray**.

We're not just using a self-help trick; we're actually asking our all-powerful Friend to step in. Encourage them that even if the hurt feels "big," Jesus is bigger, and it's *easy* for Him to fix. There's no "too big" or "too little;" ALL is easy for Jesus!

You can quote that as a catchphrase: *"Nothing's too hard for Jesus!"* Have them shout it. Therefore, no matter how bad they feel, they should always come to Him.

Closing Group Prayer:

Conclude the lesson or day by encouraging everyone to reflect on something or someone they may still need to forgive, as well as any lingering negative feelings they may have. Lead a brief moment of silence for each person to whisper their own issue to Jesus. Then, together, say out loud: *"Jesus, we give You all these hurts. We forgive everyone we need to forgive. We even forgive ourselves for mistakes because You have forgiven us. Thank You for dying on the cross to take away all our sins and hurts. We love You. Amen."* Keep it short and simple for them to follow.

REAL-LIFE EXAMPLE: The Cafeteria Chronicles
(JASON)

In prayer, I remembered one such day with painfully cinematic clarity. There I was, mid-bite and mid-debate with my buddy Jerry, arguing the essential things in life, like which local pizza joint was the best, when the unthinkable happened. A rogue pint of milk suddenly took flight from across the cafeteria like it had a personal vendetta. It soared through the air as if in slow motion, spinning like a dairy-fueled ninja star before landing with a glorious splat right on the side of Jerry's unsuspecting face.

It was like time froze. Jerry didn't move. His face went full statue mode, somewhere between shock and "Did I just get baptized in 2%?" And then came the explosion, not of milk, but of laughter. That raw, caustic, teenage kind of laughter. You know, the type that pierces your soul and shatters whatever shred of dignity you were hoping to hold onto.

What amazed me, though, was how calm Jerry stayed. No rage. No retaliation. Just stunned silence and maybe a blink or two. I didn't have a ton of close friends back then, but the ones I kept close were the peacemakers, the laid-back, humble types who could take a milk grenade to the face and still remain calm. Jerry was definitely one of them.

I felt nervous now. From that moment on, I felt unsafe and completely vulnerable. Not just vulnerable to weaponized dairy products but genuinely afraid of the other kids.

At another moment, I remembered, amid the daily school chaos, there was this kid I secretly nicknamed "Smasher Shawn."

In my very official, top-secret *Get to Know Your Bully Notebook* (GTKYB for short), I kept track of every playground menace I ever crossed paths with.

Smasher Shawn didn't waste his talents by throwing milk cartons or getting into cafeteria fights.

Nope.

His specialty was way more personal: flattening my brown bag lunch like clockwork.

But here's what I didn't realize until years later:

A bitter root had been planted. I didn't know it then, but underneath the laughs were deep, unpleasant feelings I had never dealt with: powerlessness, shame, the sting of being laughed at and not defended. I felt it in my gut, but I didn't know how to let Jesus heal it.

So, one day, years later, Jesus brought it back to me when I prayed.

I told Him, "Jesus, I remember that cafeteria. I still feel the yucky shame inside from being embarrassed and picked on, and for feeling unsafe. And I receive Your forgiveness for holding onto that pain all this time."

Then I sat with Jesus, and I let Him go through that feeling, allowing it to be carried away. I let His peace come in. I forgave Shawn. I forgave the people who laughed at Jerry and me.

Then I asked, "Jesus, what's the truth You want me to know?"

And I heard Him whisper to my Heart: "You are not alone; I am with you. You are protected, seen, and strong in Me."

That's when the shame left. I felt light. Clean. Free. The memory didn't sting anymore. I could laugh, not in bitterness, but in healing.

KEY PRINCIPLES TO REMEMBER

- Forgiveness is not just a nice thing to do; it's medicine for our hearts. Unforgiveness hurts us way more than it hurts the person who hurt us.

- Children learn forgiveness best by seeing it modeled first; they absorb what they observe in the adults around them.

- Jesus is the real Forgiver in us; we yield to Him and let Him forgive through us rather than straining to do it by our own efforts.

- There's a physical component to forgiveness, helping children connect to their 'Bible-heart' (tummy), where emotions are felt.

- Peace is the confirmation of true forgiveness. When a child feels peace inside, they know forgiveness has worked.

GENTLE CAUTIONS FOR GROWN-UPS

- Don't force a child to forgive before they're ready; guide them gently, allowing them the dignity of their own process.

- Never shame a child for struggling to forgive; it's normal and human to find forgiveness difficult.

- Don't teach forgiveness as "just saying sorry;" help them understand it's an inside heart change, not just words.

- Avoid empty phrases like "forgive and forget;" teach instead that we forgive and Jesus takes the pain.

- Don't skip the "feel it" step; children need to acknowledge the hurt before releasing it, not pretend it never happened.

- Don't rush through prayer steps mechanically; make space for the child to feel and connect genuinely.

- Don't make prayer seem like a magic spell; it's a relationship with Jesus, not a formula to be recited.

- Don't criticize their prayer words; Jesus hears even the simplest expressions from a child's Heart.

- Avoid making prayer only about crises; practice these steps in calm moments, too, so they feel natural.

(GWEN)

I've noticed something revealing about children who struggle to forgive; they often have a bitter root of victimhood. A child who constantly positions themselves as being wronged has typically believed a lie that they are perpetually a victim. When this lie takes root, it creates a terrible harvest; it actually draws similar treatment from others, reinforcing and "proving" the lie.

The child who believes "everyone picks on me" often finds themselves continually picked on, not because the belief is true, but because bitter roots create the very conditions they fear. It's a painful cycle that can only be broken by the power of Jesus through forgiveness and repentance.

Forgiveness is about freeing ourselves from the victim identity that keeps attracting, as a magnet would, the very hurt we're trying to avoid. When we help children forgive from their hearts, guided by Jesus, we're not just address-ing a single offense; we're breaking a pattern that would otherwise follow them into adulthood.

I've watched children who once complained constantly about being mistreated transform through the act of forgiveness. As Jesus washes away both the hurt and the victim mentality, they begin to walk in a new identity, not as someone perpetually wounded, but as someone constantly loved by God and capable of extending that love to others.

This is the true power of forgiveness: it doesn't just heal past wounds; it prevents future ones by transforming how we see ourselves in God's story.

Remember (for Kids):

Forgiveness is how Jesus heals our hearts. When we forgive, we give the hurt to Jesus and feel happy again. Forgiveness is a gift Jesus gives us; use it as often as you need to!

We can **always** pray when we have a problem in our hearts. We **stop** to notice the feeling, **pray** to Jesus about it, and **let it go** into His hands. Jesus is strong and loving; He can carry all the unpleasant things, so we don't have to keep holding on to them. You can talk to Jesus like your best friend, any time! He will help your Heart every single time you ask.

CHAPTER 20:
Thoughts and Truth – Keeping Bad Thoughts Away

Tiny Hearts and Big Thoughts:

Even 5-year-olds have thoughts that can be negative or scary. Sometimes, these thoughts stem from hidden hurts or the enemy (the devil) trying to make us feel bad. But we can ask, "Is this what God would say, or is this a mean thought I should ignore?" We help children learn to replace lies ("I'm not loved") with the truth that bubbles up when Jesus speaks directly to our hearts. We don't just say words; we open our hearts to Him, let Him take the "yuck" away first, and then ask the Holy Spirit, "What truth do You say about me?" This chapter helps children practice choosing Jesus' truth with a heart that listens to God.

You know, sometimes I think our adult minds aren't all that different from those of preschoolers, easily distracted by shiny objects and geared toward believing the most dramatic story available. I've even caught myself as an adult having a complete internal meltdown over an email or text message that "sounded cold." Meanwhile, my actual five-year-old is handling disappointment with more grace than I am! The good news is Jesus meets us all where we are. Whether you're forty or four, He's ready to replace those runaway thoughts and take them captive with His peace. Sometimes, I think He laughs because He knows exactly what He's doing, and He loves us through it all.

FOR PARENTS (At Home)

Explain in Child-Like Terms:

Say: "Honey, not every thought that pops into your head is true or good. Some thoughts are like sneaky bugs that buzz in and try to bite you with mean words. But Jesus helps your heart know what is truly true! First, we give Jesus the mean feeling or yucky thought, and then we ask Him, 'Jesus, what truth do You say to my heart?'" Children easily understand the concept of asking Jesus directly for help.

Game: Truth or Trash:

Play a game where you say a sentence, and your child says if it's truth (something Jesus would say in their heart) or Trash (an evil thought to throw away). Emphasize that truth isn't just repeating words, but listening to what Jesus says in their heart:

- "Nobody loves me." Child: "Trash! Throw it away!" (Have them pretend to throw it in a trash can.) Then, guide them to pray briefly, "Jesus, I give You that thought. What do You say to my heart instead?" Pause to listen together. An example of truth they might hear is: "I am very loved by my family and by God."

- "I'm so important because God made me special." Child: "Truth!" (They can hug themselves or point upward.)

- "God doesn't care when I'm hurting." Child: "Trash!" (toss it); guide: "Jesus, what's the truth?" Example: "God cares about every tear I cry."

- "It's okay not to forgive someone if they were really mean." Child: "Trash!" Guide to heart truth: "Jesus always helps me forgive."

Make it fun, but emphasize listening to Jesus in their heart.

Teach a "Shoo!" Technique:

If your child says something negative about themselves ("I can't do it," "I'm dumb," "It's hopeless"), gently correct them: "That sounds like a bad buggy thought. Let's say 'Shoo!' to it." Together, literally shoo it away (wave hands). Then immediately ask, "Jesus, we give You this thought. What truth do You speak in my heart?" Wait a moment and help them recognize the positive truth they sense Jesus saying inside: "I can try again because You help me," "You love me even when I make mistakes," or "You're with me always." Always encourage them to notice what Jesus is saying in their heart, rather than just replacing thoughts with memory verses or relying on their own thinking.

Bedtime Thoughts:

At night, kids sometimes have fearful thoughts ("There's a monster under the bed," "I'm afraid of being alone in the dark"). This is a perfect opportunity to practice giving fearful thoughts or feelings directly to Jesus. Acknowledge, "I know, buddy. Let's give that scary thought to Jesus." Together, say, "Jesus, take this scary thought away." Then, encourage them to quietly listen inside and pray: "Now, Jesus, what truth do You speak to my heart?" They might feel His peace or sense, "Jesus is right here with me."

Affirmation Jar:

Create a "God's Truth Jar." Write simple positive truths about identity in Christ on small papers ("Jesus loves me," "I am a child of God," "I have a brave heart," "Jesus makes me strong"). Explain clearly, "These are reminders of what Jesus says in your heart." When your child seems down or believes a lie ("I'm bad"), have them pull a truth from the jar. Say gently, "Let's give Jesus that sad or hurt feeling first. Now let's read this truth as a reminder and listen to what Jesus says in our hearts." This emphasizes the heart posture rather than simply quoting truths. Let siblings also contribute meaningful truths about each other, encouraging heartfelt connections.

FOR TEACHERS & MINISTRY LEADERS
(In Groups)

Illustration – Guarding the Mind Door:

Tell kids: "Imagine your head has a door. Good thoughts from Jesus are welcome inside, but we shut the door on bad thoughts." Choose a child to stand as a "guard." You (or another leader) knock, playing a "bad thought:" "Hello, I say you're not loved, let me in!" Children respond, "No! Go away!" After rejection, have them pause briefly to listen inside their hearts: "Jesus, what truth do You say instead?" Example answer: "I'm loved by Jesus!" Then another knock: "Hi, I'm the thought, 'God will always help me.'" Kids: "Yes! Come in!" This helps children learn they can choose to listen to Jesus in their hearts.

Emphasize: You're the boss of your "thought door," and Jesus helps your heart know the difference.

Talk about Voices:

Explain gently that sometimes thoughts aren't our own, like naughty or mean thoughts. "We can't see an angel or devil on our shoulder, but we feel thoughts. If it's mean or bad, it's not Jesus. Jesus always speaks kindness, truth, and love in your heart." Encourage kids: "Ask inside your heart, 'Would Jesus say this?' If not, kick it out and ask Jesus for His truth instead.'"

Activity – Thought Sorting:

Draw happy or sad faces, or use baskets labeled "Good Thoughts" and "Bad Thoughts." When sorting not-good thoughts, after discarding them, teach kids to pause briefly, "Jesus, we give You this bad thought. What's Your truth instead?" They might respond with truths like "God loves me" or "I can forgive."

Memory Verse: 2 Corinthians 10:5 (simplified): "We capture every thought and make it obey Christ." Teach kids: "Catch thoughts, give the bad ones to Jesus, and ask Jesus, 'What's Your truth?'" Pretend-catching actions reinforce this idea.

Encourage Questions – GOOD COMMUNICATION:

Teach kids to ask adults or Jesus when confused: "Is this thought true?" Explain that asking for help is part of hearing Jesus' truth clearly in their hearts.

REAL-LIFE EXAMPLE:

From Bad Boy to Beloved

When our son, Jacob, was about four and a half, we began to notice some unusual things he was saying, things that didn't align with how we had raised him or how we knew he truly felt. Out of nowhere, he began saying things like, "I just feel like you don't love me," or "I think I'm a bad boy," and even, "I do too many bad things."

As his parent, I immediately reassured him, again and again, that he was deeply loved and that he was a good boy. But my words didn't seem to reach his heart. The lie had already taken root.

I remember feeling frustrated and confused. Where did this come from? Then, the Lord lit up a light bulb inside of me. Somewhere along the way, my son had taken in a lie that he was bad. It wasn't just a fleeting thought. It had slipped into his heart and started shaping how he saw himself.

So the next time he said one of those out-of-character things, I didn't just reassure him. I invited him into an encounter.

I gently asked, "Are you ready to get rid of that feeling?" He said yes. We sat together, and I placed his hand on his tummy, his heart, and covered it with mine. I guided him to close his eyes and connect with Jesus there.

I asked him to recall the moment when he first started feeling like a bad boy. I told him it was okay to feel that feeling, but that Jesus wanted to go there with him. We sat in the quiet, and I asked him to repeat after me:

"Jesus, I receive Your forgiveness for taking that lie into my heart."

I asked how he felt afterward, and he said, "Better, but I still feel bad." That was our cue to go one step further.

I explained, "Now that your heart is at peace, we can tell that lie to go."

And we did.

"I don't believe the lie that I'm a bad boy anymore," he said, repeating after me.

Then I asked him, "Now let's ask Jesus what the truth is."

He closed his eyes, soaked in the moment, and then, with a big, joyful smile, he whispered one word: "Good."

Tears welled up in my eyes. He knew. He had heard the truth, not just from my mouth, but from the mouth of the One who made him.

We giggled together, and I told him, "That's right. Jesus says you are good. Let's pray that truth gets sealed on the tablet of your heart forever."

That moment wasn't just about correcting wrong thoughts. It was about pulling out a bitter root and planting the truth of Jacob's identity deep, where it belongs, in the garden of the heart.

KEY PRINCIPLES TO REMEMBER

- Not every thought a child has comes from them; some come from wounds, others from the enemy.

- Teaching children to discern thoughts is one of the most valuable spiritual skills they'll ever learn.

- Jesus speaks truth directly to a child's heart and teaches them to listen for His voice, not just repeat memorized phrases.

- The real battle isn't about behavior control; it's about what truth rules inside

- Children can learn to recognize Jesus' voice at very young ages; they often hear Him more clearly than adults do.

GENTLE CAUTIONS FOR GROWN-UPS

- Don't just correct negative thoughts with positive thinking; teach children to yield to Jesus first and receive His truth.

- Avoid making it complicated or scary; this isn't about spiritual warfare, but about a simple connection with Jesus, the Truth.

- Don't dismiss their fears or anxieties by saying, "Don't think that" or "You shouldn't think that way." Acknowledge the feeling first, then guide them to the truth.

- Don't rush the listening part, give them space to actually hear Jesus speak to their heart before jumping to "right answers."

- Avoid making this a performance; children shouldn't feel they have to "hear" something to please you.

Remember: Not every thought that pops into your mind is truth or from God. Some thoughts try to sneak in and make your Bible-heart feel yucky, worried, or afraid. But you don't have to keep them. When that happens, pause. Pay attention to Jesus in you and say, "Jesus, this thought feels wrong. Is it true?" If it doesn't bring peace inside, give it to Him. Let Jesus take out the lie and fill you with His truth instead. That's how your mind and heart stay clean, peaceful, and full of His love. You were made to think with Jesus, from the inside out.

CHAPTER 21:
A Heart Full of Love – No More "Empty" Feelings

Understanding the Heart's True Hunger

Even young children can feel an "empty" spot, like when they really, really want attention or affection. Grown-ups might call it "emotional neediness," but for kids, it's that empty or lonely feeling that appears when something important is missing inside. Sometimes, if they don't feel they have enough of what they need, they might feel very sad or "like a hole in the heart." However, the great news is that **God's love can fill every space!**

Abraham Maslow discovered in 1943, through his ground-breaking research on human needs, something scripture had already revealed: that we are created with specific legitimate needs.[11] When these needs go unmet, children don't just feel sad; they experience a profound sense of emptiness. That emptiness drives them to try to fill it with things that were never meant to satisfy the deepest places of the heart. Only God can fully satisfy the areas of unmet needs in children's hearts.[12]

---

11 Saul McLeod, "Maslow's Hierarchy of Needs," Simply Psychology, October 23, 2025, https://www.simplypsychology.org/maslow.html.

12 Nicole Celestine, "Abraham Maslow, His Theory & Contribution to Psychology," Modified July 28, 2025, Reviewed by Jo Nash, https://positivepsychology.com/abraham-maslow/.

The Eight Heart-Hungers That Drive the "Empty Feeling"

Based on decades of research and biblical truth, here are the core needs that, when unmet, create that aching emptiness children try to fill:

1. **LOVE** - *The Need to Be Cherished*

"But God shows his love for us in that while we were still sinners, Christ died for us" (Romans 5:8, ESV). *"See what kind of love the Father has given to us, that we should be called children of God"* (1 John 3:1, ESV).

When a child doesn't feel genuinely loved, they might:

- Constantly seek approval from others.
- Act out to get attention (even negative attention).
- Become clingy or possessive in relationships.
- Try to earn love through perfect behavior.

The Empty Feeling Says: "I'm not lovable unless I do something to deserve it." **Jesus Fills It With:** The unconditional love that He freely gives, demonstrating that they are cherished beyond measure.

2. **SAFETY** - *The Need for Security*

"He will cover you with his pinions, and under his wings, you will find refuge" (Psalm 91:4, ESV). *"The LORD your God is with you, the Mighty Warrior who saves"* (Zephaniah 3:17, ESV).

When a child doesn't feel safe, they might:

- Worry constantly about what might happen.
- Try to control everything around them.
- Have trouble sleeping or experience nightmares.
- Withdraw or hide from new situations.

181

The Empty Feeling Says: "The world is dangerous, and I'm not protected." **Jesus Fills It With:** His protective covering and the security of knowing the Mighty Warrior is always with them.

3. PURPOSE - *The Need for Meaning*

"For I know the plans I have for you, declares the LORD, plans for welfare and not for evil, to give you a future and a hope" (Jeremiah 29:11, ESV). *"And we know that for those who love God all things work together for good, for those who are called according to his purpose"* (Romans 8:28, ESV).

When a child doesn't sense their purpose, they might:

- Feel directionless or confused about life.
- Lack of motivation for activities.
- Engage in destructive behaviors ("Nothing matters anyway").
- Feel hopeless about their future.

The Empty Feeling Says: "I don't matter, and my life has no meaning." **Jesus Fills It With** His perfect plans for their future and the assurance that He is working all things together for their good.

4. VALUED - *The Need to Be Treasured*

"Fear not, for I have redeemed you; I have called you by name, you are mine" (Isaiah 43:1, ESV). *"You are precious in my eyes, and honored, and I love you"* (Isaiah 43:4, ESV).

When a child doesn't feel valued, they might:

- Put themselves down constantly ("I'm worthless").
- Compare themselves negatively to others.
- Become perfectionistic to try to earn worth.
- Allow others to mistreat them.

The Empty Feeling Says: "I'm not worth much to anyone." **Jesus Fills It With:** His declaration that they are precious in His eyes, redeemed and called by name.

5. AFFIRMATION - *The Need for Encouragement*

"The LORD your God is in your midst, a mighty one who will save; he will rejoice over you with gladness; he will quiet you by his love; he will exult over you with loud singing" (Zephaniah 3:17, ESV). *"For you formed my inward parts; you knitted me together in my mother's womb"* (Psalm 139:13, ESV).

When a child doesn't receive affirmation, they might:

- Fish for compliments constantly.

- Be extremely sensitive to any criticism.

- Never feel "good enough" no matter what they achieve.

- Fear trying new things because they might fail.

The Empty Feeling Says: "I'm probably disappointing everyone." **Jesus Fills It With:** His joyful singing over them and the truth that He carefully formed them precisely as they are.

6. AFFECTION - *The Need for Physical and Emotional Warmth*

"As one whom his mother comforts, so I will comfort you" (Isaiah 66:13, ESV). *"The LORD is near to the brokenhearted and saves the crushed in spirit"* (Psalm 34:18, ESV).

When a child doesn't feel affection, they might:

- Crave physical touch or altogether avoid it.

- Feel emotionally distant from others.

- Have difficulty expressing their own emotions.

- Feel unloved even when told they're loved.

The Empty Feeling Says: "Nobody really wants to be close to me." **Jesus Fills It With:** His comforting presence that comes near to the brokenhearted with tender, motherly affection.

7. SEEN - *The Need to Be Known and Understood*

"O LORD, you have searched me and known me! You know when I sit down and when I rise up; you discern my thoughts from afar" (Psalm 139:1-2, ESV). *"Even the hairs of your head are all numbered"* (Luke 12:7, ESV).

When a child doesn't feel seen, they might:

- Act out dramatically to get attention.

- Constantly interrupt conversations.

- Feel invisible even in a crowded room.

- Withdraw because "no one notices me anyway."

The Empty Feeling Says: "I'm invisible, and nobody really knows me." **Jesus Fills It With:** His complete knowledge of every detail of their life and His constant, attentive care.

8. SIGNIFICANT - *The Need to Matter*

"Before I formed you in the womb, I knew you, and before you were born I conse-crated you" (Jeremiah 1:5, ESV). *"For we are his workmanship, created in Christ Jesus for good works, which God prepared beforehand, that we should walk in them"* (Ephesians 2:10, ESV).

When a child doesn't feel significant, they might:

- Believe they don't make a difference.

- Think their voice doesn't matter.

- Give up on goals and dreams easily.

- Feel replaceable or unimportant.

The Empty Feeling Says: "Nothing I do really matters." **Jesus Fills It With:** His purposeful design for their life and the good works He prepared specifically for them to accomplish.

Why Material Things Can't Fill Heart-Holes

Remember our story of **Little Emmy and the Strawberry Weeds** from earlier? That picture helps us see how unmet needs can sprout into all sorts of tangled patterns. When one of these eight core needs goes unmet, children instinctively try to fill the emptiness with things that were never designed to satisfy the heart. Later, we'll share a story about a little girl and a sweet treat that shows this even more clearly.

- A child lacking love might collect toys, thinking, "If I have enough stuff, maybe I'll feel loved."

- The child lacking safety might hoard snacks or control their environment obsessively.

- A child lacking significance might show off constantly or brag about their possessions.

- The child lacking **affection** might seek inappropriate attention from others.

But here's what we've learned: **physical things and even constant attention can't fill the heart completely; only God's love can reach those sacred depths.**

FOR PARENTS (At Home)

The Love Tank:

Tell your child: "Imagine your heart is like a **tank or a cup**. It must be filled with love—from family, friends, and God. If it gets low, you feel terrible. What happens when the car runs out of gas? It stops. What if your tummy is empty? You feel hungry and cranky. It is the same with your heart. If you feel you're not loved enough, you might feel very sad or mad." Then assure: "Mommy/Daddy's job is to keep your love tank full! And God is always pouring love in, too." Make it playful, and ask your child, "How's your love tank today?" Then, fill it up with a hug, a smile, or some kind words. This will help them become aware of their emotional needs in a positive way.

When a Child Feels They Need More

Sometimes, a child might act out or appear clingy because they need reassurance of love. Use simple phrases: "Do you need an extra hug? Let's ask Jesus to help you feel how much we love you and how much He loves you." Then do a family hug and a short prayer: *"Jesus, pour Your love into ____'s heart right now. We love ____, and You love ____ so much!"* When they hear you pray this out loud, it sinks deep.

STORY TIME: The Never-Ending Cupcake:

There once was a little girl named Lily who carried a hollow feeling inside that nothing seemed to fill. When that empty ache would rise, she'd ask for cupcakes, believing the sweetness of their creamy white frosting might soothe whatever was missing.

"Just one more," she'd plead, eyes fixed on the colorful treats that promised happiness with every bite.

One afternoon, after visiting the bakery with her mother, Lily managed to convince her to buy not one, not two, but three cupcakes, each one more elaborate than the last. With frosting-stained fingers and sprinkles dotting her shirt, Lily devoured them all.

But as the sugar haze lifted, something strange happened. The hollow feeling hadn't gone away. In fact, it seemed to yawn wider than before, and now Lily's tummy ached, too, a physical discomfort joining her mysterious sadness.

Later that evening, sitting in her grandmother's warm kitchen with tears welling in her eyes, Lily confessed, "I don't understand, Grandma. I got all the cupcakes I wanted today, but I still feel sad inside. And now my tummy hurts, too."

Grandma set aside her knitting and opened her arms. As Lily crawled into her lap, Grandma held her close and whispered a truth that would change everything: "Sweet child, **maybe your heart is hungry, not your tummy.**"

Those simple words landed like rain on the driest dirt. Grandma gently placed Lily's small hand over her heart and said, "Let's ask Jesus to fill up what's empty in here."

Together, they prayed, Lily's whispered words rising like incense, inviting Jesus into that hollow space. As peace began to settle over her, Lily realized what she'd really been craving all along wasn't sugar or treats; it was a connection. Attention. The gentle assurance that she was seen and treasured.

From that day forward, Lily continued to enjoy cupcakes on special occasions. But when that familiar emptiness would creep in, **she knew that a hug, a prayer, and opening her Bible-heart to Jesus brought satisfaction.** The sweetness of being loved filled her in ways sugar never could.

This truth applies to the hearts of all our children. When they frantically collect toys, demand more screen time, or become fixated on material things, they're often signaling a deeper hunger. **Physical things and even constant attention can't fill the heart completely; only God's love can reach those sacred depths.**

Remember this story the next time your child seems insatiable. Their heart might be telling you precisely what Lily discovered—that what they're really hungry for is the Bread of Life Himself.

The cupcakes Lily devoured couldn't satisfy her heart's hunger for love and significance. The toys children frantically collect can't fill their need to feel **valued** and **seen.** Only Jesus, meeting them in their Bible-heart, can pour in exactly what each empty space was designed to hold.

Fill the Empty Heart Activity:

Draw a big heart on paper. Leave it empty/white. Give your child stickers or cut-out paper "drops" in red or pink colors. Write words on them like "love," "fun," "friends," "family," "Jesus," "kind words," etc., each representing something that fills their heart. Have the child glue or stick all these into the heart until it's full. If there are any spots left, draw little crosses or hearts and label them "God's love" to show that God fills all the empty spaces.

This craft visually shows them all the good things that fill their heart and that **God can fill whatever is missing**.

Hang it up as a reminder.

Addressing Jealousy or Attention-seeking:

If your child expresses jealousy ("You love brother more than me!") or often demands attention, **don't scold the feeling**. Instead, **address the need**: "I hear you. Sometimes, your heart worries it's not getting enough love. But I have *more* than enough love for both you and your brother. And God has endless love for you!" Perhaps set aside a special one-on-one time to invest in them. This has worked with our family very well. Then pray: "Jesus, help ___ feel how loved they are so that jealousy doesn't take hold." This ties their emotional need to God's supply.

Night-time assurance:

At bedtime, reinforce that they are loved and never alone. Some kids fear being alone at night; that's an emotional need for security. You can say: "Even when Mommy and Daddy aren't in the room, Jesus is here. You can talk to Jesus if you wake up scared or lonely." Perhaps consider giving them a plush toy and saying, "This is a gift to remind you: you are not alone; you are loved." A tangible object can symbolize that love.

FOR TEACHERS & MINISTRY LEADERS (In Groups)

Warm-up – All the Things We Need:

Ask the kids: "What do you need every day?" They'll say food, water, sleep, play, hugs, and so on. Agree and add, "We also all need **love**; that's just as important!" Show pictures of a plant with water and sunlight versus a wilted plant. "See how a plant needs water and sun? Our hearts need love and care."

Heart Hole Activity:

Cut a big paper heart and also a heart-shaped hole in the middle of it (like a donut heart). Show it to the class: "Oh no, this heart has an empty hole!" Ask, "What do you think could fill this hole so it's whole (play on words) again?" Take suggestions: maybe "love" or "friends," etc. Try some silly ones first: hold up a toy and put it behind the hole. Nope, still a hole. Candy? Still a hole. Only an appropriately sized cut-out that says, "God's Love" (or just another heart piece) truly fills it. Place that in and show the heart completely. Explain: "Toys, candy, even other people's attention are nice, but they don't truly fill an empty feeling. **God's love fits just right** in our hearts." This visual reinforces what even adults struggle with: nothing substitutes for divine love when it comes to our deepest needs.

Feeling "Left Out" or "Not Enough:"

We have seen firsthand many times how kids experience moments of feeling left out. Role-play a scenario: Two kids at play didn't ask a third to join. The third feels sad and maybe thinks, "Maybe I'm not fun," or "They don't like me." Ask the class, "What do you think this child's heart needs right now?" Likely: friendship, inclusion, love. "How can God help?" Guide: "God can remind you that you are loved and important. Ask to join or find someone else to play with; you're worth playing with!" Encourage empathy: Maybe another child can say, "I'll play with you!" Emphasize that **when we know God loves us, it helps those left-out feelings** hurt less because we remember, "I'm special to God."

(GWEN)

The empty spaces in a child's heart often form when comparison takes root. I've observed that when one classmate doesn't accept children they desperately want as a friend, something happens inside. It doesn't matter if they have a dozen other friends; in that moment, they compare themselves to the children that classmate befriends and see themselves as "less than."

This creates an emotional void, a space that yearns to be filled.

Filling Others' Love Tanks:

Make it a mini-mission that each child can be a "love helper." Explain that while God can fill us directly, He also uses **people to show love**. Ask, "How can we help fill someone's heart with love?" Brainstorm: share, say kind words, hug (with permission), and include them in play. Have each child practice by turning to a neighbor and saying one nice thing or giving a high-five. The room fills with giggles and smiles, and hearts get little boosts. Point out: "See, that's how we can be God's helpers in filling hearts!" This also combats neediness by focusing on giving, not just receiving.

God's Family Provides:

If appropriate (some kids may lack a good family life), mention that God can also use the church family, teachers, and friends to meet our need for love. If a child says, "My mommy is gone a lot," or something similar, gently acknowledge and say, "But look, God gave you a caring grandma (or teacher, etc.), and He is your heavenly Father, who never leaves." This assures them that any human lack God will compensate for.

Song – "Jesus Loves Me" with Extra Verse:

Everyone knows "Jesus Loves Me." After singing the standard, add a simple verse: "Jesus fills my heart with love, sends me kindness from above. When I'm sad and need a friend, His love for me has no end." (Just a simple additional idea). Singing about being filled with love will reinforce the concept.

You'll find more information on navigating these feelings below, using our Forgiveness Flow model and the Bitter Roots Prayer in Chapter 27. "Filling" is the last step in the prayer model.

Prayer to Be Filled:

Lead the kids in a prayer-like filling up: *"Dear God, my heart needs Your love every day. Thank you to my parents and friends who love me. And thank You that You always love me. Whenever I feel lonely or empty, please come and fill my heart up. I open my heart wide to You. Fill it to the top! Amen."* You can have them perform a gesture, such as raising their arms or opening their arms wide, when saying, "I open my heart wide," a physical sign of welcome.

STORY TIME: The Playground Orphan

Six-year-old Ava often played by herself at recess. While the other children grouped in games and activities, she would wander the perimeter of the playground, occasionally stopping to watch the others with a wistful expression that broke my heart.

One day after class, I asked her if she was okay. With surprising candor, she looked up at me and said, "My heart feels empty sometimes."

That simple statement hit me like a wave. I knelt at Ava's level and asked, "Can you tell me more about that empty feeling?"

"It's like when my tummy wants food, but it's not my tummy that's hungry," she explained, placing her hand on her chest. "It's in here."

I recognized what she was describing immediately, a loneliness that went deeper than just wanting playmates. Her parents had divorced the previous year, and she split her time between two homes, where she often felt like a visitor in both.

I asked if she wanted to pray together about her "heart hunger," and she nodded. We sat in the reading corner, and I taught her something simple:

"Jesus, my heart feels empty. I need Your love to fill me up. Please pour Your love right into the empty spots?"

Ava closed her eyes and repeated the words. When she opened them, she looked surprisingly peaceful.

"How does your heart feel now?" I asked.

"Warm," she said with a small smile. "Like Jesus is hugging me from inside."

Over the following weeks, I noticed Ava began checking in with herself when she felt lonely. She'd place her hand on her heart, close her eyes briefly, and then continue playing, sometimes joining other children afterward with new confidence.

One day, I overheard her telling another child who was feeling sad, "When your heart feels empty, you can ask Jesus to fill it up. He has special love that fits exactly where you need it."

Sometimes, it's from the mouths of babes that the most profound wisdom comes. There's a love that fits exactly where we need it.

KEY PRINCIPLES TO REMEMBER

- Every child (and adult) has legitimate emotional needs for love, connection, and security that must be met.

- No material thing, accomplishment, or even human relationship can fully satisfy the deepest longing of a heart; only God's love can.

- Children often express their emotional needs through behaviors such as clinginess, attention-seeking, and collecting things rather than words.

- Teaching children to recognize their "empty" feelings helps them learn to bring those needs directly to Jesus.

- Filling others with love is part of how God designed us to function; we're meant to both receive and give love.

GENTLE CAUTIONS FOR GROWN-UPS

- Don't shame a child for needing attention or affection; these are legitimate needs, not character flaws.

- Avoid using material things (toys, treats) as the primary way to fill emotional emptiness; they create a temporary fix but not lasting fulfillment.

- Don't dismiss jealousy or neediness with logical explanations; validate the feeling first, then guide it toward a healthier feeling.

- Avoid creating competition for love; never compare how much you love one child versus another or make affection something to be earned.

- Don't leave the "God loves you" teaching abstract; make it tangible through physical touch, consistent presence, and modeling His love.

Remember (tell the kids): If you ever feel a big empty or sad spot in your heart, like something's missing, I've got the best news! **God loves filling those empty spots with His love!** I've watched so many kids (including my own) discover this. Sometimes, He sends a friend right when you need one. Sometimes, a warm, cozy feeling bubbles up during prayer. Sometimes, it's just a sudden, deep-down reminder that you are His precious child. The Bible tells us, *"The LORD has appeared of old to me, saying: 'Yes, I have loved you with an everlasting love; Therefore with lovingkindness I have drawn you.'"* (Jeremiah 31:3, NKJV). Many children have shared with me what happens when they open their hearts and pray, "God, I need Your love," and then watch how He shows up. It might not always look the way we expect, but He's so creative in how He reaches our hearts.

As we've learned, feeling empty inside can affect not just our hearts but our whole selves. We've seen how God beautifully designed us so that emotional and spiritual healing can also touch our physical bodies in surprising ways. Remember how our hearts need love, just like our bodies need food and water? It turns out that there's even more to this connection: God created us in a fantastic way, where our emotions, spirits, and bodies are closely intertwined. In the next chapter, *"Healing the Whole Person,"* we'll explore how the emotional hurts we experience, such as feeling unloved or empty, can also impact our physical health. The excellent news is that when we invite Jesus into these tender places of our hearts, His healing often flows into our bodies, bringing peace, comfort, and even surprising physical restoration.

Let's explore how God designed our hearts and bodies to work together and how His love reaches every part, both inside and out.

CHAPTER 22:
Healing the Whole Person

How Emotional and Spiritual Healing Can Restore the Body

Have you ever noticed how our hearts and bodies seem to speak the same language? When we feel joyful and peaceful inside, our bodies often feel energized and strong. But when we carry around heavy emotions, like bitterness, shame, or unforgiveness, our bodies can feel weighed down, tired, or even physically ill. Jesus doesn't just care about your feelings; He cares about your whole body, too. Every part of you matters to Him. And every part is connected.

The Heart-Body Connection: Wonderfully Made

The Bible beautifully captures the intricately connected nature of our existence: *"I praise you because I am fearfully and wonderfully made"* (Psalm 139:14). Our hearts and bodies are so closely intertwined that emotional pain can manifest as physical ailments. When we experience deep emotional hurts or trauma, our bodies can echo those pains in unexpected ways. The fantastic thing is that when Jesus heals the heart, the body often follows suit as well.

Modern Science Agrees with Scripture

Recent studies back up what the Bible has hinted at for centuries:

- **Social Isolation and Loneliness:** Research from the CDC reveals that isolation and loneliness significantly increase risks for severe health conditions like heart disease, stroke, and dementia. We've all felt the effects of this, especially after challenging seasons like the COVID lockdowns.

- **Adverse Childhood Experiences (ACEs):** Traumas from childhood, like those studied by the CDC, can plant "bitter roots" deep within us, leading to emotional distress and physical health issues later in life.[13]

It turns out that science is catching up to Scripture; when your heart hurts, your body usually feels it as well. The good news is that emotional healing can also help restore wholeness to the body.

Testimonies of Transformation

During our time in ministry, we've seen countless beautiful examples of emotional and spiritual breakthroughs leading to remarkable physical healings.

- Many people have found relief from autoimmune symptoms after releasing deep-seated bitterness and embracing forgiveness.

- Many, including myself, have discovered relief from allergies after healing hidden emotional wounds.

- Chronic backaches, neck pain, and headaches have often vanished once emotional and spiritual healing took place.

- People have seen blood pressure stabilize and insomnia disappear when they encounter deep emotional healing through forgiveness and grace.

These testimonies show us that when Jesus sets us free emotionally, our physical bodies often respond beautifully as well.

---

13 National Center for Injury Prevention and Control (U.S.). Division of Violence Prevention. "Preventing Adverse Childhood Experiences (ACEs): Leveraging the Best Available Evidence," CDC Stacks, 2019, https://stacks.cdc.gov/view/cdc/82316.

Surprising and Miraculous Healing

One of my favorite aspects of emotional and spiritual healing is its unpredictability. To me, it restores a sense of awe and wonder towards God. We may identify one area needing healing, but Jesus often does so much more! We've witnessed children transition from restless and anxious to calm and joyful, not through behavior modification but by simply inviting Jesus into their emotional pain. Often, the healing ripples outward unexpectedly, such as fear and anxiety being replaced by peace.

It isn't the same for everyone, and physical healing doesn't occur every time. In my opinion, it adds a sense of wonder and mystery to the way God designed us, with our spirit, soul, and body all intertwined. Our job isn't to figure out the outcome. He knows what to do with the pain. And the results are often much more beautiful than we imagined.

[SCIENCE SPOTLIGHT]

Emmy's healing story, following her guidance through the prayer steps, isn't just a random occurrence. It really shows a certain truth about how God designed us as integrated beings. Dr. Harold G. Koenig, director of the Center for Spirituality, Theology, and Health at Duke University, conducted a comprehensive review of nearly 3,000 studies examining the relationship between faith and health. His conclusion: "There is mounting scientific evidence that spiritual practices are associated with better health outcomes."[14]

Koenig's research found that spiritual practices that bring genuine connection and peace often bring with them improved immune function, reduced inflammation, and better stress recovery as well. Dr. Lisa Miller's neuroimaging research at Columbia University has found that spiritual awareness activates brain regions associated with emotional regulation and strength, exactly what we see when children connect with Jesus in their hearts.

---

14 Koenig, Harold G. Medicine, Religion, and Health: Where Science and Spirituality Meet (West Conshohocken, PA: Templeton Foundation Press, 2008), 42

The Power of Letting Go of Self-Judgment

One of the hidden barriers to healing is self-judgment. Thoughts like "I'm not good enough," "I always mess up," or "I'm unlovable" don't just affect us emotionally; they also impact our physical well-being. Prolonged internal condemnation creates stress that can show up physically as tension, chronic pain, or even disease. But here's the hopeful part: when we accept Jesus' forgiveness and release ourselves from harsh self-judgment, healing floods in. Romans 8:1 (NIV) says beautifully, *"Therefore, there is now no condemnation for those who are in Christ Jesus."* Grasping this truth isn't just spiritually freeing; it often leads directly to physical healing as well.

Your Invitation to Wholeness

Jesus didn't come just to patch us up; He came to give us abundant life (John 10:10), complete and whole in every area.

Wherever you're carrying pain, be it emotional hurt, spiritual wounds, or physical illness, I encourage you to invite Jesus into that place right now. You might be amazed at how He chooses to move. You might experience His peace, His joy, or even His physical healing. However it unfolds, one thing is sure: when we release our bitter roots to Him, grace flows abundantly.

I encourage you to embrace the full measure of wholeness that Jesus offers, allowing Him to restore every facet of your wonderfully made self.

As we've seen, Jesus truly cares about every part of us, our emotions, our spirits, and even our physical bodies. When He heals a bitter root or fills an empty heart with His love, something amazing often happens: children naturally open up to Jesus in ways that surprise and delight us as parents and caregivers. I must admit, I never really considered this, but it was brought to my attention by a young mother who asked, "When my child says yes to Jesus in these moments, is that salvation?"

Maybe you've wondered about this too. When our little ones eagerly pray and genuinely experience Jesus' presence, what exactly is happening spiritually?

Are these precious encounters just sweet moments, or could they be real, eternal turning points?

In the next chapter, we'll explore this heartfelt question together. We'll look at Scripture, share encouraging stories, and gain practical insights into recognizing the beautiful ways children authentically connect with Jesus. Let's discover together how these early encounters with God can truly shape their spiritual journeys for a lifetime.

FOR PARENTS (At Home)

Explaining the Heart-Body Connection:

Tell your child: "God made your whole body, inside and outside, to work together. When your heart feels happy, your body often feels good too! When your heart feels sad or afraid, sometimes your tummy hurts, or you get headaches. Jesus wants to heal all of you, your heart, feelings, and your body too."

Use simple terms to explain that emotions can affect physical health: "Have you ever had a tummy ache when you were worried? Or did you feel super tired when you were sad? That's because your feelings and your body talk to each other."

Activity – Body Mapping:

Draw a simple outline of a body. Ask your child to color where they feel different emotions: "Where do you feel scared? Where do you feel happy? Where do you feel angry?" This helps them recognize the physical sensations that come with emotions.

Then explain: "When Jesus heals the hurting parts in our hearts, He often heals our bodies too. Let's invite Him to bring His healing to all of you."

Simple Healing Prayer:

Teach your child this prayer when they have physical discomfort:

1. "First, let's check if there's a hurt feeling in your inmost place."
2. "Let's tell Jesus about both the hurt feeling AND the body hurt."

3. "Jesus, I invite You into my sad/scared/mad feeling AND my hurting (name body part)."

4. "Thank You for healing me all the way through."

When they practice connecting physical symptoms with emotions and bringing both to Jesus, they learn holistic healing from an early age.

Peaceful Sleep Routine:

Many children experience physical manifestations of anxiety at bedtime, such as stomachaches, headaches, or general restlessness. Create a nightly "whole-body blessing"

- Place your hands on their head, saying, "Jesus, fill (child's name)'s mind and heart with peace, and their whole body, head to toe."

- Continue: "Fill their eyes with your light, their ears with your truth, their heart with your love..."

- End with: "Let their whole body rest in your perfect peace tonight."

This practice teaches them that Jesus cares about every part of their being.

FOR TEACHERS & MINISTRY LEADERS (In Groups)

The "Peace Spreads" Demonstration:

Use a clear container of water with food coloring to show how healing spreads:

1. The water represents our bodies.

2. Add a drop of dark food coloring: "This is like having sad or hurt feelings inside."

3. Then add clear, pure water (or a drop of bleach if safe): "This is like Jesus' peace coming in."

JASON & GWEN CLARK

4. Watch how it gradually spreads throughout: "When Jesus heals our hearts, His peace can spread all through our bodies, too."

Children visually understand how inner healing can affect their whole being.

The Bible Says Game:

Create cards with "The Bible Says..." statements about whole-person healing:

- "The Bible says...Jesus healed people's bodies AND forgave their sins" (Mark 2:1-12).

- "The Bible says...A happy heart is a good medicine" (Proverbs 17:22).

- "The Bible says...Jesus wants us to have life abundantly, that means being healthy in every way!" (John 10:10).

Children take turns drawing cards and completing a simple action, such as jumping, spinning, or giving high-fives, after reading each truth about whole-person health.

REAL-LIFE EXAMPLE:

Emmy's Unexpected Miracle

When Emmy forgave Jesus after the story of Tommy and Patches, something changed. That tender moment we shared in Chapter Two was just the beginning. What came next took us entirely by surprise.

For many months, Emmy struggled with severe constipation, sometimes going days, even up to a week, without relief. We were on the verge of scheduling a doctor's visit, concerned that something more serious might be going on. But what happened next wasn't found in a prescription bottle.

After identifying and praying through the bitter root that had taken hold in her heart about being abandoned, Emmy experienced not just emotional release but also physical release. Yep, she could finally go! Regularly. Naturally. Peacefully.

It was a simple reminder that our emotional and spiritual well-being are deeply connected to our physical health. When Jesus brings healing to the heart, the body often follows. And in Emmy's case, freedom looked like a healthy digestive system and a happy, dancing little girl.

I suppose when Jesus said He came to set captives free, He meant every part of us, including the bowels. I bet you didn't see that coming...I sure didn't.

KEY PRINCIPLES TO REMEMBER

- God designed us as integrated beings; what happens in our spirit affects our emotions, and what happens in our emotions affects our bodies.

- Physical symptoms in children often have emotional roots; persistent stomach aches, headaches, or sleep problems can signal emotional distress.

- When praying for healing, address both the heart and the body; Jesus cares about the whole person.

- A child's testimony of physical healing after emotional prayer builds their faith in powerful ways.

A FEW GRACE-FILLED WARNINGS

- We're not saying every tummy ache is emotional or spiritual, but some are. And the more we learn to listen, the better we'll know what our kids really need.

- Avoid creating shame around physical symptoms; never imply a child is "causing" their illness through bad feelings or doings (i.e., you have a cold because you didn't clean your room).

- Don't make promises about immediate physical healing; focus on bringing Jesus into the whole situation.

- Don't brush off physical symptoms as "just emotional." Both emotional and physical pain are real and deeply connected. Research indicates that the brain processes emotional pain, such as rejection, in a similar manner to how it processes physical pain. Each one deserves care and attention.

- Avoid creating a performance expectation around healing; the focus should be on connecting with Jesus, not getting results.

Remember: When Jesus heals our hearts, amazing things can also happen in our bodies. We're like a beautiful garden that Jesus tends; when the roots get healthy, the whole plant can flourish. Always bring ALL of you to Jesus, your thoughts, your feelings, AND your body. He made all of you, He loves all of you, and He can heal all of you!

This wholeness Jesus brings, this restoration of our entire being, raises an important question for many parents and teachers: When a child experiences Jesus in this way, when they feel His peace replace their pain and their heart connects with His, is that salvation? Is that the moment they 'become a Christian'? It's a question worth exploring because how we understand a child's spiritual journey shapes how we nurture their walk with God.

The importance of addressing emotional wounds early in childhood is supported by extensive research from the Centers for Disease Control and Prevention (CDC) on Adverse Childhood Experiences (ACEs). CDC research indicates that traumatic events in childhood can alter brain development and affect how the body responds to stress. Their studies show that addressing emotional wounds early can help prevent long-term health consequences, as children who experience multiple ACEs without appropriate intervention face significantly higher risks of developing depression, substance abuse disorders, and even physical health conditions like heart disease later in life. Prevention and early intervention, particularly approaches that strengthen family relationships and build emotional resilience, have been identified as crucial for breaking cycles of trauma. For more information, see "Preventing Adverse Childhood Experiences (ACEs): Leveraging the Best Available Evidence"[15]

---

15 Preventing Adverse Childhood Experiences," CDC, October 8, 2024, https://www.cdc.gov/aces/prevention/index.html.

CHAPTER 23:
Is That Salvation? – When Children Say Yes to Jesus

A Child's Joyful Declaration

(JASON)

It was a pleasantly sunny afternoon when a dear friend from church shared a beautiful moment with me. She was driving home with her four-year-old son in the back seat, just chatting about their day. The young mother inquired of her son if he was ready to ask Jesus into his heart yet. After a brief period of silence, her little boy piped up enthusiastically, "Mom, Jesus is already in my heart!" Surprised, she asked him what he meant. With all the confidence of a child secure in love, he explained, "We (as a family) pray and invite Jesus into our hearts all the time, especially when we do the forgiveness prayers from the heart. So He's there, Mommy!" My friend laughed softly, feeling a mix of joy and wonder. Her son's excitement was genuine. He truly believed Jesus lived in his heart because every day, they practiced receiving Jesus' forgiveness to overcome raw, heavy feelings and welcome His peace and presence.

As both a pastor and a parent, I couldn't help but smile when I heard this story. I could picture that little boy in the back seat, feet swinging, face lit up with joy, absolutely confident that Jesus was his friend. But afterward, his mother shared a question that had been quietly tugging at her heart: "Is that salvation?" She wondered, could a child's invitations for Jesus the Forgiver to come into their heart, through daily moments of forgiveness and connection, actually count as the real thing?

We all know Jesus loves the little ones. Scripture makes that abundantly clear. But how do we discern when a child's "Yes" to Jesus is not just sweet but saving? Not just emotional, but eternal?

If you take nothing else from this book, let it be this: Jesus lives within you.

And from that sacred place, your Bible-heart, every healing, every breakthrough, every new beginning flows. He doesn't merely patch things up from the outside. He heals from the inside out.

That's why we often ask children (and grown-ups, too): Would you like Jesus to come to that place of pain and bring His peace?

So, is that salvation? We may need to rewrite this question. The real question is: Is Jesus being invited in? And if so, that might be precisely where the miracle of salvation is already beginning to unfold.

In this chapter, I want to explore that question with a hopeful, pastoral heart. I'll share some of my own family's experiences, what Scripture says about childlike faith, and how emotional healing through forgiveness can be part of a child's journey with God. My prayer is that you find reassurance and practical encouragement here as you guide the precious children in your life toward emotional and spiritual wholeness.

Let the Little Children Come to Me

Whenever we're unsure about children and salvation, Jesus' own words point the way. In the Gospels, we see a beautiful scene: parents were bringing their little children to Jesus for Him to bless them. The disciples, thinking they were doing Jesus a favor, tried to shoo the children away as if Jesus had more important "adult" work to attend to. However, Jesus stopped them and corrected them. *"Let the little children come to me, and do not hinder them, for the kingdom of heaven belongs to such as these"* (Matthew 19:14). In another Gospel, it says He was even indignant that they wanted to keep children away (Mark 10:14). Jesus then took the children in His arms, laid His hands on them, and blessed them.

What a powerful affirmation from the Son of God! Jesus wants children to come to Him freely. He holds them up as examples of the kind of heart required to receive His Kingdom. *"Truly I tell you, unless you change and become like little children, you will never enter the kingdom of heaven"* (Matthew 18:3, NIV). Childlike faith, with its trust, honesty, and open heart, isn't just something God accepts. It's something He calls all of us to embrace.

So when a little one, like that four-year-old boy, lights up and says, "Jesus is in my heart," we begin with the heart of Jesus. We welcome them. Instead of dismissing it as cute or not quite real, we treat it as something precious, because to God, it truly is, and Jesus Himself does. He said the kingdom belongs to hearts like theirs. We can safely assume that heaven takes a child's faith very seriously, even if it's simple or still developing. "Do not hinder them," Jesus warned. That means we should be careful not to place unnecessary obstacles or skepticism in the way of a child who is reaching out to God.

Childlike Faith and Simple Salvation

Kids are incredible at believing. They don't overcomplicate things like we do. When they hear Jesus loves them, they usually accept it wholeheartedly.

That simple acceptance is what salvation is about: trusting Jesus Christ with your heart. Now, a toddler or young child will not articulate theology or fully grasp concepts like atonement or lordship. Still, they do understand love, and they know when they've done wrong and need forgiveness. It doesn't get much simpler than that. But we believe it's precisely the kind of posture the Holy Spirit is always ready to respond to.

Let me share from my own life: I said yes to Jesus at a very young age. I was about five years old. My dad, a pastor, sat with me and gently guided me through a salvation prayer. I still remember how eager I was; I really wanted to invite Jesus in. Sometimes, people assume a child that young can't know what they're doing. I indeed had a lot more to discover about God later on, but in that moment, I was fully aware of one thing: I needed Jesus, and I wanted Him in my life. By God's grace, it took hold. That childlike decision grew roots in my heart.

From then on, Jesus was a very real friend to me throughout my childhood. I didn't have a dramatic outward change. No one expects a kindergartner to become a saint suddenly; they're already pretty innocent! Still, I felt an inner happiness and security. My family went through some tough times when I was small. My dad had just answered a call to ministry, and we had very little money. Some days, our dinner was just crackers and jelly. Yet I look back on those years as some of the happiest times of my life. Why? I had my family, and I had God living in my heart. That simple faith gave me contentment even when circumstances were challenging. I believe that was the fruit of genuine salvation working in me as a child. I experienced joy and peace that didn't come from material comfort but from knowing Jesus was with me.

So, can a child's repeated "invitations" to Jesus be real? I would say yes; a child can genuinely open their heart to Jesus even in their preschool years. Salvation is a gift, not a graduate-level course of study. It's received by faith, not by intellectual achievement. And children often excel in the kind of humble faith that comes from God. They may say "Jesus, come into my heart" multiple times as they grow (partly because children love repetition and routine). But each time could be a sincere expression of love and trust. Rather than viewing it as "they didn't get it the first time," consider that perhaps the child is enjoying ongoing fellowship with Jesus in the way they know how. In their mind, why wouldn't they invite their favorite friend, Jesus, to be with them every day? It's a wonderful thing.

Daily Invitation vs. One-Time Decision

In many Christian traditions, we emphasize the moment of conversion—that one-time decision to follow Christ. Adults often recall a specific day or event when they surrendered their lives to Jesus. For some kids, salvation doesn't feel like a lightning bolt; it feels more like a sunrise. Slow, steady, and real. If a little boy prays nightly with his mom, "Jesus, I receive your forgiveness for being mean to my sister today. Please come into my heart and help," is there a single moment of salvation? Or is he being gently led into a relationship with Christ day by day?

It may be both. Perhaps there was a first moment the little boy reached out sincerely (even if he was only four and didn't remember it clearly). Jesus certainly heard him and responded. After that, each "invitation" is not Jesus leaving and re-entering his heart repeatedly; it's the child's way of saying, "I still want You here, Lord." Think of it like a daily "yes," in a sense. Isn't that what we all should do? Even as grown-ups, we are called to "take up our cross daily" and continually yield to Jesus. We often reaffirm our love for Him. A child doing so in simple terms, saying, "Come into my heart again today," is practicing a beautiful form of abiding in Christ, even if they don't know that term.

Now, as children mature, we can gently teach them that Jesus doesn't run away every time they make a mistake. He promises, *"I will never leave you nor forsake you"* (Hebrews 13:5). So they can have assurance that once they've honestly asked Jesus to be Lord of their life, He is faithful to stay with them. Therefore, continuing to pray and receive Jesus' forgiveness remains an excellent habit. It keeps their conscience tender and their relationship with God active.

In the story that opened this chapter, the mother and her four-year-old son had already been practicing the kind of heart-healing prayers we teach in this book. What they called "forgiveness prayers" wasn't just about saying sorry or trying to fix behavior; it was about connecting with Jesus in the heart (belly), naming the crummy emotions, and letting Him do what only He can do: remove the pain and fill the child with peace.

This family had a rhythm. Whenever something went wrong during the day, whether it was an argument, a meltdown, or just a heavy negative emotion, Mom would gently help her son place his hand on his tummy, pause, and feel what was happening inside. Then, together, they'd walk through the prayer steps:

- Feel the emotion: "What are you feeling in your belly?"

- Receive Jesus' forgiveness: "Now let's ask Jesus to wash this feeling clean and fill you with His peace."

- Forgive the person: "With Jesus' help, let's forgive them."

It wasn't about striving to be good or earning something spiritual; it was about yielding. It was about letting Jesus in.

And when that mom asked her son if he wanted to "invite Jesus into his heart" one day, his response was genuine; it was certain. "I already have Him in my heart!" To him, Jesus was already there. He knew it. Not just because he'd prayed a formal sinner's prayer but because he had experienced Jesus again and again, in the quiet moments, in the tears, and in the peace that always followed.

Rather than replace or compete with the traditional concept of a salvation moment, this kind of daily connection reinforces the reality of salvation. It's the walk that Colossians 2:6 (BSB) describes: *"Just as you have received Christ Jesus as Lord, continue to walk in Him."* Children who grow up practicing forgiveness in this way may not be able to pinpoint the first time Jesus came into their lives; they might say, "He's always been with me."

And that's okay. The children's salvation experience may be different than yours. The most important thing isn't whether they remember a specific date but that their heart is truly yielding to Him. They've learned, in the most natural and childlike way, to recognize His voice and receive His presence.

When Jesus is welcomed daily, not just in a ceremony, but in the real emotional moments of life, that's fruit that remains.

Emotional Healing and a Child's Salvation

One aspect we shouldn't overlook is how emotional healing and forgiveness are tied to a child's salvation journey. Salvation, after all, isn't only about going to heaven instead of hell. The word the Bible often uses for "save" is the Greek word *sozo,* and it means far more than just rescuing someone from sin. *Sozo* also means "to heal," "to make whole," and "to preserve." It reflects the kind of complete, inside-and-out restoration that Jesus offers. Jesus cares deeply about the whole person, including a child's hidden hurts, fears, and fragile emotions. So when a child learns to bring their feelings to Jesus, they're not just saying a prayer; they're stepping into the saving, healing power of His love in real time.

In our ministry, my family often teaches a simple practice: when you are hurt, angry, or afraid, invite Jesus into the moment and receive forgiveness. Even a child can do this. If someone is mean on the playground or if they have a nightmare, we guide them: "Let's ask Jesus to come and take away the hurt, filling your heart with His peace. Now, let's forgive that person who hurt your feelings." I've seen little ones close their eyes and pray in their own words, and then their tears stop, and a smile comes. That is Jesus at work in their tender heart! It may not look like a traditional altar call, but it's undoubtedly an encounter with the Savior.

Consider this: when children connect with Jesus in their Bible-heart and forgive someone, they are responding to one of Jesus' core teachings (see Mark 11:25). They are acting on the gospel by releasing others from offense, and, in doing so, they feel God's comfort. It's usually in those simple, honest moments that Jesus becomes real to them. Not just something they've heard about, but someone they experience and feel. His love moves into the place that hurts, and the yucky feelings start to lift. Peace takes their place. Sometimes, a child will quietly say, "Jesus, I want You in my heart forever." And you know they mean it. It all flows together. They're turning to Him, forgiving, letting Him come close, and their heart begins to heal.

So, can emotional healing be part of a salvation moment for a child? Absolutely. Sometimes, a child's first genuine connection to Jesus will happen in the context of needing comfort. For example, a seven-year-old who is anxious at night might pray, "Jesus, I'm scared. Please help me. I receive your forgiveness for taking in the fear. Please hold me like a warm hug inside." When Jesus answers by giving peace, that child's faith blossoms. They'll remember "Jesus helped me when I was afraid," and that becomes a foundation for believing "Jesus is my Savior."

I recall, even as a young boy, how Jesus' presence was with me, even in my sleep. When I was around eight years old, God spoke to me through a fantastic dream that I still carry with me today. In that dream, I saw myself walking up a set of blue steps to a large pulpit with a huge Bible on it. I was very shy and hated speaking in front of people. In the dream, as I reluctantly began to speak from the Bible, fruit started floating out of my mouth like tiny helium balloons—apples, oranges, bananas, you name it! Wherever the fruit landed on people in the congregation, their hearts melted and were healed. I woke up from that dream with tears of joy, sensing that Jesus was showing me something special. Looking back, I realize He was confirming my calling even as a child, showing me that sharing His Word would bring healing to others' hearts. That dream was an emotional healing moment for me, as well. It melted away some of the fear I had about public speaking and gave me the courage to know that God could use even a kid like me.

Not every child will have a dramatic dream like that, but many do experience God's voice or presence in personal ways. The key is that Jesus can minister directly to children, touching their hearts where they need it in ways they can understand. These experiences of His love and power are part of how a young heart is saved and nurtured.

The Role of Parents: Spirit-Led Parenting and Spiritual Covering

Yes, children really can experience Jesus on their own. They often can hear Him, feel Him, and respond in ways even deeper than we can. However, that doesn't entirely remove us from the picture. As parents, teachers, and caregivers, we've been given a sacred role. God placed us there for a reason. Our role as a steward is to create a safe space for them so that their hearts remain open and connected. Think of it as tending a garden: the child's heart is the soil, and we help plant seeds of truth, water them with prayer, and guide them to Jesus to pull up weeds of confusion or fear.

Spirit-led parenting is about inviting the Holy Spirit to guide you as you guide your kids. It means praying for insight into what each child needs and how to reach their heart. Sometimes, the Holy Spirit might nudge you that a particular Bible story would really speak to your child or that at bedtime one night, your child has a question they're afraid to ask. When you follow those nudges, beautiful opportunities to lead your child to Jesus can open up.

One mother I know felt prompted to start playing gentle worship music in her home in the evenings. It wasn't something she'd normally do, but she obeyed that inner leading. To her surprise, her restless toddler soon began to calm down at night and even hummed along. That atmosphere of worship became the backdrop for many sweet conversations about Jesus as the children grew. They were intentionally inviting Jesus into the household through prayer and worship and, yes, those daily times of forgiveness.

Parents also have a God-given authority to pray for protection and blessings over their children. We can intercede for their salvation even before they understand the concept. In the Bible, there is an interesting verse that implies the faith of a parent brings a covering of holiness over their child (see 1 Corinthians 7:14). We certainly recognize this principle when a parent dedicates their baby to the Lord or prays over a sleeping child at night. Those prayers matter! By doing so, you're effectively setting the spiritual atmosphere around your child to be one where Jesus is welcome and the enemy is barred. Think of it as pointing Jesus toward the door of their hearts and saying, "Whenever you see an opening, Lord, go for it!" When your little one is ready to consciously say "yes" to Jesus, they'll find He's already right there, waiting with open arms. In truth, He's been there all along, gently drawing them through your faithful influence.

Spirit-led parenting also means modeling the life of a Jesus follower in front of your kids. Children notice everything. When they see Mom or Dad praying, forgiving others, reading Scripture, and depending on God in tough times, it speaks volumes. A child raised in that environment often naturally wants what their parents have. How many times have we seen a toddler pretend to "preach" like daddy or sing a worship song like mommy does? They imitate what they admire. If they admire your genuine love for Jesus, they'll lean into that same love. God designed the family as the primary place for discipleship. As it says in Deuteronomy 6:7, we are to teach God's ways to our children diligently, talking of them at home and on the road, morning and night. When you do this consistently, you are actively cooperating with the Holy Spirit in your child's salvation journey.

What if They Stray? – A Journey, Not Just a Moment

Even when a child sincerely accepts Jesus early on, it's possible (and unfortunately common) that they will face a season of testing or drifting in later years. Many parents worry: "My daughter prayed to receive Christ at six, but now she's sixteen and seems so distant from God. Was her childhood decision real? Is she still saved?" These kinds of worries weigh heavily on a parent's heart. You're not alone in that. But I want to offer some hope and a fresh perspective.

As children grow into teenagers and then into young adults, something changes; well, let me rephrase that, lots of things change. However, they eventually reach a point where they must decide for themselves; what we believe as parents can no longer carry them. Their faith has to become personal. What started as a child's trust now needs to mature into a relationship that can hold them through every season ahead.

As they mature, their faith must deepen as well. And more often than not, that happens through testing. Through questioning. Through hard choices. Through needing to reach for Jesus on their own.

And here's a key truth we've discovered: you'll never grow spiritually beyond where your emotions are stuck. You can memorize Scripture and attend church, but if bitterness, fear, or shame still live buried in the Bible-heart, those roots will quietly hold you back. That's why teaching children to walk in daily forgiveness and heart-healing matters so much. It lays the foundation not just for salvation but for spiritual growth.

I went through a period as a teenager where, despite having loved Jesus since I was five, I became sullen, angry, and "too cool" for God. I never outright denied Christ, but I sure wasn't living for Him. I thought I knew better than my parents and rebelled in attitude. Looking back, I see that I was wrestling to figure out my identity apart from Mom and Dad, and sadly, I put God in that "childhood things" bucket I was pushing away. However, the foundation laid in my early years remained intact. Even as I tried to run from it, I couldn't escape the truth that Jesus was real and that I belonged to Him. His grace kept tugging at my heart through those turbulent years. When I finally got over myself and surrendered as a young adult, it was like coming home. In fact, I didn't need to get "re-saved;" I needed to repent and re-dedicate myself to the Lord I already knew. Oh, the relief and joy when I did! I realized Jesus had never let go of me, even when I'd wandered.

For many children who accept Christ at a young age, a similar pattern often occurs. They may drift in the teen years, then have a fresh encounter with God in a youth retreat or a crisis that brings them to their knees. Parents, if you're facing this, please take heart. The seeds you planted are not wasted. Scripture promises, *"Train up a child in the way he should go, and when he is old he will not depart from it"* (Proverbs 22:6, ESV). "When he is old," notice it doesn't specify what happens in the middle! The proverb acknowledges that, ultimately, the early training will produce fruit, even if there is a detour or delay. Keep praying, and keep loving your prodigal child. Remember that God loves them even more than you do, and He is actively working to bring them into full relationship with Himself.

Sometimes, as part of that journey, a young adult who was "saved" at the age of 5 may choose to publicly reaffirm their commitment through baptism or a personal prayer of rededication. That can be a beautiful milestone. It doesn't mean they weren't saved before; it simply means they are intentionally embracing the faith for themselves with a mature understanding. We should celebrate that rather than viewing it as a failure of the first experience. In my case, I eventually stood up and gave my full consent to God's call on my life, and I even entered full-time ministry. However, I will never discount the fact that I met Jesus at the age of 5. I often say I've known Jesus as far back as I can remember. His saving hand has been on me from childhood through adolescence into adulthood. It's all part of my salvation story, and I suspect in eternity, I'll see how seamlessly His grace was woven through each stage.

Humility in the Midst of Theological Differences

Whenever the topic of children and salvation comes up, it's natural for differing theological perspectives to enter the conversation. Some traditions hold to the idea of an "age of accountability," believing that young children, before a certain level of understanding, are not held fully responsible for sin and, therefore, are covered by God's grace until they're capable of making a conscious decision for salvation. Other traditions practice infant baptism as a sign of covenant, entrusting the child's future faith to God and the nurturing care of a believing community.

At our church, we follow the biblical model of child dedication, like Hannah did with Samuel. In 1 Samuel 1:27-28 (ESV), she declared, *"For this child I prayed, and the LORD has granted me my petition that I made to him. Therefore, I have lent him to the LORD. As long as he lives, he is lent to the LORD."* Baby dedication is both a declaration of our parental stewardship and a sacred act of giving our children back to God in trust and blessing. It's an act of faith and intentionality that says, "Lord, this child belongs to You, and we are stewards of their life for Your glory."

We also look to the wisdom of Psalm 127:3-5 (ESV), which reminds us that *"children are a heritage from the LORD, the fruit of the womb a reward."* Deuteronomy 6:6-7 charges us to impress God's commandments upon our children, *"when you sit at home and when you walk along the road, when you lie down and when you get up."* Proverbs 22:6 (ESV) encourages us to *"train up a child in the way he should go; even when he is old, he will not depart from it."*

Still others, especially within evangelical circles, encourage children to make a personal decision for Christ as soon as they're able to understand, sometimes as early as four or five years old. And while the ways we approach those moments may look different, most of them come from the same place: a deep love for God and a longing to honor what He's doing in a child's heart.

That's why we don't come to this with pride or certainty. We come with humility. We're not here to argue over methods. We're here to recognize the many ways God reaches for children and to honor the part we get to play in helping them respond. Whether we're parenting, teaching, or simply walking alongside them, our role matters.

I want to approach this with respect for those varied viewpoints. Godly people and Bible scholars have arrived at different conclusions regarding the mechanics of childhood salvation. I don't claim to have all the answers. What I can share is my conviction and experience: I have seen the fruit of salvation in very, very young children, so I will never say it's "impossible" or meaningless for a child to invite Jesus into their heart. At the same time, I acknowledge that a child's faith will look and operate differently from an adult's. And I believe that's okay.

Rather than getting stuck on questions like "Exactly when is it official?" or "Is the child really saved or just safe until later?" I believe our focus should be on cultivating that faith, teaching them to abide by it, and watching for the fruit. Jesus said, *"You will recognize them by their fruits"* (Matthew 7:16). This applies to any believer, including a child. So, what is the fruit of a child's salvation? We've touched on some of these already: joy, peace, love, a tender conscience, and an affinity for the things of God. You might notice your little one demonstrating compassion beyond their years or a desire to pray for others who are hurt. They might express sorrow when they've done wrong and genuinely seek forgiveness (even if it's for something as minor as snatching a toy or telling a small lie). They might have an interest in Jesus, love Bible songs, ask profound questions about God, or even share with siblings, "because Jesus wants us to love each other." These are beautiful fruits that indicate God's Spirit is at work in their young heart.

One of the sweetest fruits I see is pure praise. Children are naturally worshipers. Give a three-year-old a simple song about Jesus, and they will belt it out with all they've got. When Jesus rode into Jerusalem, and children in the temple courts shouted, "Hosanna to the Son of David!" the religious leaders were indignant. But Jesus responded by quoting Psalm 8:2: *"From the lips of children and infants you, Lord, have called forth your praise"* (Matthew 21:16). God delights in the praises of children. Their worship may be noisy or off-key, but it's sincere. When you see a child truly praising God, you're witnessing the kingdom of heaven in action. That is the real thing, no matter how simply it is packaged.

Maybe your church gives a certificate when a child makes a decision for Jesus. Maybe your tradition waits until they're older before recognizing certain steps. Either way, the heart of it is the same. Watch for the fruit. If you see signs of Jesus at work in their life, tend to it. Water it. Help it grow. And if things feel unclear, keep planting seeds. Keep showing up. Trust that God knows how to bring it all to light at the right time.

We can afford to be gracious about the theological timing because we know God is gracious with our kids. He isn't looking to exclude sincere little hearts on technicalities. On the contrary, He seems to "bend the rules" in favor of including children in His family at the earliest opportunity.

In ministry, we've had the privilege of walking with parents from many backgrounds, all with one central desire: to lead their children into a real relationship with Jesus. Often, they'll ask us, "Am I doing it right? Should I wait until they fully understand salvation?" We've come to believe that when you teach your children to meet with Jesus daily in their Bible-heart, you're already nurturing the very connection that leads to true salvation.

The model we've shared in this book isn't about rushing kids into a formal "sinner's prayer" moment. It's about inviting Jesus into the very places they feel hurt, afraid, angry, or ashamed and doing it consistently. It's about modeling how to yield their emotions to Him and watch His peace replace their pain. And when that becomes their normal, you're not just preparing them for a salvation prayer. You're walking them into a lifestyle of intimacy with God.

So if your son begins asking questions about heaven, or your daughter wonders where Jesus lives, those aren't just cute moments. They're holy invitations. Seize them. Respond with grace and joy. Let your child lead the pace, and let the Holy Spirit be the One drawing their heart. Don't worry if they don't use all the right words. If a child knows how to forgive Jesus, feel His peace, and say, "Jesus, come into this part of my heart," then something sacred is already happening. The roots of the relationship are growing deep.

And if your child is shy, unsure, or still exploring, don't force it. Just keep sharing Jesus in everyday moments, such as when you forgive each other at bedtime, when you invite Him into a sad feeling, or when you talk about His kindness. You're creating an environment where connection with Jesus isn't just an event. It's a way of life.

Every child is different, but every child can recognize peace and can experience what it means to let Jesus in, even before they fully understand the theology. That's what we've seen over and over again: when forgiveness becomes a lifestyle, the heart becomes soft and ready for Jesus to dwell there permanently.

Encouragement for Parents and Caregivers

To all the parents, grandparents, teachers, and mentors reading this: be encouraged. Guiding a child's soul is a sacred, sometimes daunting task, but you are not alone in it. The Lord is deeply invested in that little one's life even more than you are. He will give you wisdom when you ask, and He'll supply grace for the journey. Here are a few practical thoughts to encourage you as you nurture a child's faith:

Keep the Conversation Open:

Make talking about Jesus an ordinary part of life. Share your own little testimonies ("God helped me find my keys today" or "Jesus gave me peace when I felt worried"). This shows children that God is real and actively present in their daily lives. It also invites them to share their own thoughts or experiences with God, thereby maintaining a two-way dialogue.

Pray Together Regularly:

This can be at bedtime, mealtime, or at any other convenient time. Let your child hear you pray for them ("Thank you, God, for Johnny, please help him in school tomorrow"). Also, encourage them to pray in their own words.

Don't interrupt their prayer with a correction of their theology; let it be a genuine expression of their faith. If they pray, "Jesus, come back into my heart again today," just smile and know what they mean, and maybe later gently assure them Jesus has heard, and He's staying put!

Use Scripture and Stories:

Children love stories, and the Bible is full of stories of God's faithfulness. Read age-appropriate Bible stories together. Emphasize the character of Jesus— His kindness, power, and His love. Verses like *"I am with you always"* (Matthew 28:20) or *"I will never leave you"* (Hebrews 13:5) are great promises to teach a child. Also, let them know about young people in Scripture: Samuel heard God's voice as a boy (1 Samuel 3), David trusted God as a youth facing Goliath (1 Samuel 17), and Timothy learned Scripture as a child (2 Timothy 3:15). These examples validate their own ability to know God at a young age.

Model Forgiveness and Grace:

When you, as an adult, make a mistake, apologize and pray in front of the child. For instance, if you lost your temper and yelled, you might say, "I'm sorry I yelled. That wasn't right. Will you forgive me? Let's ask Jesus to help me be more patient." This humility teaches them that everyone needs Jesus' forgiveness and help. It reinforces that their relationship with Jesus is based on grace, not performance.

Applaud Their Spiritual Growth—Even the Small Wins:

If your child shows kindness, remembers a Bible verse, or decides on their own to give a toy to a friend in need, affirm it. "I see Jesus in you when you do that!" This helps them identify the work of the Holy Spirit in their life. If they express a desire to be baptized or take a new step in faith when they're a bit older, support and celebrate that wholeheartedly.

Above all, pray, pray, pray for your child. Our prayers invite God's power into their lives in ways we can't always see immediately, but trust that not a single heartfelt prayer for your child is wasted. Pray for their salvation, for protection from the enemy, for God's presence to fill their heart and your home. When you pray, you are waging spiritual warfare on their behalf and creating a highway for the Holy Spirit to travel straight into their heart.

The Faithfulness of God in Little Lives

To return to the question we started with, is it salvation when a child eagerly says Jesus is in their heart? I believe the answer, more often than not, is a joyful "Yes!" It may be salvation in seed form, but God sees the full-grown tree that the seed can become. Our job is to water and nurture it, trusting Him for the increase. Jesus is the Good Shepherd, and He knows how to shepherd the tender lambs. He knows how to speak to them at their level, how to hold them close through family and church community, and how to carry them when they stray and bring them back on His shoulders.

I think about that little boy declaring Jesus in his heart. In his simple world, saying forgiveness prayers daily means Jesus is near and always around to clean his heart, and indeed He does. What a lovely picture of sanctification at work in innocence. As that boy grows, his understanding will increase. One day, he'll realize Jesus never left his heart at all during those years; He was growing up inside him. And perhaps one day, that boy will tell his own child, "You can ask Jesus into your heart any time—He loves the little children!"

Friends, let's have faith like our kids. Let's believe that God is truly meeting them when they pray. Let's not overcomplicate it. Salvation is ultimately God's work from start to finish. Suppose He's touching a child's heart. In that case, we can be sure that He will finish what He starts (Philippians 1:6). Our heavenly Father is incredibly faithful across generations. *"His mercy is from everlasting to everlasting on those who fear him, and his righteousness to children's children"* (Psalm 103:17, ESV). What a promise! The blessings of our faith today extend to our children and even our grandchildren.

In closing, as a fellow parent and as someone who was a "saved child" myself, Jesus hears every sincere "Yes" from a child's lips. He welcomes it, treasures it, and records it in the Book of Life. There may be additional yeses down the road, and that's fine. Each one is another step closer to Him in relationship. But not one of those childlike prayers goes unheard by God.

So...is this way of praying, of connecting to our Bible-hearts, yielding to Jesus, and receiving His forgiveness, an actual salvation experience? Honestly, I don't claim to have all the answers. But I do know this: *"Just as you received Christ Jesus as Lord, continue to walk in Him"* (Colossians 2:6, NIV). If that's the model, then maybe we've been seeing something profoundly sacred all along.

Because what does it mean to receive Jesus? Isn't it about opening our hearts to Him, truly opening, not just in theory, but in Spirit and truth? Yielding our will, our pain, our shame, and allowing Him to come in and wash us clean? Isn't it choosing to believe that His presence makes all things new, even the parts that feel messy or broken? And isn't it, most of all, about receiving the deep, healing love of God, the love that covers, restores, and never leaves?

When a child places their hand on their tummy and says, "Jesus, I receive Your forgiveness," or "Jesus, come into this owchie feeling, and wash it away," something eternal is happening. They're not just saying words. They're receiving Jesus. They're receiving His love. They're experiencing, in their own tender way, the very heart of salvation: Christ coming to dwell within. And whether it's the first time or the hundredth, they're learning what it means to walk with Him, heart first, Spirit-led, and full of grace.

So maybe the question isn't, "Was that moment a salvation moment?" Perhaps the better question is, "Is Jesus being welcomed in?" And if He is, then yes, I believe we're standing on holy ground.

So the next time you hear a little voice say, "Jesus is in my heart!" smile big. Encourage that little one. Answer their questions. Pray with them often. You are watching the most precious kind of miracle unfold—a person discovering Jesus at the dawn of life. There is no greater joy than to know our children walk in truth. Let the children come to Him, for they show us what the kingdom of heaven is made of. And yes, hallelujah, that is salvation!

Truths to Carry with You

This chapter was a longer one, but it carried weight I could feel deeply. Here's a quick summary of the key things that stood out to me:

Salvation isn't just a moment; it's a lifelong "walking it out" that starts with a "yes" in the Bible-heart.

- What part of this chapter reframed how you see childlike faith and salvation?

- Did you recall your own first "yes" to Jesus and how it felt?

- What did the Spirit highlight about how salvation unfolds over time?

Let's Walk This Out

This chapter is not only about kids. It's a kind reminder to keep your "yes" alive and planted.

1. How have you defined salvation in your own life? Was it a prayer, a moment, or a slow unfolding?

2. In what ways has your understanding of salvation expanded or deepened over time?

3. Where might you and your children benefit from a more relationship-focused view of salvation?

4. How might your family's spiritual conversations change if you focused on living with Jesus rather than just praying a prayer?

Quick Takeaway:

- Look for the fruit of knowing Jesus, not just the words.

- Create space for children to encounter Him, not just learn about Him.

- Remember that your own "yes" to Jesus is still unfolding.

CHAPTER 24:
Growing Together, Walking in Freedom as a Family

(JASON AND GWEN):

Gwen and I want to take a moment and say from the heart—well done. Really. By now, you probably have a testimony or two of your own. You've walked with your child or students through something sacred. You've invited Jesus into the messy places and made space for healing to begin. That matters.

You've helped open the door to emotional honesty and spiritual growth. And even if some of the fruit is still beneath the surface, it's growing. Every time you helped a child forgive, spoke the truth with love or simply stayed present in a hard moment, you planted a seed. And no one grows those better than God.

One powerful thing you may have noticed along the way is just how much your own heart shapes the hearts around you. As a parent, teacher, or caregiver, your emotional health matters more than you think. When you choose to let God heal something in you, it doesn't just change your story. It changes the atmosphere around you. Little by little, it opens a path for the ones coming after you to walk lighter, to carry less, to grow up whole.

Take a breath. Let that sink in. This is how legacies are made.

- "What has God shown me about my own heart during this journey?"

- "Are there lingering hurts or bitter roots I need Jesus to heal so I can better support the kids entrusted to me?"

Being wholehearted doesn't mean getting it all right. It means letting Jesus shape our thoughts, feelings, and love from the inside.

When *you* find healing, your children witness the power of forgiveness first-hand. Remember, every healed heart becomes a healing presence in a child's life.

Walking in the Light, Sustaining Freedom Daily

Healing doesn't happen all at once; it grows through little moments, such as bedtime prayers, checking in, and pausing when big feelings rise. Try this:

- Daily emotional check-ins ("How is your Bible-heart today?").

- Bedtime forgiveness prayers: Keep the "Stop, Pray, Let Go" routine alive.

- Celebrate the small moments when forgiveness happens. Let those times of healing and restoration become a regular part of your home or classroom. When children see grace often, it becomes a regular part of their lives.

Freedom doesn't usually come from one big moment. It grows through steady, consistent work. The way you offer love day after day, the way you gently guide and stay present, builds something lasting.

Building a Forgiveness Lifestyle, A Legacy Worth Passing On

The greatest lessons you impart come not merely from words but from your life. Children learn best through observing real-life examples:

- Consider starting something, such as a family or classroom forgiveness wall or a journal where you can jot down those little moments when someone chose to forgive. Nothing fancy, just real stories that demonstrate grace in action. Over time, it becomes a visible reminder of "This is what love looks like in our home." It's a way to trace the heartprints Jesus is leaving in your everyday life.

- Share openly (appropriately) about your own experiences of forgiving and being forgiven, demonstrating the beauty of humility and restoration.

As you model forgiveness, you're shaping hearts that understand, appreciate, and naturally extend grace. This is how we change a family line, one moment of grace at a time.

[SCIENCE SPOTLIGHT]

The generational impact of emotional healing we discuss is supported by fascinating advances in epigenetics, the study of how experiences can affect how genes are expressed without changing the underlying DNA. Dr. Rachel Yehuda has found evidence that trauma can affect gene expression in ways that are passed down to children.[16]

But here's the hopeful news: positive experiences and emotional healing can also create beneficial patterns. Dr. Dan Siegel and Dr. Mary Hartzell note in their research: "When parents make sense of their own childhood experiences, they are better able to provide the kind of consistent, emotionally responsive care that leads to secure attachments and resilient children.[17]

This affirms what we've observed spiritually: when parents heal from their own bitter roots through connecting with Jesus inside, they create a new path forward. The peace, forgiveness, and emotional awareness we cultivate aren't just personal transformations; they become gifts we pass to our children both spiritually and biologically.

Jesus, the Constant Companion in Parenting and Teaching

Parenting and teaching are sacred work. That work is also not easy. Some days will leave you tired, questioning whether you're doing anything right. When those moments come, hold on to this simple truth: you're not doing it alone.

---

16 Yehuda, Rachel, and Amy Lehrner." Intergenerational Transmission of Trauma Effects: Putative Role of Epigenetic Mechanisms." World Psychiatry 17, no. 3 (2018): 243-257.

17 Siegel, Daniel J., and Mary Hartzell. Parenting from the Inside Out: How a Deeper Self-Understanding Can Help You Raise Children Who Thrive, 10th Anniversary ed. (New York: Tarcher/Penguin, 2013), 4.

He tends his flock like a shepherd: He gathers the lambs in his arms and carries them close to his heart; he gently leads those that have young. – Isaiah 40:11, NIV

Jesus is your constant companion and your ever-present help. He sees your dedication and gently fills in the gaps. You're deeply loved, profoundly supported, and abundantly blessed.

As we come to the end of teaching, perhaps you've begun to see pieces of your own story in the stories we've shared. Maybe a moment from your childhood has come rushing back, a memory long buried but still tugging on the edges of your Bible-heart. Or maybe, as a parent or teacher, you've recognized one of these roots growing quietly in the heart of a child you love.

That's not a coincidence.

Jesus is gently revealing what's been hidden, not to shame or overwhelm you, but to invite you into freedom. This is the beauty of our walk with Him: when we come like little children, with open hearts and empty hands, He never turns us away. He bends low, comes close, and begins pulling out the weeds we didn't even know were there.

And so I would like to share one last story with you. It's a story that holds laughter and pain, vulnerability and healing. It reflects not just the heart of a child but the healing journey of many grown-ups who are still learning to bring their yuck to Jesus.

Because freedom isn't just for adults, and it's not just for kids.

It's for anyone willing to come to Jesus with a heart wide open, ready to surrender, receive His love, and grow again.

Labels, Lies, and the God Who Sings

Looking back, I wasn't a troubled kid. I was quiet. Observant. Thoughtful. I liked things neat. I colored inside the lines, followed the rules, and found a strange joy in order and precision. But in the eyes of my teachers, these qualities weren't signs of strength or maturity; they were red flags. Indicators that something was off.

In kindergarten, I was the child who took my time. I didn't shout over others or dance on tables. I just colored carefully and meticulously while the rest of the room spun in organized chaos. But instead of celebrating my peaceful presence, my teacher pulled my mother aside and said, "He's a perfectionist. That's a concern." A concern. And so, home came a book from Focus on the Family about how to "help" children like me.

A few years later, the incident occurred again. This time, I was in fourth grade, quietly working in the back of the classroom while others carried on. My teacher, noticing my stillness and lack of rowdy enthusiasm, handed my mother a copy of The Stoic. Another subtle nudge. Another literary intervention. Another attempt to "fix" what wasn't broken.

To a child, these types of things can leave a lasting impression.

And while I didn't know it then, a lie slipped in quietly through those well-meaning diagnoses: There must be something wrong with me. Not loud enough to scream but loud enough to echo. Not sharp enough to cut, but deep enough to shape. The message I received was: **You're not like the others, and that's a problem.**

It wasn't just that I was different; it was that I needed to be different from how I was. The root of shame didn't spring up overnight. It crept in slowly through the back door of my identity. Quietly, like me.

What Took Root?

I carried that shame for years. It showed up in the way I second-guessed my instincts. It shaped the way I held back in group settings. It distorted the lens through which I saw others and, more dangerously, the way I assumed others saw me. It painted the world in suspicion. If they see the real me, they'll disapprove. It became increasingly difficult to trust that I was okay, just as I was.

That subtle root of shame grew into full-blown identity distortion. What started as a quiet lie that I needed to talk more eventually shaped the way I navigated the world. I didn't want to take up too much space. I didn't want to be noticed. I learned to wear the proper masks and manage my presence in various settings, relationships, and even prayer.

But praise God, the Holy Spirit is a skilled gardener. And one day, in prayer, He brought it up. The memory. The feeling. That quiet little moment in fourth grade when I sat in the back of the classroom, just being me, and was labeled a concern.

The Holy Spirit wasn't there to analyze me. He was there to heal me.

Praying Like a Child

I didn't reason through it. I didn't journal it to death. I prayed like a child.

I sat still and let myself feel that ache in my belly. That old, stale shame. That lie that had wrapped itself around my worth. And like a kid whispering to Jesus, I asked Him: "Will You take this ache from me?" And with the power of the Holy Spirit, I received cleansing, and then I forgave. I forgave the teacher. I forgave the system that couldn't see me rightly. I received Jesus' forgiveness for agreeing with the lie.

And then He did it…

I felt the peace flood in, the kind that doesn't come from trying harder or reading the next book on emotional health. It was deeper. Quieter. Stronger. Like Jesus was wrapping His arms around the little boy I used to be, looking him in the eyes and saying, You are not broken. You are my delight.

I am His delight. Wow. I opened my heart wide and allowed His acceptance and love to wash over me and fill all the empty places where the bitter roots once were. And for the first time in a long time, I believed it.

The Healing Brings Forth Truth

I still come back to Zephaniah 3:17 (ESV), *"The Lord your God is in your midst, a mighty one who will save; he will rejoice over you with gladness; he will quiet you with his love; he will exult over you with loud singing."*

That verse isn't just poetic. It's my anchor. It's the truth that rewrites the labels and rips out the roots of shame that once tried to define me. He rejoices over me, not because I became someone else, but because He made me exactly this way. He sings over the quiet kids. The perfectionists. The slow processors and deep feelers. He sings over me.

Now, as a pastor, I see the same lies in others: "You're too much" or "You're not enough." "You need fixing." "You're broken." These lies are familiar, but so is the truth.

So I remind them: You are the delight of your Father. He's not trying to fix you; He's trying to free you.

Final Thought

Maybe you've carried quiet wounds for years, labels spoken in passing, glances that made you feel "less than" the expectations you could never seem to meet. Maybe you've learned to survive by shrinking back, staying small, or trying to earn approval one performance at a time. But here's the truth: you were never created to be fixed; you were designed to be known, loved, and celebrated.

The parts of you that were labeled "too quiet," "too intense," or "too different" may be the very fingerprints of God's design on your life. He never asked you to change who you are to be worthy of love. Instead, He invites you to come as you are so He can show you who you've always been in His eyes, chosen, cherished, and delighted in.

When the voice of shame whispers, "You're broken, " listen for a deeper voice, the voice of the Father singing over you. His song silences every accusation. This is not self-help. This is soul-healing. And it's available to anyone willing to come back to the place of childlike trust and let the Holy Spirit touch what's buried.

You don't have to wear those old labels anymore. The shame, the labels, the words that stuck to you—they're not your identity. God has called you something better. He's written a new name over your life: Beloved. Let go of the lies.

Trust what He says is true. Lift your eyes. The One who made you still delights in you. He hasn't stopped singing.

A Blessing:

May peace settle into every corner of your home and every space where you teach. May the love of Jesus flow through you in ways that reach beyond what words can express. Whether you are parenting, teaching, or simply showing up with a willing heart, know this: you are shaping lives. You are helping raise peace-makers and planting truth in the hearts of future healers and leaders. God sees every part of it. He notices the small acts of love, the long days, and the quiet prayers you whisper when no one else is around. None of it is lost on Him. He's with you, and He will honor what you've poured out. Be encouraged. What you're doing is holy, and it's never wasted.

CHAPTER 25:
Walking in Truth Together: Confronting Dilemmas and Navigating Relationships

But the wisdom that comes from heaven is first of all pure; then peace-loving, considerate, submissive, full of mercy and good fruit, impartial and sincere. – James 3:17 (NIV)

When Heart-Focused Parenting Meets Tradition

I've sat across from countless parents who've whispered the same concern with tears welling up in their eyes: "I believe in this approach with my whole heart, but my spouse thinks I'm being too soft," or, "My church teaches discipline differently. Am I going against Scripture by focusing so much on emotions?"

Suppose you've felt that tension; you're not alone. Whenever we step into a new way of seeing, especially when it comes to raising children, we inevitably encounter established patterns and deeply held convictions.

This chapter is for the midnight moments when your heart wonders if you're the only one doing it this way. For those Sunday afternoons when Grandma's raised eyebrow makes you question everything. For those parent-teacher conferences, when you feel like you're speaking an entirely different language.

As John Eldredge says in his book *Experience Jesus. Really,* our souls are wired for connection.[18]

---

18 John Eldredge, Experience Jesus. Really: Finding Refuge, Strength, and Wonder through Everyday Encounters with God (Thomas Nelson, 2025), 16.

Is This "Biblical Enough?" Addressing Theological Concerns

We touched on this in Chapter Three, but it warrants a closer examination. Our culture often prioritizes feelings over truth, so I understand. The concern is real. However, The Bible-Heart Model never elevates emotions above Scripture. It simply invites God's Word to reach the places where feelings live, allowing His truth and the child's heart to work together.

It's about recognizing how God intentionally designed our inner world to work and learning to meet Him right there, the way He always intended.

Throughout Scripture, we see that God is deeply concerned with our inner life, not just our outward behavior:

- *"Above all else, guard your heart, for everything you do flows from it"* (Proverbs 4:23, NIV).

- *"People look at the outward appearance, but the LORD looks at the heart"* (1 Samuel 16:7, NIV).

- *"For from within, out of the heart of man, come evil thoughts"* (Mark 7:21, ESV).

- *"Create in me a clean heart, O God, and renew a right spirit within me"* (Psalm 51:10, ESV).

"In Christianity, human emotions are often considered to be misleading and untrustworthy, a lingering part of our fallen nature that distracts us from God's truth. But our emotions were created by God, and though the enemy may seek to manipulate our hearts, Jesus sets us free!" – Mark Virkler[19]

The Bible consistently emphasizes that the heart is the source of our actions, attitudes, and spiritual condition. What we're doing with The Bible-Heart Model is simply giving children practical tools to bring this biblical truth into every-day moments.

---

19 Virkler, *Unleashing Healing Power Through Spirit-Borne Emotions*, back cover.

Biblical Foundations for the Bible-Heart Approach

Consider these foundational elements of our approach:

1. Spirit-to-Spirit Connection, Jesus taught that *"God is spirit, and his worshipers must worship in the Spirit and truth"* (John 4:24). When we help children connect to their Bible-heart, we're teaching them to recognize the place where their spirit interacts with God's Spirit. As Paul wrote, *"The Spirit himself testifies with our spirit that we are God's children"* (Romans 8:16).

2. Inner Transformation Over Behavior Management, When Jesus confronted the Pharisees, He didn't critique their behavior; He addressed their hearts: *"You clean the outside of the cup and dish, but inside they are full of greed and self-indulgence"* (Matthew 23:25). The Bible-Heart Model prioritizes inner transformation, just as Jesus did.

3. Truth Planted in the Heart, David understood that God *"desires truth in the innermost being"* (Psalm 51:6, NASB). When we help children listen for Jesus' truth in their Bible-heart, we're teaching them to live from the inside out. This approach isn't just compatible with Scripture. It's drawn directly from it.

4. Forgiveness as Jesus Modeled It, Jesus taught forgiveness that comes *"from your heart"* (Matthew 18:35), not just from our words or actions. The Forgiveness Flow provides children with practical steps to put Jesus' teachings on forgiveness into practice.

What some might mistake as mysticism is actually biblical literacy, learning to read not just the written Word but the Living Word within (Hebrews 4:12). It's not about following feelings instead of Scripture; it's about allowing Scripture to transform us from the inside out, exactly as God designed.

When Family Members or Teachers Don't Understand

One of the most challenging situations parents face is when those closest to them, spouses, grandparents, or even trusted teachers, misunderstand or oppose this heart-focused approach. Here's how one mom described it to me:

"My husband thinks I'm being manipulated when our son has a meltdown. He wants immediate consequences, not 'hugs and Jesus talks.' It's creating tension between us, and I don't know how to help my son when my husband and I are on such different pages.'"

These situations require wisdom, patience, and a whole lot of grace. Here are some practical ways to navigate these relationships while staying true to what you're learning:

With a Spouse or Co-Parent

1. **Share the Why, Not Just the How**. Instead of just explaining these techniques, share how this approach connects to Scripture and the values you both hold. For example: "I know we both want our kids to have real faith, not just good behavior. What I'm learning is helping me connect the two."

2. **Invite Observation, Not Just Participation**. Sometimes, seeing the fruit is more convincing than hearing the theory. Ask your spouse to observe what happens when you help your child process emotions with Jesus. Results speak volumes. Testimonies are like gold.

3. **Find Common Ground**. Even if your spouse isn't ready to fully embrace this Bible-centered approach, look for aspects on which you both agree. Perhaps you both value honesty, respect, or spiritual growth. Start there and build bridges, not walls.

4. **Pray Before You Persuade**. Before trying to convince your spouse, spend time in prayer. Ask God to give you both wisdom and unity. Remember, transformation is His work, not yours, in your children and in your marriage.

I recall a couple I counseled once; the husband was deeply skeptical about what he called "emotional parenting." But after watching his wife walk their daughter through the Forgiveness Flow during a particularly difficult tantrum, he was amazed. "She was a different kid after five minutes," he told me later. "I don't understand it all yet, but I can't argue with what I saw."

With Grandparents or Extended Family

Grandparents often parent from a different generational perspective. Many were raised in an era when children's emotions weren't considered particularly important. "Kids are resilient," they might say. "They'll get over it."

Here's how to bridge that gap with love and respect:

1. **Honor Their Intentions**. Most grandparents want what's best for their grandchildren. Start by acknowledging their love and good intentions, even if their methods differ from yours.

2. **Share Your Journey**. Instead of presenting this approach as "the right way," share it as part of your personal growth journey: "I've been learning something that's really helping me understand our kids better..."

3. **Offer Simple Explanations**. You don't need to explain the entire Bible-heart model. Start with concepts they might find more familiar: "We're helping the kids talk to Jesus about their feelings, and it's making such a difference in how they handle tough situations."

4. **Set Loving Boundaries**. If necessary, establish clear, kind boundaries: "We're working on helping Jamie process his emotions differently now. Would you be willing to call me when he gets upset instead of handling it the way you usually do?"

One grandmother told me, "I didn't get it at first. All this talk about feelings seemed unnecessary. But when I saw my grandson close his eyes, put his hand on his tummy, and then look up with pure peace on his face...well, who am I to argue with that? Now I ask him, 'Do you need to talk to Jesus about that?' and he knows exactly what I mean.'"

With Teachers or Ministry Leaders

School and church environments often rely on behavior management systems, such as sticker charts, color-coded warnings, or reward-and-punish approaches, also known as carrot-and-stick methods. These aren't inherently wrong, but they usually focus more on external compliance than heart transformation.

When engaging with teachers or ministry leaders:

1. **Approach with Humility**. Start conversations with curiosity rather than criticism: "I'm curious about how you handle emotional outbursts in the classroom. Would you be open to hearing what's working for us at home?"

2. **Offer Resources, Not Demands**. Share this book or specific chapters as a resource, not a mandate: "This approach has been so helpful for our family. I thought you might find some useful insights for your classroom, too."

3. **Partner, Don't Pressure**. Remember that teachers and ministry leaders often manage many children with limited time and resources. Offer to partner with them: "Would it help if I shared some specific phrases that help Lucas calm down when he's overwhelmed?"

4. **Be the Bridge.** If your child is struggling in a setting with different expectations, be the bridge of translation. Help them understand the various environments while maintaining your heart focus at home.

REAL LIFE EXAMPLE: Sunday School Breakthrough

I recently opened an email from a pastor friend and found a story too good to keep to myself. While teaching Sunday school, she decided to look past the surface of a child's behavior and ask what was really happening inside the heart. What followed was nothing short of a transformative experience. Her testimony shows that this approach is far more than just a lesson plan.

The pastor noticed that seven-year-old Doris, a sweet girl with a "heart of gold," had become increasingly disruptive in class. She constantly interrupted the lesson with questions and struggled to follow directions. Rather than just implementing more behavior management, the teacher decided to connect with Doris's heart.

After class one Sunday, she invited Doris to sit with her privately. "I asked her why it was so hard for her to sit still and to listen," the teacher shared. "She said that she really wants to listen, but she just can't sit still."

As they talked, Doris revealed something deeper; she was afraid of dying. "She wants to become a scientist so she can find a cure that will help people live 200 years," she recalled. Then came an even more vulnerable confession: Doris was terrified of monsters and too afraid to shower alone.

This is where the Bible-heart approach transformed the situation. The teacher had previously taught the children about connecting with Jesus "heart to heart," so she asked Doris if she wanted Jesus to help her with her fear.

"I asked her to close her eyes and to put her hands on her belly," the teacher explained. "Then I asked her if she could picture that time when she was so scared in the shower. Then we asked Jesus to come into her Bible-heart and take the fear and all those ugly feelings away."

Without hesitation, Doris followed along. After a quiet moment, she said, "Better."

But God wasn't finished. As they continued talking, a bitter root suddenly surfaced, unresolved anger toward her grandmother, who had blamed Doris for getting them lost two years earlier and never apologized.

"I asked Doris if she was ready to ask Jesus to take away the hurt and anger," the teacher shared. They prayed together, but Doris still felt anger lingering. At that moment, the teacher realized that Doris needed justice.

"Doris, how about handing grandma over to Jesus?" the teacher suggested. "Let Him take care of her. I know she lied, and it wasn't fair, but shall we ask Jesus to take it from here?"

Doris agreed and, after a few moments, said, "It's good." The transformation was remarkable. "She was totally calm," the teacher observed. "The whole atmosphere around her had changed."

This story powerfully illustrates that what we often label as "behavior problems" are actually heart issues waiting to be addressed. Doris wasn't being deliberately disruptive; she was carrying fears and hurts that made it impossible to sit still and focus. Once Jesus met her in those places, peace naturally followed.

And notice what the teacher didn't do. She didn't scold Doris for her past behavior or implement a stricter behavior management system. She created space for Doris to encounter Jesus in her Bible-heart. The result wasn't just momentary compliance; it was genuine transformation.

That is why the Bible-heart approach isn't just another method. It opens a door for children to meet Jesus right in the thick of their everyday challenges. When they do, everything starts to change.

When You're the One with Doubts

Sometimes, the most significant resistance doesn't come from others; it comes from within us. Perhaps you've experienced moments of doubt:

- "Is this really working, or am I just avoiding proper discipline?"
- "My child still has tantrums. Maybe I need to be firmer."
- "What if I'm raising soft kids who can't handle the real world?"

These doubts are normal. They're part of the journey. **Proper discipline, I believe, isn't about making children compliant. It's about making disciples.** And disciples aren't formed through fear or force. They're formed through a relationship with Jesus.

When doubts creep in, return to your own Bible-heart. Ask Jesus to remind you of His truth. And remember, you're not raising children for today's behavior alone. You're raising them for a lifetime of knowing how to bring their whole selves, including their emotions, to the One who created them.

Practical Steps for Walking Together

Here are some practical ways to navigate relationships while maintaining your commitment to Bible-heart parenting:

1. Create a Common Language

Help others understand your approach by translating it into terms they can relate to:

- Instead of "Bible-heart," you might say "inner life" or "conscience" with some people

- Rather than "bitter roots," you could call them "emotional wounds" or "hidden hurts."

- When explaining the Forgiveness Flow, focus on the outcomes: peace, reconciliation, and emotional regulation

2. Focus on Fruit, Not Just Methods

When discussing this approach with skeptics, emphasize the results you're seeing:

- "She's learning to calm herself down when she feels overwhelmed."

- "He's becoming more aware of how his actions affect others."

- "They're developing a genuine, personal relationship with Jesus."

These outcomes are hard to argue with, even for those who prefer different methods.

3. Model It Before You Teach It

Nothing speaks louder than your own transformed life. When family members or teachers see *you*:

- Pausing to connect with Jesus in tense moments

- Speaking from peace rather than frustration

- Extending grace while maintaining appropriate boundaries

...they witness the power of this approach in action.

4. Be Willing to Compromise on Method, Not Principle

There may be times when you need to meet others halfway. Perhaps Grandma insists on her traditional approach during visits, or a teacher has classroom policies that differ from those at home. In these situations:

- Hold firm to your core values (emotional safety, heart connection with Jesus)

- Be flexible about specific techniques or language

- Process differences with your children afterward: "At school, we follow those rules, and at home, we can talk to Jesus about our feelings too."

5. Pray for Those Who Don't Understand

Instead of arguing or trying to force others to see your perspective, commit to praying for them:

- "Lord, help them see the children's hearts, not just their behavior."

- "Jesus, show them through results what I can't convince them of through words."

- "Holy Spirit, give us unity even in our different approaches."

Prayer changes situations, and it also changes us, softening our hearts toward those who don't yet understand.

Addressing Specific Concerns

Let's address some of the most common concerns you might hear from others (or even yourself):

"Isn't this just permissive parenting?"

The Bible-heart approach isn't permissive parenting, and it isn't soft on discipline. It asks what is happening under the surface, then sets clear, loving limits. Boundaries matter. They make a space where children can feel safe enough to face their emotions.

Jesus balanced grace with truth (John 1:14), and that is our aim as well. When someone questions the method, you can say, "Our expectations are still clear. The rules haven't changed. We're simply going after the heart behind the behavior, not just the behavior itself."

"Children need discipline, not endless emotional processing."

Proper biblical discipline isn't about punishment; it's about discipleship. The word "discipline" originates from the same root as "disciple," meaning to teach, guide, and train.

When others raise this concern, you might respond: "We absolutely believe in discipline. But effective discipline changes the heart, not just the behavior. That's what we're after, heart change that lasts."

"Kids need to toughen up for the real world."

This perspective assumes that emotional awareness makes children weak. In reality, the opposite is true. Children who learn to recognize, name, and process their emotions with the help of Jesus develop remarkable emotional strength. They don't fall apart when challenges come. They know exactly where to take their pain.

I often tell parents, "We're not raising fragile kids. We're raising emotionally intelligent children who know how to handle life's difficulties by taking their emotions to Jesus. I believe that's true strength."

"Behavior management works faster than all this heart stuff."

Yes, punishments and rewards can produce quick behavioral compliance. But at what cost? External compliance without internal transformation creates either rebels or performers, neither of which reflects the heart of Christ.

The Bible-heart approach might take longer at the moment, but it builds a foundation that lasts a lifetime. As Jesus said, the wise builder constructs their house on rock, not sand (Matthew 7:24-27).

A Letter to the Concerned Grandparent, Teacher, or Spouse

Perhaps you're reading this book because someone you love has shared it with you. You have questions, concerns, or even strong disagreements with this approach. If that's you, I'd like to speak directly to your heart for a moment:

Dear Friend,

Thank you for caring enough to engage with these ideas, even if they feel foreign or uncomfortable to you. Your willingness to read this far shows your deep love for the children in your life.

I understand your concerns. Perhaps you were raised differently. You may have seen effective results through more traditional methods. Possibly, you worry that too much focus on emotions will create entitled, undisciplined children.

These are valid concerns from a loving heart.

May I gently suggest that what might appear to be a soft approach is building something powerful? These children know how to bring their authentic selves to Jesus. **Children who don't just behave well because they fear punishment, but who choose right because they've encountered love Himself.**

The **fruit** of this approach is **peace**. Not weakness, not emotional indulgence, but emotional maturity.

You don't have to adopt every aspect of what you've read here. But I invite you to watch for the fruit. Jesus said we would know what's true by its fruit (Matthew 7:16). When you see a child close their eyes, connect with Jesus in their Bible-heart, and emerge from that moment visibly changed, that's not a technique. That's transformation.

And isn't that what we all want for the children we love?

With respect and grace, Jason

Closing Reflection: Unity in the Essentials

As we navigate relationships with those who may see things differently, let's remember this ancient wisdom: "In essentials, unity; in non-essentials, liberty; in all things, charity."[20]

The essential is this: we want children to *know* Jesus, not just know about Him, but to experience His transforming presence in their everyday lives.

The methods may differ. The language may vary. However, suppose we keep our eyes on this central purpose. In that case, we'll find enough common ground to walk together in love, even when our approaches don't perfectly align.

Helping your child connect with Jesus in their belly-heart might make you feel weird around certain people, but it's worth every awkward moment. You're not just parenting differently. You're planting a legacy. And that kind of change rarely comes without resistance.

"Let us not become weary in doing good, for at the proper time we will reap a harvest if we do not give up" (Galatians 6:9, NIV).

Truths to Carry with You

Resistance to this heart-focused approach often reveals what others value most: sometimes control, sometimes tradition, and sometimes a sincere concern for children's well-being. But opposition doesn't mean we're wrong; it might mean we're onto something transformative.

- Have you encountered resistance to this approach? From whom?

---

20 aniel Stegeman, "In essentials unity, in non-essentials liberty, in all things charity," The Sentinel, 4 September 2021, https://www.lewistownsentinel.com/news/religion/2021/09/in-essentials-unity-in-non-essentials-liberty-in-all-things-charity/.

- Which concern or objection resonates with your own doubts or questions?

- What fruit have you already seen that confirms you're on the right track?

Let's Walk This Out

1. What relationship feels most challenging as you implement this approach? Spouse, grandparent, teacher, friend?

2. Which explanation or strategy from this chapter might help bridge the understanding with that person?

3. Where might you need to set a gentle boundary to protect your child's emotional and spiritual growth?

4. How can you invite Jesus into these relationship tensions, not just to change others' minds, but to keep your own heart at peace?

CHAPTER 26:
Bitter Roots in Little Hearts: Finding and Healing the Yucky Stuff Inside

(For Parents, Teachers, and Ministry Leaders)

Healing the Heart of a Child

> *"See to it that no one falls short of the grace of God and that no bitter root grows up to cause trouble and defile many." – Hebrews 12:15 (NIV)*

By now, you've walked through the stories of real families. These children weren't taught to suppress their emotions or "fix" themselves, but instead learned how to connect with Jesus in their Bible-hearts. You've read about fear surrendered, rejection

"What you're holding isn't meant to just sit on a shelf. For so many families we've walked with, the information on these pages has become like a doorway, an opening to experiences with Jesus they never thought possible."

lifted, and anger melted. Shame washed away, not by better behavior or clearer thinking, but by Jesus, the real, present One who shows up right in the middle of the mess and brings peace to places we didn't even know were hurting.

Now it's time to focus specifically on how these bitter roots manifest in the youngest hearts among us, because children's emotional worlds may look different from those of adults, the principles of healing remain beautifully the same.

We've been walking adults through healing for years. Marriages restored. Emotional pain is released. Shame uprooted. Fear and unforgiveness surrendered to Jesus. And over and over again, the Lord showed us something we could no longer ignore: most of the bitter roots that we helped people to forgive **began in childhood.**

However, the turning point came one day with our own five-year-old daughter.

What started as a piercing scream from the backyard turned out to be something entirely different—no broken bone, no injury—just heartbreak. Emmy sobbed, "They left me." That moment shattered our assumptions.

One quiet question opened a door I hadn't expected: 'Did something inside you feel icky or yuck when that happened?' Her answer told me that what we were dealing with wasn't just behavior. There was something deeper going on inside her little heart. At that moment, I sensed the Lord showing me something I'd never fully grasped before: children can develop bitter roots, too! It was like Hebrews 12:15 (NKJV) jumped off the page with new meaning: *"Looking carefully lest anyone fall short of the grace of God; lest any root of bitterness springing up cause trouble, and by this, many become defiled."* I'd always thought of this verse in terms of adults, but here it was, playing out before my eyes in my own child! (GWEN)

That realization lit a fire under us. Jason had been sensing it was time to write a book, but he didn't know which book until it poured out in a matter of days. The stories. The structure. The prayers. The Spirit-led tools. And now, what was once an idea is this complete text.

This is a guide for every parent, teacher, mentor, and ministry leader who wants to interrupt generational pain before it becomes permanent. As you have probably learned by now, it's about whole hearts. This is spiritual parenting, kingdom discipleship, and genuine restoration all woven together in one place.

Roots of bitterness don't stay small. Left unchecked, they twist the way a child sees God, themselves, and others. But when those roots are addressed early, when a child learns to feel, forgive, and invite Jesus into their Bible-heart, something powerful happens. The cycle breaks. The reaping stops.

(OUR SHARED PERSPECTIVE):

You've also seen by now that this isn't just for kids.

What surprised us most? As we taught our children how to bring their hearts to Jesus, He began healing ours as well.

"We teach our kids how to brush their teeth to prevent cavities. How much more should we teach them to tend their hearts to prevent bitter roots?"

As we taught bedtime forgiveness prayers and illustrated healing with strawberries and weeds, we started to see something in ourselves. Kids bury pain in behavior. Adults bury the pain in explanations. Nevertheless, buried pain still grows, and whether it's a tantrum or a shutdown, the solution is the same: **Jesus inside the Bible-heart.**

Some of our most profound personal healings happened while explaining these steps to children. The simplicity of childlike faith opened the door to our own restoration. If you're reading this as a caregiver or leader, you're not here just to help someone else heal. You're here to encounter Jesus, too.

Matthew 18:3 (AMPC) says: *"Unless you…become like little children [trusting, lowly, loving, forgiving], you can never enter the kingdom."* Jesus didn't say become childish. He said to become childlike. The gateway to the kingdom is found not in striving but in trust, not in knowing more, but in yielding more.

Many believers are trying to walk from "faith to faith and glory to glory." Still, they often start from a place of exhaustion, not from a position of victory. Here's the truth: you can't go from glory to glory unless you begin from the place where God started.

Victory begins before the trauma. Before the diagnosis. Before the abandonment. It starts in the place where God said, *"I knew you before I formed you"* (Jeremiah 1:5).

This book has always been about returning to that truth for the sake of our children and ourselves.

Let's raise a generation of clean-hearted kids. Let's stop the weeds before they choke the fruit. Let's begin again, this time from victory.

The Healing Prayer Model for Kids. This next section offers the Spirit-led steps we use to help children heal emotionally, spiritually, and relationally. These are the exact steps we walk out with adults, reimagined with language and flow that children understand and respond to.

Gentle Reminder:

You're not here to force a breakthrough or fix a problem. This isn't about thinking, *"I've got to fix this kid."*

The mindset is entirely different.

You're here to make space for Jesus to do what only He can do.

Your role is to invite, to listen, to stay present... and let Him be the Healer.

What Is the Bible-heart Again? This inner place is what we refer to as the human spirit when teaching children. Scripture often translates the word "koala" as "belly." Still, it actually means "innermost place," referring to the spiritual core of who we are. It's not imagination. It's the place where Jesus lives inside us.

• Out of his belly shall flow rivers of living water" (John 7:38, KJV). *"The spirit of man is the candle of the Lord"* (Proverbs 20:27). *"A spring of water welling up to eternal life"* (John 4:14, ESV).

A Kingdom Legacy Worth Sharing

You've come a long way, so pause for a moment.

Let what you have learned settle in. A key to the kingdom now rests in your hands. It is not just another program. It is the way Jesus moves. One child. One prayer. One tender moment at a time.

What you're holding isn't meant to just sit on a shelf. For so many families we've walked with, the information on these pages has become like a doorway, an opening to experiences with Jesus they never thought possible. I can't promise exactly what your journey will look like because God is too creative for cookie-cutter experiences. Still, I can tell you that when children learn to bring their emotions to Jesus instead of burying them, something remarkable tends to happen. As Scripture says, *"Taste and see that the LORD is good."* (Psalm 34:8, NKJV). That's my invitation to you through these pages.

So, let's teach our kids to listen to Jesus in their Bible-hearts. Let's show them how to forgive quickly and love deeply. Let's not wait until they're grown to hand them the tools of emotional healing. We were never meant to parent from behind, always chasing behavior. We were made to lead from within, partnering with the Holy Spirit and the Living Word.

And what if the next revival isn't loud?

What if it begins in living rooms and bedtime prayers and tearful whispers like, "Jesus, I open my Bible-heart to You"?

What if healing becomes the family legacy?

Share the Heart, Not Just the Book

Would you like to pass this on to another parent or leader? Try these statements:

- "This book helped me realize my child's emotions are a doorway, not a detour."

- "I finally found a way to help my kids heal that's Biblically sound, Spirit-led, and not pressure-driven."

- "The language of the Bible-heart unlocked something in *me*, not just my kids."

- "This isn't about raising perfect kids. It's about raising whole-hearted ones."

Let's Raise a Generation that Knows Peace

Now, turn the page. The prayer steps are next. But look how far you've come. You opened the door for the Lord to create new mindsets, grow with a deeper connection, and developed a heart for what's next.

Let this be a line in the sand, not just for your children, but for your legacy.

Healing can begin early, it can begin here.

And it can start **with you.**

CHAPTER 27:
The Bible-Heart Model

Forgiveness Flow: Forgiveness Prayer Steps

Before we begin the prayer steps, please note that people use various words to describe their connection with Jesus. Some call it heart healing. Others say "abiding" or "Spirit-led prayer." The language may differ, but the truth remains the same: Jesus meets us in the deepest places and brings peace where pain once lived. Throughout Church history, believers have experienced Christ's peace replacing their inner turmoil, whether they called it "heart healing," "sanctification," "the exchanged life," or simply "abiding in Christ." These steps work because they're simple and real and because Jesus always shows up when we invite Him in. As the Psalmist wrote, *"The LORD is close to the brokenhearted and saves those who are crushed in spirit"* (Psalm 34:18, NIV). This promise is for all who seek Him, regardless of how we articulate the journey.

What This Is:

A prayer model that helps kids actually feel what's going on inside and bring it to Jesus. Not just with words but with their heart. Why It Works:

- It connects through their innermost being, not just the mind.
- It lets Jesus do the heavy lifting.
- It helps kids forgive others, forgive themselves, and, if they're upset with God, bring that to Him too.
- It lays a lifestyle foundation of inner healing as an everyday healthy walk, not just a rare moment.

What You'll Need:

- A peaceful moment.

- An open spirit, not just in the child, but in you.

- A willingness to go slow and listen together.

Tips for Leading Children Through the Steps:

1. **Go Slow.** Let the Holy Spirit set the pace.

2. **Don't Push for Words.** Presence matters more than precision.

3. **Use "Tummy" and "Bible-heart" Language.** Help them locate where they feel it.

4. **Validate Their Emotions.** "You are allowed to feel big things, and Jesus would like to help you with them."

5. **Be Present.** The goal is connection, not performance.

When someone hurts you, or when you feel mad, sad, left out, or even disappointed with yourself or God, these steps help you do something compelling: they help you let Jesus forgive you and through you. When He does, peace comes rushing back into your heart.

Gwen and I keep coming back to these steps. They may seem simple, yet this is all you really need to allow for real healing in most cases. Bitter roots, though, call for something deeper. Here, we invite Jesus to delve into the hurts we've buried long ago and rewrite our stories in a way that reflects how we see the world.

▶ Forgiveness Prayer Steps (Jesus the Forgiver)

1. **Feel the Feeling**

   Put your hand on your tummy. Do you feel anything sad, mad, or yucky in there? Let your child pause and name the feeling.

   It's okay to sit quietly and just wait for a bit.

2. **Open Your Bible-heart to Jesus the Forgiver**

   Jesus, I open my Bible-heart to You. Come into the yucky part of my tummy. Let them pause. You can say, "Feel Jesus giving your belly a hug from the inside."

3. **Forgive (Three directions as needed)**

   a. **Receive Forgiveness for Myself:** Jesus, I receive Your forgiveness for holding on to this crummy stuff for so long.

   b. **Forgive Others:** Jesus, I let You forgive [name] through me (or with me).

   c. **Forgive God:** Jesus, I receive your forgiveness for being mad at You.

   I know You love me. I open my heart to trust You again.

   Wait quietly. Let the not-good stuff wash out. Feel His peace rise inside you. That peace means the forgiveness worked!

   Gratitude is usually the first thing that bubbles up when Jesus truly transforms something. It's the most natural response to a supernatural moment. Sometimes, it feels like joy. Sometimes, a heaviness lightens up, turning into a smile.

Bitter Roots Healing Prayer Steps

When a feeling or memory keeps resurfacing,
or something has been buried for a long time,
these steps help Jesus go to the root. We don't
want to just trim the leaves or prune the
branches; we want to do it properly. We want
to allow Him to heal all the deep places inside.

For root issues that present themselves, these additional steps are needed:

4. **Give Jesus the Yuck and Receive His Peace**

   Jesus, I give You this crummy stuff in my heart. I don't want to hold it anymore.

   Please take it all out. Pause. Let them feel the letting go, then say, "Now feel Him pouring in His peace and love."

5. **Fill Up with Love**

   This step is really important. After you dig up the bitter root and allow Jesus to remove the unpleasant feeling, you have now made space for the Holy Spirit to fill those areas of your heart. If it was a lie they believed, He could fill it with His Truth. If it was an unmet need, He can fill it with His nature; His love.

Pray: Jesus, I open my heart where the hurt used to be, fill my Bible-heart with Your love, peace, and joy. Let them sit for a short time with their hand on their tummy, breathing slowly.

[SCIENCE SPOTLIGHT]

The Forgiveness Flow steps we outline align with what researchers call "emotion coaching," an approach proven to help children develop emotional intelligence and resilience. Dr. John Gottman's groundbreaking research has tracked children for over twenty years. It showed that when parents took time to validate a child's feelings and walk them through the process of handling those feelings—rather than brushing them aside—the results were striking.

Children who received this kind of guidance stayed focused longer, earned higher grades, had fewer behavioral issues, and formed stronger friendships. Best of all, they grew up with what researchers call "emotional self-efficacy," a quiet confidence that says, "I know what I'm feeling, and I can handle it."

The Bible-Heart Model's steps—feel the feeling, open your heart to Jesus, forgive, and receive peace—create this exact kind of emotional processing pathway. We're not just teaching children spiritual practices; we're helping them develop the emotional skills research has identified as crucial for lifelong well-being.[21]

21 Gottman, John M., Lynn Fainsilber Katz, and Carole Hooven. Meta-Emotion: How Families Communicate Emotionally (Mahwah, NJ: Lawrence Erlbaum Associates, 1997), 163-165.

PART FOUR:
Troubleshooting and Testimonies

CHAPTER 28:
Troubleshooting, When Life Doesn't Follow Your Script

The truth is, real life rarely sticks to a script. You're in the kitchen, trying to get dinner on the table, when suddenly your child erupts, screaming, then collapses to the floor in tears. What just happened? Maybe little bro grabbed the cup they wanted or made a face at them from across the table. And just like that, a civil war breaks out. You freeze for a moment, caught off guard. It seemed like such a small thing, but clearly, it wasn't. It's not about the cup or the silly faces.

This chapter is for those moments. Not the easy ones. Not the polished ones. The messy, holy, unpredictable ones where your training feels like it falls short, and we need to rely entirely on God's grace.

Before we dive into these sections, I want to speak to you, not just as a fellow parent or teacher but as someone who has stumbled through many of these lessons myself. This book isn't a rulebook for "perfect parenting," nor is it meant to leave anyone feeling judged or weighed down.

We wrote this guide with tears running down our faces and prayer-filled hearts right in the middle of real parenting moments.

So, if you see yourself in some of the "what not to do" examples ahead, please don't let guilt or shame creep in. Gwen and I made many of these same mistakes more than once. And honestly, we're still learning. Compassion for our children and ourselves

"When we help children identify those root systems early and invite Him into that sacred space, transformation doesn't have to wait until adulthood. It can happen in a bedtime prayer. During a car ride. Even in the middle of a meltdown."

is what this is all about. Without Jesus, we can do NOTHING.

Core Principles of Spirit-Led Response

Instead of providing a checklist of every situation, we want to share the one thing that transforms all of them: a spirit-led presence.

1. **Presence Over Performance** – In the chaos, your steady presence does more than the best parenting tip for controlling misbehavior. Children don't need us to fix them; they need us to find them in their pain, stay steady, and lead them out of it with Jesus.

2. **Connection Before Correction** – Even during moments of discipline, seek heart connection first. A child's behavior often reveals a deeper need that cannot be addressed solely through consequences.

3. **Listening Beyond Words** – Children's behaviors are messages from their hearts. When we listen with spiritual discernment rather than just parental anxiety, we hear what is truly being communicated.

4. **Yield First, Guide Second** – Your yielding to the Holy Spirit must precede any attempt to lead a child. The peace they need flows through you, not from you.

Common Challenges and Spirit-Led Responses

Now we'll address specific scenarios, organized by the emotional patterns they represent rather than as separate sections:

When Emotions Feel Overwhelming (Meltdowns, Shutdowns, or Withdrawal)

When a child's emotions flood beyond their capacity to manage, their nervous system shifts into survival mode. The logical reasoning part of their brain goes offline. Asking them to "use their words" or "calm down" in these moments is like asking someone who is drowning to calculate their buoyancy based on their weight and volume instead of throwing them a lifeline.

Whether a child is exploding with big emotions or retreating into isolation, the root need is the same: safety, connection, and gentle guidance back to peace.

Spirit-Led Approach:

- Create a quiet, safe space without demanding immediate processing.

- Use gentle breathing together while maintaining a physical presence.

- Offer comfort through touch if welcomed or a nearby presence if not.

- Speak slowly and softly: "I'm right here. Jesus is here, too. We're not going anywhere."

- Wait for the emotional storm to pass before attempting heart-healing.

What to Avoid:

- Don't threaten abandonment ("If you don't stop crying, I'm leaving").

- Don't force immediate processing ("Tell me what's wrong right now").

- Don't dismiss emotions ("It's not that big a deal").

- Don't rush to distract rather than process.

When Shame or Self-Judgment Takes Hold

Gwen and I have found that most of the time, children who isolate themselves, punish themselves, or speak negatively about themselves are experiencing shame rather than mere disappointment.

Spirit-Led Approach:

- Recognize self-isolation as self-protection, not defiance.

- Draw near gently without demanding engagement.

- Offer grace-filled words: "Jesus loves you even when you make mistakes."

- Model vulnerability by sharing age-appropriate stories of your own mistakes and God's grace.

- Create "return rituals" that welcome them back to the connection without shame.

What to Avoid:

- Don't interpret withdrawal as manipulation.

- Don't force confession before offering comfort.

- Don't lecture about behavior during moments of shame.

REAL-LIFE EXAMPLE:

When I Isolated

This doesn't happen too often with our kids. Still, every now and then, we see children removing themselves, not because we sent them away, but because they're punishing themselves.

And every time it happens, it takes me straight back to a moment in my childhood. One I remember vividly, and not exactly proudly.

I couldn't have been more than six, maybe seven years old. My neighbor and I were pretty good friends, regular backyard buddies, the kind of friendship where you'd trade snacks one minute and then argue over who cheated in hide-and-seek the next, a real solid foundation.

One afternoon, I discovered a tiny grasshopper in the backyard. I was mesmerized by it, as if I'd uncovered a magical treasure. So I gently cupped it in my hands and sprinted around to the front yard to show my friend.

"Let me see! Let me see!" he said. So I knelt down and placed it carefully in the grass between us…and without hesitation, before I could blink, he stomped on it.

Splat. Just like that. My magical moment? Gone. Dead in the grass.

And in that exact instant, I did something I had never done before. I punched him. Hard. Right in the stomach. He threw up.

I ran straight into the house, straight to my room. I slammed the door and sobbed on the bed.

I wasn't just heartbroken about the grasshopper; I was devastated about what I had done in response. I didn't need a parent to correct me; I was already handing out my own sentence. I went full courtroom-judge-and-jury mode and gave myself the maximum penalty: isolation.

I didn't have the words for it back then, but I know now I was ashamed. I knew my reaction was wrong. I expected punishment, so I beat everyone else to it. I punished myself.

And here's the thing: I didn't need more disconnection at that moment. I needed gentle restoration. I needed someone to come sit on the edge of my bed and say, *"I see your heart, and even when you mess up, I'm still here."*

But I didn't know how to receive that or even ask for it. So I just sat in the silence.

That moment shaped something in me, a bitter root that whispered, *"When you mess up, go hide."*

It's part of why I'm so passionate now about helping kids learn a different way. Self-isolation in a child isn't always rebellion; it's often a form of self-judgment. It is shame, and if we don't show up with love and presence in those moments, it can quietly become a way of life.

Addressing the Messages Behind Behavior

We've also noticed that when children act out repeatedly or in patterns, they are expressing something deeper than just poor choices.

Spirit-Led Approach:

- Ask heart-focused questions: "What does your tummy feel like right now?"

- Name possible emotions: "I wonder if you're feeling invisible or not good enough?"

- Invite Jesus into the real issue: "Let's ask Jesus to help us understand what's happening inside."

- Listen for bitter roots: "Did something happen that made you feel this way before?"

What to Avoid:

- Don't address only the behavior while ignoring the emotional root.

- Don't assume bad intentions ("You're just trying to manipulate me").

- Don't compare siblings or peers ("Why can't you be more like...").

Creating a Heart-Safe Environment

We have also discovered that the atmosphere we create determines whether children feel safe to open their Bible-hearts or feel the need to protect themselves.

"Sometimes what we see on the outside is not the whole story. Many of those outward reactions are messengers pointing to something deeper."

Spirit-Led Elements of Safety:

- Consistent emotional availability.

- Quick repair after conflicts.

- Permission to express all emotions without shame.

- Invitation rather than demand when processing feelings.

- Modeling vulnerability and your own connection with Jesus.

Building Ongoing Trust:

- Daily heart check-ins.

- Gentle bedtime forgiveness practices.

- Celebrating moments of Bible-heart connection.

- Modeling your own emotional authenticity with Jesus.

A Prayer for Parents and Leaders

Heavenly Father,

In these spaces between understanding, where Your ways of reaching children's hearts sometimes differ from tradition, we come seeking Your perfect wisdom.

Lord Jesus, You spoke to the hearts of children while the disciples tried to manage their behavior; teach us to see as You see.

For the spouse who doesn't yet understand, we ask not for persuasive words but for visible fruit that cannot be denied.

For the grandparent whose love runs deep but whose methods differ, we ask for bridges of grace and moments of revelation.

For the teacher or pastor trying to manage many hearts at once, we ask for divine glimpses of what transformation truly looks like.

And Father, for our own doubting hearts, in those midnight moments when we wonder if we're getting this right, we ask for the gentle reminder that You are the One who transforms. We are merely vessels, conduits of Your presence.

Spirit of Truth, help us to stand firm where we must and bend where we can. Give us discernment to know the difference between principles worth defending and methods that can flex.

May we be quick to extend grace, slow to take offense, and ever aware that the children watching us learn more from how we navigate our own disagreements than from the words we speak?

And in all things, Lord, may we be found walking in that heavenly wisdom that is "first of all pure; then peace-loving, considerate, submissive, full of mercy and good fruit, impartial and sincere" (James 3:17).

The legacy we're building is about raising generations who know how to bring their authentic selves to Jesus' real presence.

In the name of Jesus, the One who always sees the heart, amen.

CHAPTER 29:
Real Stories from Real People –
A Garden of Healing

"All of the stories in this chapter flowed from children using the simple forgiveness steps we outline in Chapter 27."

(JASON)

The following stories are phenomenal to me. They are honest, raw, and unashamed. They're not polished or packaged. They are moments from families that Gwen and I know personally, where the Prince of Peace Himself stepped in and transformed tiny hearts. What follows is a garden of healing stories, semi-grouped by the types of emotional roots they represent. Let these stories remind you that healing doesn't have to wait for a certain age or a significant life event. It starts in small, quiet moments, right where the hurt resides. It can happen in the middle of bedtime, in the back seat of a car, or while playing with a favorite yo-yo.

When Fear Tried to Stay, but Jesus Came In

Jesus Made Me Brave

(Connects to Lesson 3 – A Tale of Two Kingdoms and the God Emotions)

This story shows how fear can become a doorway, not a dead end. His Bible-heart learned to trade fear for courage right in the middle of the moment.

When our soon-to-be adopted son was four years old, he had to go to the hospital for a preparatory procedure before a larger surgery scheduled a few months later. After we returned home, we needed to remove a large medical-grade bandage using a special solution provided by the hospital. He already disliked Band-Aids and the pain of peeling them off. This one was bigger, stickier, and far more intimidating.

There were lots of tears. He didn't want me to touch it at all.

So we sat down together, and I gently encouraged him to focus on Jesus. I reminded him, "With Jesus, we can do hard things. You don't have to be afraid of the bandage; Jesus is right here, and He can help you not feel so scared." Slowly, he agreed to let me apply the solution to loosen the bandage, but he wanted to be the one to take it off himself.

As he sat there, I showed him how to place his hand on his tummy, his Bible-heart, and give his fear to Jesus. He closed his eyes, opened his little hands like he was handing the fear away, and whispered his surrender. Then, we paused to receive Jesus' peace together. Something shifted in him.

Bit by bit, he began to peel the bandage off. It took almost ten minutes, but he did it. And when he was done, he looked up at me and said with confidence, "Jesus made me brave."

Two months later, we returned to the hospital for his more serious surgery. On the day of discharge, he had a few more bandages on his chest that needed to be removed before we could leave. The fear returned, this time bigger and louder. He was visibly shaken and didn't want to go through it again.

I held him close and gently reminded him of what happened before: "Remember two months ago? You were scared then, too. But Jesus helped you, didn't He? When you're ready, you can give Him your fear again, and He'll help you be brave just like last time."

After a little while, he nodded. He put his hand on his belly and gave his scared feelings to Jesus once more. As His peace settled in, the panic faded. He was calm, and, on his own, he removed the bandages.

That timeline and those two experiences became a living testimony for our family. Our little boy didn't just learn how to take off a bandage. He knew how to invite Jesus into moments of fear, receive His peace, and do the hard thing anyway. That memory lives inside him now, not as trauma, but as truth: Jesus makes me brave.

Jesus in the X-Ray Room

(Connects to Chapter 6 – Fear's Disguise and the Voice of Peace)

This is one of those powerful snapshots of what it looks like when a child chooses peace in a scary place. A real-time Bible-heart connection.

This incredible seven-year-old had been battling a persistent cough for weeks during a difficult winter virus season. After monitoring her symptoms, her dad took her to urgent care one morning to have her chest checked. When they arrived and were guided toward the dark, unfamiliar x-ray room, fear began to rise quickly inside her.

The dim lights, the large machine, the unfamiliar sounds, it was all overwhelming. As the technician prepared to begin, she began to panic. But instead of shutting down completely, she turned to her father with urgency and said, "I need to connect with Jesus in my Bible-heart, Dad!"

Without hesitation, he nodded and gently guided her to close her eyes and place her hand on her belly. Together, they invited Jesus into the fear. "Jesus, we give You this scared feeling. Please come into this place and fill it with Your peace." They paused. Waited. And Jesus came. The fear lifted, and peace flooded her little heart.

Shame, Guilt, and Identity Lies

From Bad Boy to Beloved

(Connects to Chapter 7 – The Battle of Thoughts and Lies)

I love this. A lie got planted early, but Jesus' truth prevailed, and that truth took root.

When our son, Jacob, was about four and a half, we started noticing some unusual things he was saying, things that didn't line up with how we had raised him or how we knew he truly felt. Out of nowhere, he began saying things like, "I just feel like you don't love me," or "I think I'm a bad boy," and even, "I do too many bad things."

As his parent, I immediately reassured him, again and again, that he was deeply loved and that he was a good boy. But my words didn't seem to reach his heart. The lie had already taken root.

I remember feeling frustrated and confused. Where did this come from? Then, the Lord lit up a light bulb inside of me. Somewhere along the way, my son had taken in a lie that he was bad. It wasn't just a fleeting thought. It had slipped into his heart and started shaping how he saw himself.

So the next time he said one of those out-of-character things, I didn't just reassure him. I invited him into an encounter.

I gently asked, "Are you ready to get rid of that feeling?" He said yes. We sat together, and I placed his hand on his belly, his Bible-heart, and covered it with mine. I guided him to close his eyes and connect with Jesus there.

I asked him to remember the time he first started feeling like he was a bad boy. I told him it was okay to feel that feeling, but that Jesus wanted to go there with him. We sat in the quiet, and I asked him to repeat after me:

"Jesus, I receive Your forgiveness for taking that lie into my Bible-heart."

I asked how he felt afterward, and he said, "Better, but I still feel bad." That was our cue to go one step further.

I explained, "Now that your heart is at peace, we can tell that lie to go."

And we did.

"I renounce the lie that I'm a bad boy," he said, repeating after me.

Then I asked him, "Now let's ask Jesus what the truth is."

He closed his eyes, soaked in the moment, and then, with a big, joyful smile, he whispered one word: "Good."

Tears welled up in my eyes. He knew. He had heard the truth, not just from my mouth, but from the mouth of the One who made him.

We giggled together, and I told him, "That's right. Jesus says you are good. Let's pray that truth gets sealed on the tablet of your heart forever."

That moment wasn't just about correcting wrong thoughts. It was about pulling out a bitter root and planting the truth of his identity deep where it belongs, in the Bible-heart.

Now, whenever I see him walk in confidence or speak life over himself, I remember that one lie tried to take hold, but Jesus stepped in and told him who he really was. And now he knows it, too.

Jesus Did WHAT?

(Connects to Chapter 10 – The Healer in the Hidden Place)

One of the most unforgettable moments we've experienced in our family was when our son, just four years old at the time, prayed and saw Jesus heal his baby sister. It was a moment so sacred, so real, that I still carry it with reverence in my heart.

Landon, at age four, was a firecracker of a kid, full of energy, movement, and imagination. He kept us on our toes every day. One evening, as we were wrapping up the night, he accidentally shut the bathroom door on his baby sister Emmy's thumb. She was just beginning to toddle around at age one and had followed him too closely. But the door didn't just close. It slammed shut on the hinge side, with her tiny thumb caught in the narrowest gap, barely an eighth of an inch wide.

Her little squeal pierced the air, and I rushed to open the door. Emmy's thumb looked twisted and crushed. No blood, but it was badly indented and crooked like something you'd expect would need urgent care. Gwen scooped her up immediately and took her into the bathroom to examine her hand under better lighting. Emmy was screaming, and the whole situation felt overwhelming.

Meanwhile, Landon had run upstairs by himself. When I went to check on him, I found him lying on his bed, crying and punishing himself for what had happened, even though it was an accident. He was crushed by the guilt.

It was bedtime, so I sat down next to him and gently helped him settle. I invited him to connect with Jesus in his Bible-heart so he could give the pain, fear, and guilt to the Lord. As we prayed, I reminded him that Jesus was with him and with Emmy, too, and that we could ask Him to bring peace and healing.

Landon's whole countenance shifted. He sat up, completely calm, with his eyes wide and full of wonder. Then he said something I'll never forget.

"Daddy," he whispered, "I see my Jesus coming out of my belly."

I blinked.

He continued, with complete peace and sincerity, "I see my Jesus coming out of my belly, walking across the room, going through the wall, going down the stairs, through the kitchen, and into the bedroom. He's touching Emmy's thumb right now, and He's making it all better."

I was stunned. The presence of the Lord was thick in the room, so real, so holy. I just started to cry. I didn't fully understand what I was witnessing, but I knew Heaven was in our home. I gently helped Landon finish his bedtime prayers, thanking Jesus for His peace and for healing Emmy's thumb.

Then I went downstairs.

To my amazement, Gwen told me Emmy had completely calmed down. Her thumb, which had looked so mangled just minutes before, was already looking better. The swelling had gone down dramatically, and within a few hours, it was as if it had never happened at all. No lasting marks. No doctor visit. Just peace and healing.

That moment is seared in my memory, not just because of the miracle but because of how God used a child to demonstrate the reality of Christ in us. Landon didn't imagine Jesus up in the clouds or far away. He knew exactly where Jesus lived, inside his belly, his Bible-heart. And when he yielded to the Spirit and released what he saw, the result was healing, peace, and transformation.

I may never witness another miracle like that again in my lifetime, but I'll never forget that one. The power of instilling truth in our children, that Jesus is always with us, in us, and works through us, is priceless.

That one moment showed me what it really means when Jesus said, "Let the little children come to Me."

And this time, He came through a child.

An unforgettable moment. Landon recognized where Jesus really lived and let Him move from the inside out. That's the heart of this book, right there.

Rejection, Insecurity, and Comparison

Love Letters and Rejection

(Connects to Chapter 9 – The Three Directions of Forgiveness)

We've all felt the sting of rejection, but this moment shows how even that can become a setup for knowing you're deeply loved.

Lennox had a pretty big crush on the little boy next door. She wrote him love letters and thought about him constantly. One day, she saw him outside and asked him if he, too, had a crush on her. He replied, "No." She came back into the house feeling so defeated and rejected.

She moped around all day and kept asking me why he didn't like her. I could tell this was more than just a fleeting feeling. It had taken root. I gently asked if she would like to connect with Jesus about it in her Bible-heart. She said yes. We sat together, and she brought her feelings of rejection to Jesus. She gave it to Him and waited to receive peace.

What came back was the truth. She was filled with the knowledge that she was loved, accepted, and chosen by the King.

Now, she can play freely with that little boy next door again, with no sadness or insecurity between them. Just peace and joy.

Listening Past the Outbursts

(Connects to Troubleshooting 2: Listening for the Real Message Behind Behavior)

Such a beautiful example of not reacting to behavior, but listening underneath it. The fruit? A child felt seen, and the root got healed.

As a new parent, there were many times in my daughter's early years, especially around age five, when I found myself labeling her behavior as "strong-willed" or "difficult." I'd take her meltdowns personally, assuming it must be my fault or a reflection of poor parenting. I've made plenty of mistakes, but as I began to understand bitter roots, I started to see her reactions differently. I realized that many of her outbursts weren't rebellion or defiance; they were signals of emotional pain. There was something deeper going on under the surface.

The more I invited the Holy Spirit into those chaotic moments, the more I began to see her through God's eyes. Her explosions weren't just "bad behavior." They were cries of the heart, rooted in fear, in not feeling seen or understood. As the Lord began to convict and gently rewire my thinking, I learned to pause, kneel, look her in the eyes and ask, "Honey, what's happening inside?" And then I'd say things like, "Did you feel like Mommy wasn't listening or caring just now? That must feel so yucky. Let's take that feeling to Jesus and let Him hug your heart. Let's invite Him to fill you with His love."

One pattern that really challenged us was her habit of constantly interrupting, especially when my husband and I were having serious conversations. She would jump in, sometimes shouting or even crying, to make sure she had our attention. Over time, this became exhausting. We tried consequences, explanations, reminders, and everything in between. However, nothing stuck because we were only addressing the behavior, not the root cause.

One day, in prayer, I asked the Lord for insight. His gentle whisper came: She feels like she's not seen. She's afraid she doesn't matter when you're not looking directly at her. That revelation changed everything.

The next time it happened, I pulled her close and knelt down. I asked gently, "Sweetheart, do you feel like when we're talking and not looking at you, you're not important?" Her eyes welled up. She nodded. I held her close and said, "Even when we're not talking to you, you are still important. You are still seen. You are still loved. Can we take those sad feelings to Jesus now?"

Together, we prayed. I helped her place her hand on her Bible-heart. We said, "Jesus, I give You the feeling of being unseen and not important." Then we asked, "Jesus, what do You say to my heart instead?" She paused… smiled… and said, "Jesus told me not to interrupt anymore!"

It was one of the clearest moments I've ever seen of the Holy Spirit healing a heart, right there in the middle of real life.

We had explained the importance of respecting others when they're speaking so many times before, but this was different. When Jesus touched her root emotion, fear of being invisible, He replaced it with peace. And that peace changed her. She wasn't just learning a rule; she was receiving healing. The interruption habit didn't vanish overnight, but the frantic, desperate need to interrupt did. That moment marked a shift. And it's stayed.

This is just one example, but there have been many like it. I'm so grateful for the tools we've learned through the Bitter Root teachings, tools that help us parent from the inside out. Our daughter is becoming more emotionally aware, more Spirit-connected, and more confident in who she is. I genuinely believe this will shape her entire life.

And as for me, I'm learning not to react out of frustration, but to respond in faith. To slow down and ask, "What is her heart saying right now?" Because often, when we listen past the outburst, we discover a precious opportunity to lead our children right into the arms of Jesus.

Flying Squirrels and Yo-Yo Wars

As a family, we treasure spending intentional time together. But sometimes those sweet, cozy family moments take a sharp left turn. What began as peaceful fun can unravel into meltdowns, bickering, and emotional chaos. In those moments, we're learning to pause and remember: this is our opportunity, not to control behavior, but to reconnect hearts. These are the moments where we get to help our kids return to the Heart of Jesus.

We're learning more and more that connection with Jesus, not flawless parenting, is the answer. Our best efforts fall short without the power of His forgiveness, His truth, and His peace flowing through our home. This is where the Gospel comes alive in real-time.

One recent afternoon, our four-year-old was having a particularly tough day. Grumpy. Sabotaging play and instigating conflict.

The final straw came when all three kids, ages 7, 4, and 2, got yo-yos as a surprise. The 7-year-old caught on quickly, which only deepened the frustration in our 4-year-old. He couldn't get the hang of it and took the disparity personally. Instead of asking for help or taking a break, he began grabbing the yo-yo out of his older sibling's hands mid-play. He spiraled into angry outbursts and disruptive behavior. As you can imagine, it didn't take long for joy to disappear and tensions to rise. I found myself wanting to toss every yo-yo in the trash and declare the afternoon a total loss.

But something in me said, "This isn't about the yo-yo."

I called our four-year-old into the bedroom for a quiet moment. Years ago, the Lord had gently shown me that this child struggled with feeling "less than" his older sibling. I had prayed about it, and now it seemed like that deep-down belief was showing its face again.

I knelt beside him and asked, "Do you feel like because your brother is better at the yo-yo, that means he's just better than you?" He lowered his head, whimpered, and nodded. My heart ached.

I said softly, "Just because someone's better at something doesn't mean they're better than you. That's not what God says. Are you ready to let Jesus help you with this?"

After a moment of hesitation, he gave a little nod. He opened his heart, and we walked through it together, giving the yucky feeling to Jesus and asking Him to come close and speak the truth.

And what happened next was joy. Instant, full-body joy. He jumped up and started bounding across our bed like a flying squirrel, laughing, shouting, totally free. The heaviness left. The sabotaging behavior stopped. And friends, it hasn't returned. He's been generous and lighthearted ever since. Thank You, Jesus!

I was stunned by how quickly the healing came. But as I reflected, I realized: this wasn't sudden. This healing was built on a foundation that had already been laid over time. From the time our kids were little, just old enough to speak, we've been creating moments where they can practice opening their hearts to Jesus. We talk to Him when we're sad. We tell Him the truth when something feels yucky inside. And we invite His peace to come in.

Moments like this one are the fruit of that history. When they've practiced welcoming Jesus in small things, they're ready to meet Him in the bigger moments too.

I remember when my husband first got to walk one of our boys through a heart-healing prayer. He was so moved, he emailed me right afterward so we wouldn't forget the moment. That email is still saved.

We try to create space in ordinary days to marvel together: "I'm so glad I can feel Jesus in my heart right now. Do you feel Him too?" or "Do you want to feel Him even more?" These little check-ins are like planting seeds of connection. And the fruit shows up when it matters most, like when someone feels second-best because of a yo-yo.

The nods, the quiet smiles, the peaceful sighs… they're the outward signs of what's happening inside. What a privilege it is to parent this way, to pause the hustle, and help our children open their hearts and experience Jesus right in the middle of real life.

Peaceful Practices and Connection at Home

Love That Lingers

Some nights, bedtime used to be a challenge for our little guy. The separation, even just the transition to his room, brought up a lot of anxiety. It wasn't just restlessness; it was that quiet emotional ache that can creep in when a child feels alone.

So we asked the Lord for a way to help Jacob feel connected and secure. What came from it turned into one of the sweetest routines we've ever had.

Every night, right before bed, we pause and sit close. We each put our hands on our tummies, our Bible-hearts, and for one minute, we release love to one another. No talking. Just a shared moment of quiet, Spirit-led connection. We tell him, "We're gathering in Jesus' name, and that means He's here with us" (Matthew 18:20). And you can feel it. A warm peace settles over both of us. The love flows, the anxiety fades, and the bedtime struggle melts away.

That one-minute heart exchange has become a sacred rhythm. It fills him with comfort and safety. It reminds him he's not alone, not just because I'm near, but because Jesus is present and active inside him.

Sometimes, even during the day, he'll look at me and say with a big smile, "I'm still releasing to you!" It's his way of saying, "We're connected. Love is still flowing."

On the nights when something still stirs, if he calls out from his bed because of a not-good thought or a sudden worry, I'll gently walk him through a forgiveness prayer right over the monitor. "Let's give that thought to Jesus," I'll say. "Now, ask Him to wash it away and fill you with His peace."

Within moments, his spirit settles, and he drifts off peacefully. No fear. No heaviness. Just peace.

This is what emotional discipleship looks like in our home. It's not flashy. It's not long. But it's real. He's learning that Jesus isn't just a bedtime story; He is the one who brings peace when we need it most. And that's a truth he's learning not just in his head, but deep in his heart.

Bedtime Healing Moments

At night, both of my girls hop into bed and, after their short devotion time, they look forward to connecting with Jesus in their Bible-hearts. Lennox once told me, "I don't like feeling icky." This is her way of describing how toxic emotions make her feel inside.

There have been nights they won't go to sleep until they've brought those "icky" feelings to Jesus. Whether it was a moment of sadness, frustration, or something that didn't feel right from the day, they've learned to go to Him, to give Him their heavy feelings and receive His peace in return.

What a gift to see them growing in their awareness that uncomfortable emotions aren't just something to stuff down or avoid, they're signals that it's time to open their hearts and let Jesus bring healing. Even at bedtime, they're learning what it means to live with clean hearts and a clear connection.

Bailey's Little Heart Learns Peace

Bailey, our three-year-old, has been a witness to Lennox going to the Lord with her feelings. She has picked up on the transforming peace and forgiveness that Jesus exudes through Lennox. Bailey begs to do a belly-heart prayer whenever she gets upset, especially after being disciplined in her growing three-year-old ways.

Forgiveness, Release, and Reconnection

When Forgiveness Comes First

(Connects to Chapter 8 – Jesus the Forgiver)

This one is simple but so powerful, it shows how forgiveness can become a rhythm, not a rescue mission.

Our four-year-old is learning to go directly to Jesus with his negative emotions, before they have a chance to turn into roots of bitterness. We've made connecting with Jesus in the Bible-heart and practicing the forgiveness steps a regular part of our daily rhythm. And I can say with confidence, it's changing everything. Helping him cultivate a real relationship with Jesus at such a tender age has been one of the most priceless gifts of parenting.

Jacob's First Healing – Age about 3 years old

One evening after returning home from a friend's house, I was getting him ready for bed and noticed something alarming: bite marks on his leg. His little friend had bitten him hard. I could see every single tooth's imprint. As soon as I brought it up, he recoiled, refused to talk about it, and began to cry.

My heart ached. I could sense the trauma setting in, and I didn't want that pain to take root. I asked the Lord for help.

I centered myself first, connecting with Jesus in my own heart, and then gently asked my son, "Do you want to get rid of this feeling?" He tearfully nodded yes. I guided him to place his hand on his belly, and I covered it with mine. I asked him to close his eyes and connect with Jesus in his Bible-heart.

We sat quietly for a moment while I invited him to feel what had happened, not just the bite, but the feelings it brought with it. Then I asked him to let Jesus come close and go to that place of pain. He repeated after me: "From my belly, I release forgiveness. I forgive the one who hurt me. I receive Jesus' forgiveness for taking that fear and pain into my heart." We soaked there for a few extra seconds, letting the peace settle in. Then I asked, "How do you feel now?"

He opened his eyes wide, lit up with a huge smile, and exclaimed, "It's gone!"

And it was. The tears stopped. His body relaxed. He was able to talk about the event calmly, without being overwhelmed by the emotion. He forgave his friend, and the offense didn't get buried; it got released.

That night was more than just a bedtime routine. It was his very first experience of emotional healing with Jesus. And it was beautiful.

Backseat Revival

(Connects to Chapter 11 – Fruit That Grows on the Vine)

One of our good friends reached out to us with this wonderful testimony:

After a long, laughter-filled but exhausting playdate at Grandma's house, the car ride home was filled with tired little voices on the edge of meltdowns. The three children, ages 7, 4, and 3, were all feeling it. The air in the car was thick with frustration, weariness, and sibling-style tension.

As we pulled out of the driveway, I felt a gentle nudge from the Holy Spirit: "This is a moment for connection." So I turned down the music and asked, "Would anyone like to talk to Jesus and let Him take these yucky feelings away?"

One of them looked up, puzzled, and asked, "What does that mean?"

I smiled and said, "It just means we let Jesus into our Bible-hearts to help take away the mad or sad feelings we're carrying. He knows how to make our hearts feel peaceful again."

Without hesitation, all three children closed their eyes right there in the back seat. I quietly guided them, "Put your hand on your tummy. Let's tell Jesus how we're feeling. Now let Him come and take it."

Within moments, their tense little faces softened. One of the cousins opened his eyes wide and exclaimed with a huge grin, "Whoa! That worked!"

The car was filled with giggles and peace as if Jesus Himself had climbed into the back seat and wrapped them all in a giant heavenly hug. That spontaneous prayer time didn't just shift their moods. It showed these young hearts that Jesus isn't just someone we talk about at church. He's real. He's close. And He wants to meet us right where we are, even in the back seat of a minivan after a long day.

Jesus showed up in the minivan, just because the invitation was there. Now that's the Gospel in motion.

"Let's raise a generation that doesn't wait until their 30s or 40s to heal. Let's build homes and classrooms and ministries where peace reigns. Let's give the children we love the one thing that changes everything: connection with Jesus in their Bible-heart."

After the Garden: Your Story Belongs Here

You've heard real stories from real families, kids who didn't have to pretend everything was okay or stuff their feelings deep down or "fix" themselves, but instead learned how to connect with Jesus in their Bible-hearts. You've seen kids let go of fear. You've read about rejection falling off, anger softening, and shame losing its grip. And none of it happened by better behavior; it happened because Jesus showed up.

And now, it's your turn.

This is your invitation. A place to breathe. To listen. Maybe even to let Jesus interrupt the story you thought was settled.

Because you have a story too. And it's not too late to let Jesus into it.

As we come to the end of this journey together, remember that every time you help a child open their Bible-heart to Jesus, you're creating a heartprint of hope that time cannot erase. You're raising wholehearted children whose identity flows from the inside out, from the place where Jesus dwells. The bitter roots you help them uproot today won't have decades to distort their vision. The peace you help them plant will sustain them through storms you may never see. And the legacy you're growing, one prayer, one forgiveness moment, one heart connection at a time, will outlast your lifetime. Because the seeds you plant in their hearts today truly do shape the story they'll carry forever. And that story is just beginning.

GLOSSARY OF HEART HEALING TERMS

Bible-Heart

The belly—the spiritual center of a child (or adult)—is often described as the innermost place where the Holy Spirit communes with our spirit. It is where peace is felt and bitterness is uprooted.

"The spirit of man is the candle of the LORD, searching all the inward parts of the belly."

– Proverbs 20:27 (KJV)

Bible-Heart Check

A simple practice of pausing to notice what's happening within your spirit, especially when feeling overwhelmed. A check-in with Jesus to see if any forgiveness, peace, or presence is needed right now.

"Search me, O God, and know my heart; Try me and know my anxious thoughts."
– Psalm 139:23 (NKJV)

Bitter Root

This toxic, emotional, and spiritual belief forms when unresolved pain becomes internalized. It often originates from a time of emotional wounding or trauma, and it impacts how one perceives God, self, and others.

"See to it that no one fails to obtain the grace of God; that no 'root of bitterness' springs up and causes trouble, and by it many become defiled." – Hebrews 12:15 (ESV)

Blurry Heart Glasses

When emotional wounds distort how we see ourselves, others, and God, like looking through smudged glasses, bitter roots cause us to misinterpret situations and respond from pain rather than truth. When Jesus heals our hearts, our vision clears, and we can see people and situations as they truly are.

"Blessed are the pure in heart, for they shall see God." – Matthew 5:8 (NKJV)

Emotional Memory

A spiritual-emotional imprint left by past experiences, especially from childhood, that may still affect how we feel or respond today, even if the event is forgotten mentally. Jesus often brings these to the surface so they can be healed, not relived.

"He has sent me to heal the brokenhearted, to proclaim liberty to the captives, and the opening of the prison to those who are bound." – Isaiah 61:1 (NKJV)

Emotional Triggers

Current emotional reactions that are stronger than the situation warrants. They often indicate past unhealed pain or a bitter root being activated.

Forgiveness Flow

The gentle, Spirit-led prayer process that helps children and adults identify feelings, receive forgiveness, forgive others, and experience peace. Not a formula, but a pathway to encounter Jesus in our innermost being.

"And when you stand praying, if you hold anything against anyone, forgive them, so that your Father in heaven may forgive you your sins." – Mark 11:25 (NIV)

God Emotions

The feelings produced by the Holy Spirit are the Fruit of the Spirit. These include love, joy, peace, and other soul-healing emotions sourced in heaven.

"But the fruit of the Spirit is love, joy, peace, patience, kindness, goodness, faithfulness, gentleness, self-control; against such things there is no law." – Galatians 5:22-23 (NASB)

Heart Connection

The practice of shifting your focus from busy thoughts to your Bible-heart, where your spirit meets God's Spirit. This isn't just a technique but a way of life, creating space for intimate communion with Jesus throughout your day.

"Be still, and know that I am God." – Psalm 46:10 (NKJV)

Heart Safe Environment

A relationship or space where emotions can be expressed honestly without fear of judgment, dismissal, or punishment. Where children (and adults) feel secure enough to open their Bible-hearts to connection with Jesus and others.

"Perfect love casts out fear." – 1 John 4:18 (NKJV)

Hell Flags

A term used to describe toxic emotions that reflect the fallen emotional nature of man. Recognizing these helps identify when a bitter root may be present. This acronym includes the most common ones; however, there are a myriad of toxic emotions that crept in at the fall of man (Full acronym found in Chapter 5).

Jesus the Forgiver (in Me)

Children are taught they don't have to force forgiveness; Jesus, who lives inside them, does the forgiving through their Bible-heart. It's not their willpower. It's His presence flowing from the inside out.

"I have been crucified with Christ. It is no longer I who live, but Christ who lives in me."

– Galatians 2:20 (ESV)

Legacy Healing

When a parent, caregiver, or teacher pursues their own healing for the sake of the next generation, it can have a profound impact. It breaks cycles of bitterness, shame, or silence, and creates space for children to inherit connection, safety, and truth instead.

"Therefore know that the LORD your God, He is God, the faithful God who keeps covenant and mercy for a thousand generations with those who love Him and keep His commandments."

– Deuteronomy 7:9 (NKJV)

Peace as a Person

True peace isn't just an emotion; it's Jesus Himself. When peace rises in the Bible-heart, it's not because a problem went away, but because the Prince of Peace came near. It's His presence that quiets the storm inside.

"For He Himself is our peace." – Ephesians 2:14 (NKJV)

Spirit-Led Yielding

The posture of surrendering to Jesus from the inside out, not just thinking about Him, but allowing Him to lead you from within your innermost being, your Bible-heart. Yielding is felt, not forced. It invites Jesus to guide the healing, rather than trying to manage it ourselves.

"Trust in the LORD with all your heart, and do not lean on your own understanding. In all your ways acknowledge him, and he will make straight your paths." – Proverbs 3:5-6 (ESV)

Spirit-to-Spirit (Big 'S' to Little 's')

A way of describing how God's Spirit communicates directly and is combined with the human spirit, beyond intellect or behavior. It's the foundation for heart-based healing.

"The Spirit Himself bears witness with our spirit that we are children of God." – Romans 8:16 (NKJV)

Stop, Pray, Let Go

The simple three-step rhythm that helps children process emotions with Jesus: **Stop** and notice feelings, **Pray** and invite Jesus in, **Let Go** of the hurt and receive peace. This creates a pattern that even young children can learn to practice in everyday moments.

"Let all bitterness, wrath, anger, clamor, and evil speaking be put away from you, with all malice. And be kind to one another, tenderhearted, forgiving one another, even as God in Christ forgave you." – Ephesians 4:31-32 (NKJV)

Three Directions of Forgiveness

The complete forgiveness process that brings full healing: forgiving others who have hurt us, receiving forgiveness for ourselves (including for holding onto hurt), and releasing any disappointment or anger you may have toward God.

"And be kind to one another, tenderhearted, forgiving one another, even as God in Christ forgave you." – Ephesians 4:32 (NKJV)

Tummy/Belly Prayer

A child-friendly term for praying from the spirit or Bible-heart. Children are taught to place their hands on their belly and talk to Jesus from that inner place.

"He that believeth on me, as the scripture hath said, out of his belly shall flow rivers of living water." – John 7:38 (KJV)

Yucky Feeling

Kid-language for emotions that feel off: sadness, anger, guilt, fear, rejection. These feelings are not bad. They're signals. When we listen to them with Jesus, they lead us to healing, not hiding.

FOR MORE RESOURCES

Visit **heartprintsofhope.com** or scan the QR Code to see all the available content on this subject and more!:

For Printables and Downloads like the Extended Troubleshooting Manual, Sample Lesson Plans, and More.

www.ingramcontent.com/pod-product-compliance
Lightning Source LLC
Chambersburg PA
CBHW051414090426
42737CB00014B/2661